Affordable Housing Preservation in Washington, DC

Affordable Housing Preservation in Washington, DC uses the case of Washington, DC to examine the past, present, and future of subsidized and unsubsidized affordable housing through the lenses of history, governance, and affordable housing policy and planning.

Affordable housing policy in the US has often been focused at the federal level where the laws and funding to build new affordable housing historically have been determined. However, as federal housing subsidies from the 1960s expire and federal funding continues to decline, local governments, tenants and advocates face the difficult challenge of trying to retain affordability amid increasing demand for housing in many American cities. Now, instead of amassing land, financing and sponsors, affordable housing stakeholders must understand the existing resident needs and have access to the market for affordable housing.

Arguing for preservation as a way of acknowledging a basic right to the city, this book examines the ways that the broad range of stakeholders engage at the building and city levels. This book identifies the underlying challenges that enable or constrain preservation to demonstrate that effective preservation requires long-term relationships that engage residents, build trust and demonstrate a willingness to share power among residents, advocates, and the government. It is of great interest to academics and students as well as policy makers and practitioners internationally in the fields of housing studies and policy, urban studies, social policy, sociology and political economy.

Kathryn Howell is an assistant professor of Urban Planning at Virginia Commonwealth University and is the co-director of the RVA Eviction Lab. She investigates ways to interrupt ongoing patterns of migration, displacement and segregation in cities. She focuses specifically on affordable housing and public spaces to explore redevelopment, displacement and governance. Over the past decade she has looked at the preservation of affordable housing in Washington, DC, examining the intersection between policies, governance and the built environment. Most recently, she has partnered with community-based and policy advocacy organizations to collect and analyze eviction data to address housing instability and ongoing displacement in communities of color in Richmond. Before earning her PhD, Dr. Howell was a practitioner in local government, developing housing and community development policy in Washington, DC and Maryland agencies.

Explorations in Housing Studies

Series editors:

Janet Smith, *University of Illinois, Chicago*
Keith Jacobs, *University of Tasmania, Tasmania*
Mark Stephens, *University of Glasgow*

Explorations in Housing Studies is a series of high quality, research monographs which aims to extend and deepen both theoretical debate and empirical research in the housing studies field. The series is being introduced at a time when housing, in its various dimensions, is particularly closely intertwined with the impact of demographic change, economic instability, the shaping of life chances and wealth distributions and with the uncertain impacts of environmental and technological change. This series aims to engage with these and related issues from a variety of perspectives and methodologies.

Housing in Post-Growth Society
Japan On the Edge of Transition
Yosuke Hirayama and Misa Izuhara

Neoliberal Housing Policy
An International Perspective
Keith Jacobs

Housing, Neoliberalism and the Archive
Reinterpreting the Rise and Fall of Public Housing
Kathleen Flanagan

Evictions in the UK
Power, Housing, and Politics
Joe Crawford

Affordable Housing Preservation in Washington, DC
A Framework for Local Funding, Collaborative Governance, and Community Organizing for Change
Kathryn Howell

Affordable Housing Preservation in Washington, DC

A Framework for Local Funding, Collaborative Governance and Community Organizing for Change

Kathryn Howell

Routledge
Taylor & Francis Group
NEW YORK AND LONDON

First published 2021
by Routledge
52 Vanderbilt Avenue, New York, NY 10017

and by Routledge
2 Park Square, Milton Park, Abingdon, Oxon OX14 4RN

Routledge is an imprint of the Taylor & Francis Group, an informa business

Library of Congress Cataloging-in-Publication Data
Names: Howell, Kathryn, author.
Title: Affordable housing preservation in Washington, DC : a framework for local funding, collaborative governance, and community organizing for change / Kathryn Howell.
Description: New York, NY : Routledge, 2021. | Includes bibliographical references and index.
Identifiers: LCCN 2020052006 (print) | LCCN 2020052007 (ebook) | ISBN 9780367333096 (hardback) | ISBN 9780429319129 (ebook)
Subjects: LCSH: Housing rehabilitation--Washington (D.C.) | Housing rehabilitation--Finance. | Housing policy--Washington (D.C.)
Classification: LCC HD7304.W3 H69 2021 (print) | LCC HD7304.W3 (ebook) | DDC 363.5/83--dc23
LC record available at https://lccn.loc.gov/2020052006
LC ebook record available at https://lccn.loc.gov/2020052007

ISBN: 978-0-367-33309-6 (hbk)
ISBN: 978-0-367-77180-5 (pbk)
ISBN: 978-0-429-31912-9 (ebk)

Typeset in Sabon
by Taylor & Francis Books

To my parents Eric and Rhoda who never stop learning.

Contents

Figures

Preface

Washington, DC has a rich history of tenant-based housing policy that is visible in the policies actively used, the culture of advocacy and organizing, and the buildings that line some of the city's most highly gentrified corridors in neighborhoods like Shaw, Columbia Heights, H Street NE and Gallery Place/Chinatown. My work in both government and academia have given me a window through which to view this history. I walk or bike around the city, and as I do, I have the stories of almost 200 affordable buildings in my head. I see a building, and I remember that it was built in the early 20th century for wealthy white residents, it was first preserved in the 1970s after the African American families who had been living in poor conditions staged a rent strike, or it is owned by a group of Salvadoran and Guatemalan immigrants who bought it in the 1990s. There are few neighborhoods where I cannot talk about the history of affordable housing – specific buildings, zoning decisions, rent strikes, buildings that have been demolished, buildings that have been converted, buildings where low- and moderate-income communities have come together to resist and buildings where bad actors have exploited tenants. It is a part of DC history and present that are almost impossible to untangle.

Learning that history has helped me to understand the national picture for affordable housing and the nuances of federal policy. It has also helped me understand the conflicts and commonalities in a city that has been changing since it was built. The District has become a leader in the preservation of affordable housing at the same time that it has been tagged as one of the fastest gentrifying cities in the country[1]. After spending the past 13 years working with organizers, tenants, city government, lenders, developers and policy advocates to develop policy and understand the challenges, I have learned a lot about the relationships between different places where planning and policy-making happen, specifically community, advocacy and government. Preservation engages all three of those arenas for a simple reason: people live there, the building has been in place for at least a couple of decades and affordable housing finance is never done in a vacuum.

Affordable housing preservation is contested. Residents argue that they should have a right to determine their futures. At the same time, high-level "experts" argue that they know how to finance the building and will do their best for the residents. Government agencies look to various forms of efficiency and compliance as they navigate political decisions about funding and policy. Thus, the building itself becomes a battleground for larger fights over community power, gentrification and cultural displacement across the jurisdiction in the context of diminished federal support for affordable housing development and preservation.

Over the past decade, many cities and states have begun to take seriously the reality that policies leading to global growth in housing prices, declining real wages and rising inequality have resulted in displacement of low- and moderate-income households. To combat this, many are developing policies to reduce displacement and create new units in neighborhoods that have been closed since the advent of zoning. They are trying to address both the displacement of today and the results of segregation over the past century or more. Yet the approaches to the creation of new affordable housing – which requires land, developer and funding – do not always respond effectively to working equitably in existing buildings, neighborhoods and communities.

In the past two years, colleagues – organizers, government agency staff, developers and advocates – in DC have received phone calls and emails from places like Oakland, Minneapolis, Boston and elsewhere asking how they can do similar work. My hope is that this book helps to tell the story of DC's move toward a preservation policy and the long-term struggle to use policy to acknowledge the rights of tenants in a gentrifying city. I hope it illuminates more than just the end policies – which are helpful. But I hope that this book tells the larger story of the process and fight of residents, organizers and advocates, the collaborations with a broad range of stakeholders and the changes that had to be made to do the work that is underway. In spite of these strides, DC is not perfect and faces ongoing race-based displacement – both in housing and in public spaces. The long-time advocate, pastor and director of DC's office of the Local Initiatives Support Coalition exclaimed at a rally, "We're doing better than other places – that's great. But we aren't comparing ourselves to others." No matter where your city has landed, I hope this book gives you the tools to look to your own community history and knowledge to solve a critical problem.

Note

1 Jason Richardson, Bruce Mitchell, and Juan Franco, "Shifting Neighborhoods: Gentrification and Cultural Displacement in American Cities", Washington, DC: National Community Reinvestment Coalition, March 18, 2019, https://ncrc.org/study-gentrification-and-cultural-displacement-most-intense-in-americas-largest-cities-and-absent-from-many-others/.

Acknowledgements

This book – and indeed preservation in DC – would not be possible without the decades of work by activists who have withheld rent, testified at the DC Council, organized their neighbors, built coalitions, held bake sales, told their stories, bought their buildings and asserted their right to be a part of the District. They have expanded the ways we think about what affordable housing is and should be through the brave decisions they have made. My hope that this book honors the work they have done and, as I explained during interviews, it helps others to hear their voices and see what might be possible.

I also want to acknowledge that affordable housing in the District would not be at the forefront of the minds of so many people in DC without the tireless work of the late Robert Pohlman, founding Director of the Coalition for Nonprofit Housing and Economic Development. Without meaning to, Bob taught a generation of strong leaders in affordable housing development, organizing and advocacy about the importance of knowing the tools, showing up, having a vision and remembering the big picture over political wins. Without his leadership, the DC Preservation Network would have likely died a quick death, and the government tools for affordable housing would be diminished.

This book has been in my head – and therefore coming out of my mouth – for a decade. And so I also want to acknowledge the wonderful women advocates I have worked with over the years who have allowed me to bounce ideas, follow them around, interview their clients and show up to their meetings. Particularly, I thank Martha Davis, Elin Zurbrigg, Farah Fosse and Aimee McHale who have connected me with residents, been open in their own experiences and remained passionate activists for many years. I also thank Allison Ladd who hired me for the first time and has continued to look out for me, cheer me on and be on my side since 2004. These amazing women are leading the charge on different fronts and also believe in the long game of affordable housing and equity. The DC housing governance network has been a wonderful home for me, and so I also thank Peter Tatian, Andrew Martin, Scott Bruton, Leila Finucane, Jose Nuñes and Leslie Steen.

I also thank those who have been my intellectual sounding boards and inspiration as I fumbled for the language, stumbled into bigger questions and kept talking and listening as I evolved over the past decade. Andrea Roberts, Kristine Stiphany and Barbara Brown Wilson who share a mission of justice and push me to open my eyes, imagination and abilities wider through their work, support, questions and laughter. I appreciate the ongoing support of my PhD advisor Liz Mueller. Thanks to Brandi Summers for talking DC, inequality, space, race and theory – I feel so privileged to work with and learn from you and your work. For my VCU Urban Planning colleagues: I am so incredibly honored to be part of a community of academics who believe, as I do, that we have the responsibility to serve and make our work relevant to those who can use it most. Particularly I thank Meghan Gough, Ben Teresa and Sarah Raskin, whose passion for community and justice is contagious. I also thank John Accordino who has been an advocate, who has opened doors in a new community and who gave me the best advice a new faculty member could get: "Are you out of ideas? You're only in trouble if you're out of ideas." This book suggests that I wasn't out of ideas yet.

While research helped me with the language of my questions, the bigger questions about roots and goals, power and voice came from my family – both those that brought me into the world and those who have chosen to travel through it with me. My parents, Eric and Rhoda Howell, who have an unfailing belief in justice and who showed me what it means to be mission-driven. To Anna and Kari who have become unintentional experts in affordable housing, Urban Renewal and gentrification in DC – and have been unfailingly kind, brilliant and fun through this process. And to Danilo, who should have known better than to get involved with an academic. But who has been a sounding board and support when I have been tired and frustrated. And who has been a behind-the-scenes change-agent in DC – and nationally – in affordable housing preservation and housing justice.

Abbreviations

AHPF	Affordable Housing Preservation Fund
AMI	Area Median Income
CDBG	Community Development Block Grant
CNHED	Coalition for Housing and Economic Development
DCHA	DC Housing Authority
DCHFA	DC Housing Finance Agency
DCHRA	DC Human Rights Act
DCPN	DC Preservation Network
DCRA	DC Department of Consumer and Regulatory Affairs
DHCD	DC Department of Housing and Community Development
FHA	Fair Housing Act
HPTF	Housing Production Trust Fun
HUD	US Department of Housing and Urban Development
IZ	Inclusionary Zoning
LEC	Limited Equity Cooperative
LIHTC	Low Income Housing Tax Credit
LRSP	Local Rent Supplement Program
NLIHC	National Low Income Housing Coalition
OP	DC Office of Planning
OTA	DC Office of the Chief Tenant Advocate
PUD	Planned Unit Development
RFP	Request for Proposals
TOPA	Tenant Opportunity to Purchase Act

Introduction

Wah Luck House apartment building sits at the corner of H Street NW and 6th Street NW in the Chinatown neighborhood in view of the Chinatown Friendship Arch, dedicated in 1997 by former Mayor Marion Barry. Since 2000, the population in the census tract where it is located has increased by more than 100%, part of a trend in the surrounding tracts where population overall has increased by more than 75%. Meanwhile, the number of housing units in the tract around Wah Luck has increased by 63%. This has been driven by rapid growth in the white population and a fall in Black and Asian populations. Notably, in 2000, Asians represented 33% of the neighborhood population, but that share has fallen to 12.5%, with the surrounding tracts seeing far lower percentages of Asian residents.

Part of the reason for that remaining population of Asians in Chinatown is Wah Luck House. It is a building housing Asian seniors that was a little out of place amidst its neighbors until almost 2010. Built as part of the Downtown Urban Renewal Area in the late 1970s the 152-unit brutalist building has Chinese accents on the balconies and at the entrance, as well as a garden in the courtyard. The building takes up a half of the frontage of 6th street NW and a quarter of the frontage of H Street NW, which, until recently was lined with low-rise row houses and brightly-lit Chinese restaurants. Now it is increasingly surrounded by glass-fronted hotels and office buildings with sleek, first floor retail and entertainment in the Gallery Place/Chinatown neighborhood. Over the past decade, the Portrait Gallery and the National Building Museum, long time anchors of the area, have been supported with entertainment, shopping and dining options. The nearby arena, which is home to the Washington Capitals Hockey Team and the Washington Wizards Men's Basketball Team, along with concerts and large-scale events, brings in tourists from throughout the region and across the country.

Wah Luck House was built on land acquired through eminent domain and disposed of as part of the Downtown Urban Renewal Plan. It also was awarded a Section 8 place-based contract. It houses primarily Asian seniors and, along with Museum Square, a 301 unit building four blocks away that has lost its Section 8 subsidy, what still continued to make Chinatown more than just a zoning overlay, that requires signage in Chinese for the chain restaurants and shops like Urban Outfitters and Legal Seafood. Along with Judiciary House, a public housing community for seniors, Wah Luck House is one of the only affordable buildings in a neighborhood that now houses a Tesla showroom and a Hermes store, among other high-end retail.

Wah Luck was also one of the first modern fights over the preservation of affordable housing in Washington, DC. It illustrated the power interaction of "dirt" law, history, advocacy and the US Department of Housing and Urban Development's (HUD) legacy programs – or those that largely sunset in 1983. In 2008, while I was a policy specialist with the DC Department of Housing and Community Development (DHCD), the owner marketed it without any affordability requirements, in spite of the Section 8 covenant on the property. When this information was reported by a mission-driven for-profit affordable housing developer with his ear to the ground at a meeting of the DC Preservation Network (DCPN), a monthly meeting of preservation practitioners, the participants in the network discussed potential action. The Section 8 contract was still in place, but it was unclear if there were any additional affordability requirements due to its inclusion in the Downtown Urban Renewal Area.

When an organizer introduced Wah Luck at a monthly meeting, District agency staff used institutional knowledge to uncover details related to the disposition of the property in 1978. A government attorney explained that, not only was there an affordability covenant for the property due to the Section 8 contract, but also a 75-year land lease that was part of the Urban Renewal disposition agreement. While it was unclear, he argued, if the covenant ran with the building or the land, it was still effective. A community-based nonprofit was organizing the tenants to

Figure I.1 Wah Luck House and Chinatown

make sure they were ready if a fight for the building ensued. The staff retrieved the original covenant from the Recorder of Deeds, kicking off a process of preservation of the building that ended with retention of the Section 8 contract and the addition of Low Income Housing Tax Credits to fund the building's rehabilitation almost ten years later.

In my two years of work at the DC Department of Housing and Community Development and my subsequent engagement with the same practitioners as both a student and a professor, I was thrown into the relatively unique world of DC housing policy. Because the District serves both a city and a state function – particularly in terms of housing policy where Low Income Housing Tax Credits, Community Development Block Grant, HOME Investment Partnerships Program (HOME) and other federal sources are administered locally – DC offers the opportunity to see housing from top to bottom – from covenants and dispositions to sale and subsidy. Projects like Wah Luck illuminate the roots and history of the city's affordable housing infrastructure, as well as the interaction of policy, money and people that facilitated its creation and preservation. It also highlighted the role of decisions about the built environment – land leases, affordability covenants and zoning – decades beyond the decision in the ultimate goal of anti-displacement and community preservation.

At the same time, Wah Luck House demonstrates the power of policy infrastructure such as DC's Housing Production Trust Fund, the unique Tenant Opportunity to Purchase Act (TOPA), which gives tenants the right of first refusal, and rent control in allowing the impacts of a limited focus on preservation to be mitigated in affordable housing. That is to say, the foundations of these laws meant that the lack of focus on preservation by mayoral administrations until recently prevented the District from losing all of its affordable housing in some of the fastest changing neighborhoods starting in the early 2000s. Preservation in DC demonstrated the opportunities in the networks created for information sharing, advocacy and facilitating connections between residents and power. Finally, these networks made residents visible. Studying Wah Luck House has highlighted the power of the housing infrastructure, policy and governance that made preservation possible.

In one of my first days working for the DC Department of Housing and Community Development, a local advocacy organization offered a bus tour of Limited Equity Cooperatives in the District to DHCD employees – specifically targeted at the director's office and development finance division. DC has approximately 95 limited equity cooperatives representing just over 4,200 units and offering homeownership and stability to low- and moderate-income households. Resident-owners were a mix of native Washingtonians, new residents to the city and those who were new to the country. Cooperative owners at Capital Manor near U Street and Brightwood Manor in Northeast DC told us about their experiences – why they purchased, what they hoped to achieve and the challenges they face. Capital Manor owners talked about the challenge of building community relationships outside of the building and the challenge of remaining affordable as the neighborhood changed. Brightwood Manor residents explained that it was more than a building – it was a family, both figuratively and literally. They knew the importance of place in the preservation of community – the rental housing they grew up in and, in turn, raised families in – and eventually purchased after tenures of five months, five years or fifty years. The stories of residents' fights to stay in their buildings, in spite of often poor conditions and disinvested neighborhoods, facilitated a view of a changing DC beyond the blank slate often promoted as cities expand. It became clear that affordable housing had to be a cornerstone of the anti-displacement efforts underway in cities facing change – whether gentrification or decline. The tour and my ongoing engagement with tenant organizers, advocates, affordable housing developers and service providers illustrated that affordable housing was more than just a place to live. For many of the residents with whom we spoke, the building where they lived represents community, it is where their children grew up – and in some cases where their grandchildren lived.

Affordable housing preservation is more than high-level finance and federal policy. Housing preservation policy is local and contextual with strange bedfellows, individual life experiences, failures and successes (often within the same unit, building, program and day), exchange and use values. It engages at multiple scales: a single household, building, neighborhood and city all at the same time. Affordable housing preservation is messy, and typically we join the conversation mid-stream, 50 or more years late with no clue that as practitioners and advocates, we are often late to the game. Understanding preservation challenges assumptions about the value of low- and moderate-income communities – and the agency that renters can or should have, and it complicates the narrative of deconcentration of poverty as a remedy for poor neighborhood conditions. It forces planners and policy makers to rethink top-down approaches.

I began to put these pieces together while working on my dissertation research in 2012 and 2013 to understand what happens when cities and nonprofits preserve affordable housing in the midst of rapid large-scale redevelopment and gentrification in the DC neighborhood of Columbia Heights. My focus was on what happens after redevelopment when not all of the original residents were displaced due to preservation and new construction. Understanding that necessitated digging into how we arrived at that point where 20% of the units in the neighborhood were deeply income-restricted despite the $1million home sales prices, spiking market rents throughout the neighborhood and growth in demand. In the five years since completing that project work I have returned to the DC Public Library, National Archives and Library of Congress to learn about the implementation history of federally subsidized housing programs, local laws and funding in the District. I also interviewed additional residents, advocates, organizers, agency staff and technical assistance providers in DC to understand how DC's housing landscape evolved.

As housing has come to the fore in local and national political contexts, local and state practitioners have looked to federal, state and local governments for additional funding and innovation – though the contributions from the federal to state and local governments has been on a decline since 1980. To fill these gaps, many large cities are looking inward to create local funding sources, build or create tenant protections or create housing through the planning process, including rights of first refusal, local funding sources and rent stabilization. But when a former tenant organizer in DC was asked by organizers in other cities how they can get something like DC's Tenant Opportunity to Purchase Act (TOPA), which gives tenants the right of first refusal when their building is for sale, she said:

> First you need organizers and you should publicly fund them because I think that's something huge that DHCD [DC Department of Housing and Community Development] has done – and the city has done. And it isn't being done nationally and is a great use of CDBG [Community Development Block Grant] dollars and goes a really far way.

What she understood – and what I have learned – is that advocacy, and, more specifically, understanding what residents experience, is often a critical base step to changing the way preservation and affordability are understood at the local level and making it real.

Why Washington, DC?

This book examines affordable housing preservation in the United States using Washington, DC as a site of investigation. Although, as I will explain, DC has many of the same background elements of other cities, including patterns of population growth and decline, federal policy and local trends, DC has an important history of community power that has shaped the processes, policies and outcomes of preservation. As cities – led by policy, global investment and national demographic trends – face dramatic growth and displacement, DC as a case has an important set of lessons to learn that are translatable beyond its borders.

The idea of writing on DC is often critiqued, particularly if it somehow involves government, because DC's unique status – as neither a city, nor a state, but with nominal federal oversight, and no voting representation in Congress – makes it questionable as a space from which to learn. Yet from a housing policy perspective (and certainly for the purposes of this book) it is a great way to see the details of how patterns of affordable housing develop and how the options for preservation – and ultimately, the prevention of displacement – evolve. DC offers a space to untangle the impacts of different types of infrastructure: land use, grants, federal policy, local policy and community-based power in the midst of a common US story of urban growth and change. This infrastructure in DC allows us to look at both process and outcomes in housing policy in one geography.

DC, like many American cities, experienced growth from immigration, the Great Migrations of African Americans and other domestic migration starting at the end of the Civil War. It felt the effects of racially restrictive covenants, Redlining and racialized zoning in the built and social environments. The

District was also a testing ground for federal housing policy, including highway and Urban Renewal projects, Section 8 and HUD-insured mortgages for multifamily properties, and like cities across the US, the laws and practices undergirding segregation, land dispossession and inequality birthed successive organizing campaigns that built power to make change for marginalized groups in Washington.

DC is, in many ways, an ideal space to examine the conflicting and complimentary approaches to preservation. With the built-in tenant power of its right of first refusal law at sale-driven preservations, rent control and concurrent government funding for tenant organizing and preservation, tenant-oriented preservation projects are more than just one-off projects. At the same time, DC has the same types of preservation efforts in public housing and other subsidized housing as other cities where owners refinance and redevelop to preserve affordability in some way that may or may not engage tenants as priority stakeholders. Increasingly, cities across the country – driven by grass-roots organizations – are trying to understand how to engage tenants, and the policies that once were one-of-a-kind are finding homes in other localities looking for tools for preservation.

From a funding perspective, the bulk of housing preservation in the United States is a blend of federal funding (passing through states) and local land use decisions, suggesting that DC functionally is not drastically different. What are unique, are the options that have evolved in recent decades that preserve housing. However, all localities are unique within a similar national context. DC has a large affordable housing trust fund, a two-year-old housing acquisition fund and a local housing voucher program, along with the Low Income Housing Tax Credit, federal vouchers and other sources like HOME and the Community Development Block Grant that make a high volume of rental and owner-occupied housing preservation possible. But with local and state housing trust funds and other sources becoming ubiquitous in large and small cities, it seems DC is not an outlier. As such, this book is an exploration of the variation in the ways that redevelopment – and particularly the development of affordable housing in redevelopment – could be done.

DC is both a city and a state – yet has the autonomy of neither. During the pre-Home Rule period, Washington, DC's lack of local control acted both as a positive and negative force in the Urban Renewal era. While the federal government's role is challenging – as Congress has the right to veto laws, including the budget, of the District, the federal government has had limited interest in opposing housing laws in DC. But being in the backyard of the US Department of Housing and Urban Development, as well as Congress, in many ways, meant that federal programs operated as intended – for good and for ill. Members of Congress read *The Washington Post* over breakfast, meaning they knew when there was community outrage, which proved useful in a couple of cases. Washington was often used as a test case for federal programs and attracted activists from across the country who filled the District's local offices, advocacy organizations and neighborhoods.

Other than a short experience with Home Rule in the 19th century, Washington, DC was fully under the control of the federal government until 1974. By then, the lines of race and class had been drawn and redrawn multiple times. The District experienced significant post-Civil War population growth – particularly in places like Southwest DC and the Shaw neighborhood. This growth in the African American population continued with the Great Migrations into the 1970s. The post-World War II population growth followed the growth in the federal government. Although upper Northwest Washington had been (and remains) primarily white and upper middle class, the line between white and Black Washington has moved over time, enforced through restrictive covenants, community norms and discriminatory lending. By the 1970s, the line was firmly entrenched at Rock Creek Park, with the notable exception of Capitol Hill where the areas near to the Capitol have remained largely white throughout the past century.

DC's political and policy history helps to detangle the roles of process and outcomes in preservation. When Washington was granted Home Rule in 1974, the newly elected council members came from the Civil Rights Movement and grassroots community organizing – with a focus on community-based empowerment and Black political and community leadership. They passed critical legislation that opened up access to land and community-based power such as the Tenant Opportunity to Purchase Act (TOPA), which gave tenants the right of first refusal when their buildings were sold. Residents can purchase it themselves to become a condominium or cooperative, do nothing and allow the sale to proceed, or assign their rights to a developer who follow the tenants' demand through a contract with the tenants and keep the building as a rental building. The District's financial support of legal representation and tenant organizers for low- and moderate-income buildings has made the right to purchase a building realistic by facilitating technical assistance and basic knowledge of the complexities of housing development. While TOPA has provided a stopgap against displacement and a means through which to access the multifamily market, the District has also developed significant funding for affordable housing development through the Housing Production Trust Fund (HPTF). HPTF uses a portion of transfer taxes on real estate to support affordable housing.

Washington, DC offers an opportunity to investigate the need for anti-displacement focused preservation in a changing city. Since 2000, when the population was 572,000, Washington, DC has added more than 125,000 new residents, led largely by a 48% increase in white residents. Between 2000 and 2010, the growth in population was centered in Ward 1, primarily in the U Street, Adams Morgan and Columbia Heights Neighborhoods. Yet, since 2010, the growth – though still occurring in parts of Columbia Heights – has moved south to the waterfront neighborhoods near the baseball stadium, North of Massachusetts Avenue, or NOMA, and Brookland, where population has increased in some tracts by more than 100%. While the number of low- and moderate-income households has remained steady, the number of units affordable to them has decreased by 50%, and rents citywide have doubled. While the region's median income was

$97,000 in 2017, the District's median was $77,000, an increase from $58,000 in 2010. Yet this masks the variation across the District based on race. The District's white median household income topped $125,000 annually, up from $97,000 in 2010, while Black median household income remained stagnant or fell in real dollars from $38,000 to $41,000 in the same period. This income inequality is both the result of and the reproduction of a racialized landscape in DC.

The District's housing stock also grew by 5% between 2010 and 2017, and building permits have remained constant over the past nine years, averaging 4,600 new units each year. However, DC also has a significant stock of subsidized affordable housing across the city, including almost 32,000 federally and locally funded units across the city. Importantly, approximately 3.2% of the District's housing units are subsidized using Section 8 place-based subsidies that were put into place by the 1980s. The combination of existing affordable housing and rapid growth has led to a clearly-defined need for affordable housing preservation of existing subsidized housing. At the same time, Washington has become a national leader in preservation policy using local funding, collaborative governance, grassroots organizers, policy advocacy and legal tools such a covenants and tenant rights that have prevented displacement for thousands of low- and moderate-income District residents.

However, it is not merely putting those pieces together that makes preservation in the District a case study worth exploring. Understanding preservation has also required an understanding of the historical opportunities and challenges created by exclusionary zoning, Urban Renewal, progressive leadership, focused investment in affordable housing and federal engagement in local government. As a result, the ability to preserve affordable housing today is a complex puzzle built over time that has significant impact on resident access and, indeed, the current and future city form.

Methods

This project has evolved over more than a decade of research and practice in Washington, DC. I use a mixed methods approach to understand the successes and missed opportunities for affordable housing development and preservation in Washington, DC. Where possible, I try to center the discussion of affordable housing on buildings and the experiences of those living and working in the buildings that have been preserved and lost in DC. I relied on archival sources – including the National Archives, Library of Congress, the Washingtoniana section of the DC Public Library, the National Capital Planning Commission archives and online newspapers, planning documents and maps. I used these data to create maps[1] and understand the context for affordable housing in DC. I read decades of interoffice memos, constituent letters and public comment, newspaper accounts and classified ads. I interviewed individuals who worked in government and non-profits over time to develop a narrative of the history of the policy and planning interventions, including Urban Renewal and the Tenant Opportunity to Purchase Act, and the governance structures that impacted the affordable housing landscape.

The second part of this project – the modern look at where DC is now with its preservation of affordable housing – relied on mixed methods, including interviews, participant and direct observation and analysis of quantitative data. I interviewed more than 75 residents living in both rental and cooperative affordable housing as well as current and former advocates, agency staff, tenant organizers and service providers working in the affordable housing sector over the past ten years to understand the impact of these policies. I was a participant observer in public meetings and hearings held by government and nonprofit agencies and the Coalition for Nonprofit Housing and Economic Development (CNHED). I also attended and engaged in working group meetings of CNHED for eight years and participated with the DC Preservation Network (DCPN), a network of stakeholders from residents and organizers to funders and federal and local agency staff who focus on preservation at the building level through data and monthly meetings since the group's inception in 2008.

I also used current qualitative and quantitative affordable housing data collected by DCPN, local housing agencies and interviews to compare the data from 1983 to the current landscape. From this, I developed a dataset of more than 150 narratives of affordable housing developments based on the meeting notes, agendas and observations of the DCPN between 2008 and 2016. Interview data and qualitative data from the DCPN were used to understand the history of specific buildings that may have changed structure (by adding or subtracting units or by changing to a cooperative or condominium structure) or were redeveloped via HOPE VI or another large-scale development process[2].

How This Book Is Organized

The goal of this book is, first and foremost, to give a better sense what preservation is, has been and can be. To do that, I explore the complexity of the landscape for preservation using a series of embedded case studies within the District of Columbia. While DC has its own story, it became a leader in preservation, not because it has always been progressive, or because it has always been this way. The successes and failures of preservation emerged from a series of policy and planning decisions, theoretical underpinnings and grassroots mobilizations that will be explored throughout the book. Like the preservation of Wah Luck House, DC would not be where it is without Urban Renewal, organizers, bureaucrats, federal and local funding, and a network of actors who gathered data and deployed it strategically.

Throughout this book, I implicitly ask six questions based in planning theory and practice in thinking about not just what but how we preserve: What is the history of preservation at the building and city levels? What are the goals? What tools and processes are used? Who has a voice? Who has power in decision-making? Who has the power to originate ideas? These questions describe the broad arc of the book, but they also drive the ways I approach the chapters. I toggle between scales – asking questions of power and voice, while digging deep into local context, policy and practice because, while not all practitioners will engage in ongoing study of planning theory, they should be asking questions to interrogate the long-term implications at multiple scales.

Chapters throughout the book use a combination of case studies on particular buildings and policy processes, as well as citywide quantitative and qualitative data to illuminate the arguments discussed above. Chapter 1 frames the issue through existing literature and theory. I look at questions of historic and current housing policy evolution, governance, resident power and community organizing to help set the stage and understand where Washington DC's story fits. The next three chapters are devoted to understanding the mechanics that created the opportunities for preservation, specifically, the history, policy and advocacy. In Chapter 2, I investigate the evolution of the implementation of local and federal programs over time in the District that formed the physical infrastructure for our current landscape. I analyze historic affordable housing and archival data on subsidized buildings over the past 60 years to better understand the importance of this type of infrastructure to communities over time as well as the policies, networks and relationships that maintain these buildings as a critical infrastructural asset for the District. I further investigate the ways in which housing created in the diverse eras of Urban Renewal has served as the base for much of the deeply affordable housing. Finally, I explore the impact of the city's affordable housing infrastructure in gentrified and currently changing parts of the city.

Chapter 3 explores the development of unique local policy and practices that ultimately came to influence the ways local jurisdictions approach preservation. This chapter helps to set the stage for the ways that advocacy, residential and city government agencies understood the needs, opportunity and community role in the preservation of affordable housing.

In Chapter 4, I explain the advocacy and governance structures that have grown up around affordable housing generally and, more specifically, how they have evolved to address affordable housing preservation. Specifically, this chapter explores the ways that advocates have come together around preservation and – just as importantly – how they have engaged in both adversarial and collaborative organizing at different times to promote policy changes, funding structures and action on particular buildings. This chapter also investigates how data-sharing relationships have improved long term outcomes for affordable housing in Washington.

Chapter 5 examines the pathways and outcomes – or how the elements infrastructure, policy and networks – in the three previous chapters were applied and what they look like citywide in terms of location, the path to preservation or loss, building type and neighborhood characteristics. I take a deep dive beyond the national datasets to follow the 161 properties flagged by the DC Preservation Network over the eight-year period from 2008 to 2015. Through this chapter I expose the quantitative data on the neighborhood, building and historical context of buildings that were preserved and lost during that time. I use this to get a better sense of the long-range process and build on the previous chapter's look at governance to better understand the way that policy tools have been effectively (or not) employed to keep buildings affordable.

Chapter 6 discusses the resident-level impact of preservation. The tenant-led preservation that evolved out of DC's policy and advocacy framework has created significant opportunities and challenges both in the fight to initially preserve their communities and the ongoing effort to maintain them. In this chapter I discuss the needs of this type of preservation, including significant levels of access to funding, expert knowledge and time. Those tools are critical to addressing the complexity of affordable housing development, overcoming gaps in trust by residents who have been repeatedly displaced and supporting long term stability. I also explore the impact of preservation on residents of affordable housing. Specifically, this chapter investigates why residents moved to the building and remained in the midst of poor conditions and management; how the preservation process impacted their lives; and whether the way in which the preservation was achieved – subsidy, building, community, ownership structure – impacted the way they view their building and community.

Finally, Chapter 7 places Washington, DC in the existing literature and makes recommendations for local policy. This chapter brings together the lessons learned to nest them within the larger body of literature and theory. It then uses those lessons to make specific recommendations about the way that local and state governments can use an understanding of the existing build, policy and activist environments to preserve affordable housing locally.

While this book is not meant to be a specific formula for preservation at the local or state level, it serves as an unpacking of the issues, opportunities and challenges of working to maintain affordability for existing households and communities.

Notes

1 I also created shapefiles for Urban Renewal Areas through hard copy maps and descriptions of the boundaries from the relevant time period. I digitized a hard copy file of all affordable housing created or planned in 1983 – the last year of new place-based Section 8 contracts and three years before the advent of the Low Income Housing Tax Credit – developed by the Washington Area Council of Governments in 1983. I digitized, geocoded and mapped these data for the District and analyzed them using data from decennial census data between 1980 and 2010, as well as the American Community Survey from 2015.

2 Because of the need for recapitalization over the past decade, many buildings experienced some sort of change that is not reflected in the quantitative data. I also created a quantitative dataset from these narratives to determine not just if they were preserved or lost, but the ways they were preserved and the steps taken in the process by building owners, residents, advocates and public agency staff.

1 Dirt, Development and Displacement

Museum Square One is a 301-unit building developed as part of the Downtown Urban Renewal Plan. Located four blocks from Wah Luck House, the land was acquired by the city and disposed for a discounted price with affordability covenants, a HUD-insured mortgage and ongoing Section 8 contract. Though a part of the residential section of the Urban Renewal Plan intended to encourage investment in the area, Museum Square One and a children's museum located nearby failed to spur the intended redevelopment for almost 30 years. The ten-story building stood out among aging two-story row houses and parking lots that surrounded it on the edge of Downtown.

However, over the years, Museum Square One and Wah Luck House four blocks away have become the two remaining buildings where the Asian residents that maintained Chinatown's dying identity live. After several large-scale redevelopments, including a new convention center and an arena starting in the mid 1990s, the number of luxury mixed-use developments increased in the blocks surrounding the Museum Square One. Now the building is surrounded in new multifamily buildings with rents exceeding $2,500 per month for one-bedroom units. In nearby Mt. Vernon Square, a former Carnegie Library now holds an Apple Store, along with the DC Historical Society, and high-end gyms and restaurants now stand where nail salons, vacant storefronts, go-go clubs and parking lots once stood. Museum Square One is no longer a stand-out multifamily building. Yet, because the building is in a census tract with approximately five other Section 8 buildings constructed as part of the Downtown and Northwest One Urban Renewal Areas, it is still considered a high-poverty neighborhood, with median incomes in the surrounding tracts below $15,000 in 2010. Functionally, this meant that, even after preservation became a policy goal, the concentration of poverty meant that this building would be a difficult sell for preservation.

Documented back to 2002, residents complained of poor conditions in the building resulting from a lack of basic maintenance. Over the intervening years, residents also complained of fires in the building, lack of security and other issues, including, ultimately, a failed Real Estate Assessment Center (REAC) score that threatened the Section 8 contract[1]. While the owner applied to government agencies for financing, he refused to make repairs, and his requests for funding from the US Department of Housing and Urban Development (HUD) were denied. He also

Figure 1.1 K Street/Museum Square One

told residents and local government officials that he planned to opt out of his building contract more than once. He made several attempts to raze or sell the building in violation of the District's Tenant Opportunity to Purchase Act (TOPA), resulting in lawsuits by the tenants and rallies to demand city action. When he finally offered it for sale, the price averaged out to $830,000 per unit – a total of $250,000,000 – based on the potential total number of units the owner could build on the site, including a parking lot behind the building. This prompted a second successful legal challenge from the tenants, this time arguing that it was not a "bona fide offer of sale," as required by the law because the price was not reasonable. The owner withdrew his application for a raze permit. Finally, however, he opted out of the Section 8 contract, leaving residents – all seniors, many Chinese-speaking – with few options.

While the residents are technically permitted to stay using Tenant Protection Vouchers[2] they received when the Section 8 contract ended, many received misinformation about whether or not they could stay, and the housing conditions remained shaky. As a result, Museum Square One is still in limbo. There may still be an opportunity for residents or the city to purchase the building if the owner razes or tries to sell the building again, but due to the size, location and deferred maintenance on the building, the price of the building may be prohibitive for residents, affordable housing developers or the city to purchase the building and keep the residents in place. This challenge is exacerbated by the loss of the ongoing rental housing subsidy that cannot be replaced.

The future of Museum Square One is one of many complex preservation challenges across the country that is impacted by the building, neighborhood and citywide contexts in which it is located. Understanding buildings like Museum Square One helps to frame out the need, challenge and opportunities for preservation. This chapter explores themes that arise from this and many other cases in the book. Specifically, I will discuss the challenges preservation of affordable housing is meant to address; the challenges tenants, localities and housing developers face in trying to preserve; and the programs in place to preserve buildings. I also will look at the history of the built environment – or the dirt on which affordable housing stands. This includes federal programs that helped to create the buildings tenants seek to preserve, including evolution and intent; current affordable housing policies used at the federal and local level and how those policies have implicitly and explicitly defined preservation; and the role of local planning power over time. I will then look at the role of advocacy and direct service governance networks in affordable housing. Finally, I will discuss the changing role of residents in affordable housing and how policy implicitly or explicitly defines their roles.

Preservation History and Process

Over the past 20 years, affordable housing has increasingly been put at risk from both an increased demand for housing and a low demand for housing. Though seemingly contradictory, these trends originate from similar speculative roots and are often different points on the same timeline. As cities like Washington, DC, Minneapolis, Portland, Richmond and Los Angeles have attracted new higher-income households through redevelopment and as a part of larger demographic trends toward delayed household formation, many neighborhoods have become wealthy, well-amenitized neighborhoods, with public transportation, grocery stores, restaurants and access to employment. Yet, many of these same neighborhoods that previously served as a source of affordable housing, community networks and job access for low- and moderate-income households now face higher costs which have put housing out of reach for many of the low- and moderate-income households that could benefit from a central location. Rising property values and expiring subsidies are often cited as a primary factor impacting the affordable stock[3]. However, cities or neighborhoods facing economic decline also lose units from the unsubsidized and subsidized affordable stock. This is due to failing conditions inspections and subsequent demolition, or due to lack of financial and technical stability of landlords holding on to properties as reliable income or those who are speculating while not making improvements until the market for multifamily buildings improves[4]. Exploitation of scarcity by investors and landlords through the housing and land market has been long researched and observed, specifically as an opportunity from the growth in low-wage labor and limited housing options in the tenements of the late 19th and early 20th Centuries[5] and as an opportunity created through legalized discrimination of African Americans in lending[6]. More recently,

Desmond argues that landlords now are exploiting the affordable housing shortage and earning wide profit margins in low-income neighborhoods[7]. In many cases, these two trends – gentrification and decline – occur in the same housing markets, with some units failing out of the affordable stock and others redeveloping out of the stock.

One source of subsidized housing is buildings constructed or preserved in the mid- to late-20th century using mortgages insured through the US Department of Housing and Urban Development (HUD) and operating subsidies such as Section 8 and public housing funds. The affordable housing produced before 1983, through what I call Legacy Programs, has remained a critical source of deeply affordable housing, representing 20% of the total subsidized stock[8]. Yet the stock is threatened by opt-outs, expirations and failed inspections. Over the past decade, studies have evaluated the factors that threaten the subsidized stock, such as owner opt-outs and prepayments; expiration of the subsidy; and physical deterioration of the buildings, which can lead to failed inspections and the loss of the subsidy[9]. Between 2005 and 2015, 8% of all subsidized housing units were lost from the stock, compared to 19% between 1998 and 2004[10]. Nationally, there was greater variety in the characteristics of buildings leaving the subsidized pool from 2005 to 2015 than in a study from 1998–2004. This may be due to the volatility of the market during the later period and the growth in advocacy and preservation work done by nonprofit and government actors[11]. In addition, buildings serving the lowest incomes – such as those with Section 8 place-based subsidies – were less likely to remain affordable after an opt-out compared to higher-income targets that often remained close to the Fair Market Rent[12], meaning that not only are buildings in newly gentrifying neighborhoods most at risk from a subsidy opt-out, but that the poorest households are most vulnerable to displacement. This is compounded by the limited scope of current affordable housing production tools, such as the Low Income Housing Tax Credit, that target higher-income households than the legacy programs for project-based rental assistance.

However, the majority of low- and moderate-income households – more than three times the number of households in subsidized housing – live in unsubsidized affordable housing[13]. These units are often lost to redevelopment, code enforcement, abandonment or obsolescence through demolition or gut rehabilitation, or as a gradual replacement of existing tenants with higher paying new tenants. While the contexts for these buildings vary, the loss of this stock represents an exacerbation of existing shortages of affordable housing across the country where 75% of all renter households earning less than 50% of area median income are housing cost burdened, and almost half face extreme cost burden, or paying more than half of their incomes on housing[14]. Though new construction is growing the subsidized affordable stock, losses in the unsubsidized stock are creating a net loss of affordable and available units for low- and moderate-income households.

The issue of preserving the affordable housing that does remain faces critical challenges due to the same problems that precipitated the need: expensive housing markets, poor conditions and a lack of support for affordable housing[15]. The rising costs of land and the speed of the market make it difficult for nonprofits and governments to intervene to purchase and preserve both subsidized and unsubsidized housing. At the same time, limited affordable rental housing options have incentivized poor maintenance and a lack of investment into affordable buildings, giving landlords high profit margins from owners of housing in poor neighborhoods[16]. Unfortunately, preserving these buildings then requires more than just the market acquisition price, but also the rehabilitation cost for decades of deferred maintenance, necessitating large subsidies or putting the project out of reach. Before 2006, some owners of assisted buildings strategically "failed out" of the programs or engaged in demolition due to poor conditions, contributing to initial losses in low-income communities. This has resulted in market-affordable buildings where poor housing conditions and high vacancy have contributed to ongoing losses in the affordable stock[17].

In response to pressure by advocates, as well as declining federal resources, local and state agencies have made policy changes address preservation[18]. These changes have included improvements to notification requirements when an owner opts out of a subsidy; the creation of rights of first refusal in the cases of sale or the termination of a Section 8 contract; relocation cost mitigation for residents; tax abatements to convince owners to keep the building affordable; local acquisition and housing trust funds to facilitate preservation; community land trusts; and incentives or set-asides of existing funding sources[19].

The diversity of preservation efforts illustrates the complex space preservation occupies. Concurrently a question of affordable housing provision, community engagement and tenant rights and power, preservation can be undertaken in a variety of ways, depending on the goals embedded in the approach. Affordable housing preservation is more than just a policy question to answer – but a planning process with which to engage. Affordable housing policy in the United States, like many problems that deal with people, tracks, often painfully, with the evolution in planning practice. The elite-driven focus on economic efficiency of rational planners cleared the way for some of the most painful slum clearance, Urban Renewal and highway projects and facilitated the power that allowed Black neighborhoods to be razed in their wake. Future work in affordable housing policy followed Davidoff's belief that planners should advocate on behalf of the most vulnerable – yet their views were just another data point to be understood by experts who knew the best way to help[20]. These theoretical frameworks have continued to guide the way that cities redevelop neighborhoods – with affordable housing often tacked on or negotiated as part of the process, rather than central to the outcomes.

Preservation, however, takes several modern approaches to planning engagement. It can take a Just City approach that views preservation as a way of supporting the affordable housing stock, deconcentrating poverty or exposing the low- and moderate-income households to middle class norms, wider job networks and improved educational outcomes through living in mixed-income communities[21]. The goal of engaging the three pillars of diversity, equity and democracy provide space for resident engagement, but residents inform, and are not the drivers of these paths to preservation[22].

Other forms of preservation engage in a collaborative approach across multiple sites of planning – government, advocates and residents – to ensure residents are represented and have a voice in the process. Inclusive collaborative processes engage residents not as "lucky" recipients of housing – but as critical partners necessary to determining the outcome with the power to decide the outcome and process by which their buildings are preserved[23]. Alternatively, preservation can be framed as anti-displacement and radical, centered on tenants and their right to determine their collective future, building on right to the city arguments in changing neighborhoods[24]. In a more radical preservation, the goal is to change the structures of power under which residents have lived and facilitate their control over the space[25]. While the goals of preservation may be part of any of these approaches, the process of preservation can both define and change the way the diverse stakeholders in preservation think about the outcomes.

Preservation Policy and Implementation

This book approaches preservation as dependent on three primary contextual areas: existing built environment and the land on which it stands, housing governance networks, and the policies and laws in place in the state or locality. Preservation, in the context of declining affordable stock, diminished federal resources and increasing demand for housing, seems like a clear need. Operating subsidies, short of project basing Housing Choice Vouchers, are rare, meaning those that exist are worth protecting. However, in communities where conditions – at the building or community level – have deteriorated, practitioners often question why they should preserve. However, community members would argue that maintaining the community-level ties is critical. At the same time, preservation has also been linked to sustainability in maintaining existing buildings – particularly for those in older central city locations. Yet preservation has been critiqued both implicitly and explicitly for maintaining outdated forms – garden apartments, low-density development or large parking lots – in central city locations. These debates are embedded in critical questions about neighborhood and housing form and function – as well as the nature of neighborhoods and how their composition can or should be changed, the role of government and the power of advocacy. As such, I will frame this section by exploring the development of housing resources, local and state policy, and the role of networks in housing policy to better understand DC within the broader US context for preservation and housing policy.

The Built Environment

Like most policy and practice, the outcomes of preservation are dependent on the goals of the stakeholders – anti-displacement, subsidy preservation, removing eyesores or improving conditions. These approaches reflect long-held goals of affordable housing policy more broadly. Framed alternately as a social welfare policy issue, community development opportunity, macroeconomic policy and anti-displacement policy, housing has been embedded in larger philosophical debates about the deserving and undeserving poor, the proper role of government in spurring development and in the management of economic issues[26]. Starting in the late 19th century with an identification of poor conditions, housing has been used as a remedy to fear of disease and moral contagion, a way to impose order on the perceived chaos of the city and a way to improve the city's image[27]. It has, as was discussed previously, been used as a mechanism for wealth creation by building owners, aware of the profit to be made through ownership[28]. Slum clearance, public housing and Urban Renewal arose in response to the ongoing documentation of significant slum housing conditions in cities growing rapidly due to industrialization, migration and immigration, the need to employ the large number of unemployed workers as the Great Depression deepened, and the prevention of unrest[29]. At the same time, local governments hoped to clear slums to make way for projects that would promote the image of an economically viable city and remove minority communities from central city areas[30]. Because these areas were typically located near employment centers, their ongoing presence was, for city boosters, both a deterrent to investment and an opportunity for investment. The development and provision of affordable rental housing has evolved significantly since the 1930s, including the purpose of its provision, what it looks like and how it is done. Starting in 1937 with the Wagner-Stiegel Act, the federal government inserted itself into the rental home building process – and spent the next several decades trying to extricate itself[31]. Programs for public housing and Urban Renewal were debated through the mid-20th century with supporters like the American Institute of Planning arguing for expanded approaches – connecting the redevelopment power with highway construction – for a more comprehensive approach to planning[32]. At the same time, community organizations and experts alike made strong critiques of the process and outcomes of Urban Renewal, including the implications for communities, public space, historic preservation and power[33]. Public Housing was under fire before the first foundation was poured from home builders who feared unfair competition and market capitalists who felt it was not the appropriate role for the federal government[34]. This resistance to public housing was enshrined in law and budget processes by reducing support for public housing, requiring it to be built in slum clearance areas, and chronically underfunding capital repairs[35]. These debates over 20th century housing policy expose conflicts between the community's exchange value and its use value for communities; the role that residents place in determining their own futures and owning space within the city[36]; and the right residents have to safe, decent and affordable housing[37].

The critiques of public housing led to the development of new programs that brought in private sector actors. In the late 1950s and throughout the 1960s, the federal government introduced several funding programs, including Section 221 (1961), Section 202 (1959) and Section 236 (1968) loans that helped to subsidize the development and management – through reductions in the cost of borrowing – of affordable housing by private developers. While these programs created almost 700,000 units, Section 221 and 236 programs were heavily critiqued for not serving the neediest households, incentivizing cost overruns, subsidizing developers and a lack of responsiveness to the market. In response, the Section 8 program was created to address cash flow issues in existing properties and provide operating subsidy to new and substantial rehabilitation of existing buildings. Section 8 was terminated in 1983 but produced more than 850,000 new or rehabilitated units over that time. Unfortunately, many communities have lost much of this subsidized stock through sale, demolition and opt-outs from the Section 8 contract, resulting in efforts by state and local advocates and governments to preserve affordable housing through data, funding tools and neighborhood engagement[38].

Starting in 1986 the bulk of affordable housing was produced using the Low Income Housing Tax Credit[39]. It remains the largest mechanism for new production and rehabilitation. However, tax credit buildings typically serve moderate-income households and require additional subsidy to reach the lowest-income households, which had been served through the Section 8 program. As a result of the devolution of affordable housing development to local and state governments, as well as the sharp reduction of funding for community-based organizations beginning in the 1970s, affordable housing development is now built and managed by nonprofit and for-profit developers and funded by a mix of public and private sources[40]. Local housing agencies predominantly rely on federal sources of funds such as HOME, the Low-income Housing Tax Credit (LIHTC) and the Community Development Block Grant (CDBG), all of which provide subsidies to private developers for housing development for low-income tenants at various income levels. They additionally rely on the residual buildings constructed throughout the past century through project-based Section 8, HUD-Insured Mortgage Programs and Public Housing[41].

Where Is Affordable Housing Located?

The question of the location of affordable housing becomes critical during the conversation about preservation due to the ongoing fights over the deconcentration of poverty, place-based redevelopment, gentrification and resident self-determination. Historically, affordable housing has been concentrated in communities of color, those with few resources and those with least access to transportation and jobs due to community resistance to both affordable housing specifically and multifamily housing more broadly[42] as well as intentional segregationist policies[43]. The resistance to affordable housing was exacerbated by the fight against rental housing, which was famously described as a "mere parasite constructed in order to take advantage of the open spaces and attractive surroundings created by the residential character of the district" in Euclid v Ambler in 1926[44], justifying protective zoning that prevented the construction of new rental housing in new residential areas. Though these policies were explicit in law and practice before the Fair Housing Act (FHA), they have continued through other mechanisms such as single-family and large lot zoning, as well as through Home Owners Association regulation about finishes and design. As a result, affordable housing communities are rarely found in high-income communities – particularly ones that developed after the advent of zoning and the FHA lending. This made homeownership a critical dividing line between wealth and poverty – but also, the racial basis in historic and ongoing decisions racialize a seemingly "race-neutral" privilege of homeowners over renters in political discussion and power to control the future of one's community.

The boundaries of the early 20th century, reinforced through the placement of affordable housing, racist lending practices and ongoing restrictive zoning have perpetuated the patterns of affordable rental housing placement. While high-income, largely white neighborhoods exclude low- and moderate-income households through single-family detached zoning, these households are often placed in the most ecologically vulnerable locations[45] with low access to amenities like good schools, healthy food and quality infrastructure.

However, as cities have looked to redevelopment as a way of growing the population and, subsequently, the tax base, affordable housing – including public housing – has been put at risk of redevelopment and loss[46]. The protectionism in white, high-income neighborhoods – along with the concurrent high land values – have left low-income neighborhoods vulnerable to large- and small-scale redevelopment, rezoning and displacement. In addition, because areas of slum clearance were often located adjacent to business districts, so were many public housing communities and, in some cases, Section 8 buildings. As real estate values increased, the land on which subsidized affordable housing sat became increasingly valuable. As a result, these were often the first communities slated for redevelopment through programs such as HOPE VI or through opt-outs[47], repeating patterns started during the early 20th century efforts to clear slums[48].

Regardless of the type of neighborhood where affordable housing remains, preservation has become a critical need to address macro needs such as the jurisdiction-wide affordable housing stock and homelessness, as well as households' needs for housing they can afford, the long-term retention of community networks and safe and healthy housing and communities.

Laws and Policies for Preservation

Affordable housing preservation has become a critical piece of policy – particularly in cities. Federal tools have been created to try to address the loss of subsidized housing, including the Rental Assistance Demonstration Program, which opens up aging subsidized buildings to new investment; Mark up to Market, which allows for higher rents and 8(bb) subsidy transfers, which allow the movement of subsidies from one building where an owner wishes to opt out to another building that needs a subsidy. However, these tools require significant local investment in the form of information, funding and policy[49]. In the case of federally-assisted properties, such as those with investments through Section 8, the loss of these buildings results in losses of both a physical asset and an ongoing subsidy. While residents receive Tenant Protection Vouchers (TPV), fewer than half the residents displaced through a Section 8 opt-out can use them[50], and the loss of the physical unit (and the land on which it sits) is, in many cases irreplaceable.

Unfortunately, in gentrifying neighborhoods, preservation efforts face tough competition from redevelopments that are framed as natural and "vibrant" (future) remedies to the poverty and blight that have been the physical manifestations of the inequality, racism and disinvestment in cities[51]. This focus on the market determinism of redevelopment leaves the state with no perceived options to mitigate for the effects of redevelopment or demand greater community-based development to improve equity outcomes and reduce the displacement from rising rents. Thus, as neighborhoods change through dramatic investment in commercial and residential development and rising demand for urban living, affordable housing, if it is considered a piece of the redevelopment, is often created through set-asides in market-rate buildings, rather than through an intentional focus on anti-displacement and community-level preservation[52]. Within this context, new development – regardless of affordability – is framed as a way to reduce rents in gentrifying communities[53]. However, the results are mixed, typically finding that new construction moderates housing costs at the top end of the market, while doing little to mitigate the impacts of development for the bottom third of the market[54], meaning that affordable housing preservation and creation are critical to mitigating the impacts of gentrification[55].

Alternatively, an intentional focus on preservation for existing tenants suggests that in the long term some advocates support the argument that remaining in one's neighborhood constitutes a right to the city[56] or, "the right to change ourselves by changing the city," rather than just a right to passively inhabit the city[57]. The right to the city argument challenges the dominant hegemony of development and capital by arguing that, in spite of the exchange value of economic development and neighborhood construction of physical place, long-term residents' use value of the community is of greater weight. The right to housing advocates also believe that everyone, regardless of income, should have the right to safe, decent housing in a neighborhood of opportunity[58]. Both the right to the city and the right to housing theorist argue that, regardless of the type of housing (single-family or multifamily) or type of tenure (rental or homeownership), marginalized residents have an equal, if different, stake in the city[59]. As a result, translating these rights into meaningful policy remains problematic without existing residual radical policies[60].

Beyond the right to the city, preservation may offer a critical way to build strong counter-publics, remove housing from the speculative market and build community. Huron has argued that preservation – specifically through the formation of limited equity cooperatives removes housing from the speculative market and enables low- and moderate-income households to have control over their daily lives, similar to other forms of homeownership[61]. The stability and control through a tenant-oriented preservation approach also supports the maintenance and development of community norms and power, making them real places for both those living in and outside of these buildings. The creation of place can facilitate the development of counter-publics that support organizing, political power and visibility[62].

While some jurisdictions, local nonprofit organizations and nationwide foundations have focused on preservation of these buildings, they face an uphill battle in the face of the dual problems of ongoing disinvestment and gentrification in US cities[63]. The federal government's support for affordable housing has retreated rapidly since 1980, but the bulk of funding and tools for many jurisdictions still come from the federal government[64]. This has left significant and growing gaps between the need for affordable housing and the resources needed to assist households. To fill the gap, cities and states have developed policy tools and funding sources to address deeper needs in housing affordability and preservation, specifically through local housing trust funds[65]. By 2016, 47 states and Washington, DC, as well as more than 700 cities and counties had created affordable housing trust funds[66].

While the funding has made preservation – including rehabilitation of existing subsidized buildings and acquisition of for sale properties – possible, cities and states have also looked for ways to slow the costs of housing. One of the ways this has happened is through Community Land Trusts (CLT). The model separates the land, which changes value based on increased demand in the surrounding neighborhood, from the improvements on the land, which typically only change when there have been major renovations. By separating the cost of land, the nonprofit CLT facilitates affordability of the units in the trust – regardless of whether the buildings are owner-occupied or rental housing. Land acquisition can come through purchase, disposition of government-owned land or voluntarily by the owner of the property. There are more than 225 CLTs across the United States, functioning in diverse, locally grounded ways[67].

Another newly growing tool is a right of first refusal laws. Rights of first refusal have been proposed and adopted in cities such as Oakland, San Francisco and Minneapolis over the past few years. These rights of first refusal operate in many different ways. One way gives tenant associations or, in the case of single-family rentals, the individual renter, the right to buy the property when it is for sale. In other cases, the right is reserved for nonprofits or the local government. The goal is to facilitate access to the market for residents, the local government or nonprofit affordable housing developers as a way to preserve the community.

Another tool used at the local level to address preservation is data. Policy makers and planners have used adaptive and collaborative approaches successfully to address complex environmental management challenges[68]. Similarly, the changing landscape of housing policy has created an opportunity for collaborative and multi-sector data sharing and collection approaches around housing conditions across the country. The shrinking sources of funding for affordable housing, increased demand for market-rate urban living and the ongoing need for affordable housing suggest that existing affordable housing – particularly in gentrifying areas – requires a complex set of actors with diverse bases of information. However, most interventions to preserve housing have been top-down, often missing opportunities at the grassroots level[69]. Housing and community development work can run on parallel tracks where siloed government agencies fund projects and work from their high-level data, while tenants and advocates use the experiential data. As a result, many parts of the story are untold, and it is difficult to find common themes across a neighborhood, portfolio or jurisdiction to understand the scale or scope of a challenge. Equity of information may create a more level playing field outside the collaborative space. The group learning that comes from sharing information in an inclusive process may allow local knowledge experts to make recommendations to agency staff, better understand their rights and resist the pressures from owners and landlords. In the early 2000s, cities and states across the country used MacArthur's Windows of Opportunity Initiative to build capacity and to develop information locally[70]. These diverse approaches reflect the complexity of the preservation process that requires funding, affordable stock and access to information from a wide variety of actors[71]. This was one reason why the National Low Income Housing Coalition (NLIHC) also developed a nationwide database of federally subsidized housing as a resource for local activists[72]. These databases have been used as a way to target preservation resources, understand the scope of the challenge and predict where buildings may be lost. However, to be effective, these data resources require a network of organizers, advocates and service providers.

Building Governance Networks

Preservation's complexity makes the coordination of strange bedfellows – residents, developers, organizers, multiple government agencies and lenders – critical. Yet, there is often very little infrastructure in place to do this – particularly when residents are shut out of the decision-making process. Sandercock argues that planners "need to be attentive to how power shapes which stories get told, get heard, carry weight" and ensure they listen to and share more than one story or narrative[73]. In contrast to the top-down way of approaching planning that has historically disempowered low-income communities, social movements of the 1960s and 1970s, as well as protests against neighborhood destruction from Urban Renewal and highway construction projects, helped to build support for the agency of low-income residents in neighborhoods across the country through the funding of neighborhood-based planning, organizing and social service efforts[74]. The result of this effort was the creation of Community Development Corporations (CDCs) and mobilization within communities to assist with job creation or the development of affordable housing, as well as providing "a political voice for poor and racialized minorities previously excluded from decision-making"[75].

However, communities remained empowered and organized in spite of the local government's reluctance to include them in the decision-making for redevelopment. These groups continued to organize to provide neighborhood-based services when the government and private sectors failed[76], protest destructive redevelopment and displacement[77], and advocate for greater redistribution of resources for low-income households[78]. Martin and Pierce suggest that some of the anti-hegemonic structures created during this era remain residuals of the radical governance and advocacy of the 1960s and 1970s and provide ongoing resistance to neoliberal power[79].

Governance networks can play a number of roles – service, advocacy and organizing – focused on being both collaborative with governmental agencies and confrontational, depending on the setting, funding and goals of the organization. In the case of preservation, governance networks are engaged in the provision of affordable housing and housing-based services, typically funded through local or state money; organizing tenants to focus attention on building conditions, displacement or proactive efforts to purchase the building; and advocacy to develop new funds and laws, provide conduits to power for residents and promote awareness of needs across the housing continuum. In the preservation context, where actually retaining the affordability of the building depends on both private and public sources of funds, the relationships between governance networks and other actors can present logistical challenges.

Organizing

Community organizing can be defined in three primary ways: confrontational as a means to system transformation, consensus organizing to improve neighborhood outcomes and community-building, which focuses on creating or remediating relationships within the community with the goal of self-sufficiency[80]. Organizing – specifically confrontational and community-building – also plays a critical role in the preservation of affordable housing by enforcing existing local and state laws, convincing owners to preserve the building or lobbying for new laws or funding to protect low-income renters[81]. Consensus organizing, conversely, focuses on working with government agencies to improve outcomes for the population served, often making it difficult to push for system transformation[82].

Organizing tenants and gaining a voice in planning processes is impacted by the available funding and support from philanthropy and government agencies[83]. Yet organizing is one of the critical ways that preservation centered on tenants can be successful in preserving their buildings and remaining in place[84]. The need to find funding for organizing can expose conflicts between engagement and confrontation – particularly if the organization receives funding from outside organizations such as banks, local or state government[85], potentially putting advocates at risk of unstable funding. An Urban Institute report argues that Community Development Block Grant (CDBG) funds have been largely used to fill gaps in housing development budgets, rather than for community engagement and development[86]. As a result, community organizations face an ongoing tension between the need to collaborate with government, or other powerful organizations, to address problems and the need to remain distant or even adversarial in order to more effectively protest or otherwise critique the policies impacting the constituents they serve.

This funding system also creates a structure where nonprofits with high levels of professional expertise in the planning and development of affordable housing have access to public and private funders and competitive government funding sources, while community-based nonprofits focused on organizing have few resources. Just as importantly, disparities in expertise and knowledge between formal planners and stakeholders can create an imbalance of power and a lack of understanding about the institutional challenges faced by those engaged in housing policy. Unfortunately, not only are there few channels through which grassroots data about tenants can be shared with decision-makers, these data are typically undervalued in planning practice.

As in earlier eras when project-based Section 8 buildings were created, housing advocates have played important roles in the preservation of buildings. In a multiple case study of anti-displacement programs, Levy et al. found that community organizing played an important role in preserving affordable housing in gentrifying neighborhoods by enforcing existing local and state laws, convincing owners to preserve the building, or lobbying for new laws or preservation funding[87]. Moreover, affordable housing is complex – requiring multiple levels of expertise in finance, public processes and policy, historic funding programs, development and data. While government actors, banks, developers and others engaged in the process are paid and trained to fill the role, residents face an inequality of knowledge in this arena. This expertise, ideally provided in part by governance networks, whether in organizing, technical assistance or advocacy can play critical role in filling inequities in knowledge between residents, government and private sector actors. More importantly, it can lead to engagement and information from multiple levels of expertise. Sandercock conceptualizes planning as a multi-sited endeavor that includes both formal, certified planners and those at the community level[88]. The engagement in inclusive processes may engender an opportunity for "coproduction of processes, policies, and programs for defining and addressing public issues"[89].

Partnerships with Government

Nongovernmental and community-based actors have historically been skeptical of the motives and methods of government agencies. This distrust of government plays an important role in the decision to support system transformation or work collaboratively with government organizations. As Laurian argues, "when non-experts have poor experiences at access points, they may become resigned, cynical or disengage from the system, meaning that poor experiences with planners can have ramifications beyond the specific planning process at hand"[90]. In her seminal piece on power and community engagement, Arnstein argued that there is a relationship between engagement and power for residents. Proposing a ladder of participation, she suggested that there are varying levels of participation, translating to access to power[91]. While programs like Choice Neighborhoods required a significant public engagement to address the shifts in housing, the bulk of changes to privately-owned affordable housing requires little to no engagement with residents about the future of the building beyond the issuance of an opt-out notice to enable the housing authority to issue enhanced vouchers[92]. This has been particularly challenging in the cases of affordable housing located in low-income neighborhoods or buildings facing poor conditions where agency staff view the destruction of the building as a net positive for residents despite community-based fights to remain and exercise a functional right to the city[93]. According to Arnstein's framework, this means that residents have very little access to meaningful decision-making and power. However, this lack of power in the midst of the increasingly financialized landscape of housing can actually function as a way of focusing and mobilizing residents to take rights[94].

Where collaboration happens between government and nonprofits or other community organizations, there are hurdles to overcome. Government actors can fear a loss of control over the process – particularly in a heated political context – while still needing the political support for policies that can be derived by developing community-based networks[95]. At the same time, community organizations can feel constrained by these same political considerations, as well as the agenda-setting of government-led collaborations. These processes can, in fact, reproduce and reinforce the power of government or powerful actors[96]. These types of collaborations can represent a type of exclusion through inclusion – or a manipulation of community organizations.

While this inclusive practice is typically examined as a part of a government-led process, the diverse and powerful roles of housing actors across sectors – government, grassroots, legal, funding, development and policy – suggest that inclusive processes do not necessarily arise from government alone[97]. Howell and Wilson argue for "Radical Collaboration," or a collaborative approach that is community-led and focused on change in power, rather than reproduction of existing power structures[98]. These collaborative processes must also be sustained to overcome distrust and be truly inclusive[99]. Quick and Feldman argue, "An inclusive 'way of knowing' a public policy problem is an ongoing accomplishment that must be sustained through the 'continuous renewal of associations' among parties and perspectives"[100]. In addition to the reluctance of government actors to engage in these types of collaborations, existing power structures – legislators or executives – may make acting on information about the experiences of marginalized groups difficult or impossible for planners in government agencies[101]. While collaborative processes are not effective for all planning activities, they can help to overcome the challenges facing actors in complex processes by using a broad range of stakeholders to engage multiple types of knowledge and use those to create and recreate policy[102]. These collaborative efforts, therefore, cannot be perfunctory or unequal to be effective.

Unfortunately, the collaborative relationship can easily be one-sided, with the government having a more powerful role in the relationship. However, while actors in processes may share goals, they differ on their methods, leading to distrust between groups[103]. This may be because trust must be characterized by similar planning values such as reciprocity, open information sharing and similar expectations[104]. Thus, it takes time to repair distrust between government and nongovernmental actors due to unproductive collaboration efforts, broken promises and a fear of cooptation that will reproduce existing power structures. The time it takes to repair that trust can impact long-term efforts to improve outcomes for the populations most impacted by policy and planning.

Conclusion: Policy, Planning and Governance in Washington, DC

The research for this book started with a question back in 2011 when I first started my dissertation research: How did DC preserve all this housing in a hot-market, changing city? One obvious reason for the city's preservation infrastructure is the Tenant Opportunity to Purchase Act (TOPA), DC's right of first refusal law. No one else had it at the time[105], and the right to determine to whom and how a building changes hands is a powerful tenant right that explicitly acknowledges the rights of tenants to remain and retain their collective stakes in the city. Further, by facilitating access to the market, TOPA provides tenants and government agencies a way to slow down the process to preserve housing. However, TOPA, while necessary, is not sufficient to make this kind of right meaningful and real for low- and moderate-income households. Renters earning less than 30% of Area Median Income could not possibly gain access to enough affordable finance to purchase a single house – let alone a multifamily building – in a city where per unit prices have soared above $300,000[106]. A second answer to how Washington, DC preserved housing was the District's annual $100 million Housing Production Trust Fund and other supporting funding, including an acquisition fund. Yet, understanding the opportunities and applying and conducting necessary compliance for affordable housing funds require specialized knowledge. Housing finance is complex and time consuming – as is building management, tenant rights and affordable housing. The idea that anyone with a full-time job who had never owned a building and was not engaged in housing finance could effectively navigate the worlds of finance, development and government successfully over time is questionable on a large scale. However, the impact of the District's funding (through the Community Development Block Grant) of tenant organizers as a critical piece of the puzzle – as well as DC's history of organizing and activism – also plays a role in preservation and, therefore, supporting the right of tenants to remain in the changing city. The network of organizers who talked to each other about the buildings, engaged with tenants and used their connection to District government to connect residents to power was not necessarily unique, but it was critical to sustained affordable housing development and support. But there had to be *affordable multifamily housing to preserve* in the first place. Whether it was just multifamily housing that was rent stabilized, market-affordable units[107] or buildings that had been subsidized over the past 80 years through Project-Based Rental Assistance, HUD-Insured mortgages, public housing or other newer programs, low- and moderate-income people needed to be living somewhere that could be preserved. Thus, there are important policy decisions that have been made through zoning, federal and local programs, and other race-based practices that helped to create this infrastructure. Woven through these interventions, however, is also a broad governance network that advocates, holds accountable, resists and proposes new policies and practices for both non-profit and public organizations. Though policy practice often seeks a simple or single answer, it is clear that DC's approach to preservation is the result of an evolving housing policy that engaged multiple actors, laws and histories. It is not a quick one-shot project that made the system function, but approaches that engage in multiple scales and times.

DC's case is unique – in the way that all localities are unique. They have cultures, governance structures, and policy and planning histories that have formed them and have made the work of anti-displacement differently challenging. But they all work with the same federal limitations that require a local or state policy framework to fill the gaps in federal funding. How they interpret and use federal funds, as well as how they fill the vast spaces left by federal funding, is part of the unique work of local policy. Throughout this book, I make the following arguments that can be understood across contexts:

- The opportunities for preservation are largely dependent on the existing built, policy and planning environments that have evolved through decades. This includes the overlay of federal and local levels of infrastructure.
- Effective preservation requires long term relationships that engage residents, build trust and demonstrate a willingness to share power throughout the process.
- The preservation of existing stock uniquely enables the long-term preservation of community-based power and ties among existing residents.

If this sounds like a messy prospect, I have communicated effectively. Affordable housing, generally, is a challenging mix of money, land and people – as well as a healthy dose of multi-level politics. Preservation elevates that to new heights. Instead of a blank site to start, preservation starts with a building full of people and community, memories and usually lead, asbestos and mold behind the walls, figuratively or literally. It is this mess that makes it worth doing. As cities change, fill in and grow, increasingly low- and moderate-income households are seeing their housing options – and community bases – disappear, and city governments are realizing their options for equitable housing are shrinking. We have to figure out how we are going to preserve what we have so that, when we pour new housing into the top of the bucket, existing units are not falling out of the gaping hole in the bottom.

The remainder of the book uses Washington, DC to explore these concepts and argue that they represent a triad of affordable housing infrastructure. I will first explore the critical role of the existing built environment. I argue in Chapter 2 that the current preservation landscape – and indeed the full landscape of affordability – was based in the infrastructure created almost 100 years ago when the District began to expand into its in-town suburbs and was solidified with decisions made in the 11 Urban Renewal Areas. I next explore the power of existing laws and funding. While this is typically the area where the focus lives in the discussion of housing policy, I examine the decisions made over decades to posit the policy framework as a type of necessary infrastructure for preservation. This infrastructure necessitates engagement of government agencies and individual actors to be effective. Finally, I argue for governance networks as the third element of a necessary housing infrastructure. This governance network must be robust, featuring not just service providers or radical organizers – but a broad range of actors who provide direct services, organize tenants to demand changes and advocate and translate among government and private sector actors. In the second part of the book, I look at what it means to work within those structures, shifting from process to outcomes for the building, the subsidy and, most importantly, for the residents who live in the communities that are preserved.

Museum Square One, like many of the buildings throughout the book, offers a one-stop-shop opportunity to dig into the embedded challenges and opportunities of preserving affordable housing: laws and policies, the built environment and governance. Though it is in a neighborhood with high costs and rapid development now, the preservation process started long before the Apple Store opened and the Go-Gos closed. The residents faced poor conditions and threats while Downtown's boom was still speculative and the neighborhood was considered high poverty. The change in the neighborhood merely serves as the backdrop for a process that happens across contexts – in subsidized and unsubsidized buildings – and relies on a broad range of actors being on the same page. More than that, Museum Square One required a robust policy and funding regime. While its story is not yet complete, Museum Square One is a complex case produced through white flight and disinvestment, Urban Renewal, organizing, policy and governance. Over the next several chapters, I will unpack these stories through the lenses of the physical, policy and governance infrastructures at play in Washington, DC to help to understand how low- and moderate-income communities can be preserved and how other communities can dig into their own histories to understand the roots and opportunities for the future.

Notes

1 REAC inspections are conducted by HUD's Real Estate Assessment Center from physical inspections of HUD-assisted properties. A failing REAC score can signal management or financial issues and can lead to the loss of subsidy on the building if there are subsequent failed inspections.

2 Tenant Protection Vouchers enable a tenant to remain in their unit, regardless of rent increases after a subsidy has been lost.

3 Vincent Reina and Jaclene Begley, "Will They Stay or Will They Go: Predicting Subsidized Housing Opt-Outs," *Journal of Housing Economics* 14 (2014): 1–16; Michael C. Lens and Vincent Reina, "Preserving Neighborhood Opportunity: Where Federal Housing Subsidies Expire," *Housing Policy Debate* 26, no. 4–5 (2016): 714–32, https://doi.org/10.1080/10511482.2016.1195422.

4 Philip M.E. Garboden and Sandra Newman, "Is Preserving Small, Low-End Rental Housing Feasible?," *Housing Policy Debate* 22, no. 4 (2012): 507–26, https://doi.org/10.1080/10511482.2012.697909.

5 Jacob Riis, *How the Other Half Lives: Studies Among the Tenements of New York* (Boston: St Martin's Press, 1890); Matthew Desmond and Nathan Wilmers, "Do the Poor Pay More for Housing? Exploitation, Profit, and Risk in Rental Markets," *American Journal of Sociology* 124, no. 4 (2019): 1090–1124, https://doi.org/10.1086/701697.

6 Beryl Satter, *Family Properties: How the Struggle over Race and Real Estate Transformed Chicago and Urban America* (New York, NY: Henry Holt & Co., 2010); Keeanga-Yamahtta Taylor, *Race for Profit: How Banks and the Real Estate Industry Undermined Black Homeownership*, Justice, Power, and Politics (Chapel Hill: University of North Carolina Press, 2019).

7 Desmond and Wilmers, "Do the Poor Pay More for Housing? Exploitation, Profit, and Risk in Rental Markets."

8 Alex F. Schwartz, *Housing Policy in the United States* (New York: Routledge, 2015).

9 Andres G. Blancoa et al., "Affordability After Subsidies: Understanding the Trajectories of Former Assisted Housing in Florida," *Housing Policy Debate* 25, no. 2 (2015): 374–94; Elvin Wyly and James DeFilippis, "Running to Stand Still: Through the Looking Glass with Federally Subsidized Housing in New York City," *Urban Affairs Review* 43, no. 6 (2008): 777–816; Anne Ray et al., "Opting In, Opting Out a Decade Later" (Washington, DC: HUD, 2015).

10 Ray et al., "Opting In, Opting Out a Decade Later."

11 Ray et al., "Opting In, Opting Out a Decade Later."; Reina and Begley, "Will They Stay or Will They Go: Predicting Subsidized Housing Opt-Outs."

12 Blancoa et al., "Affordability After Subsidies: Understanding the Trajectories of Former Assisted Housing in Florida."

13 Joint Center for Housing Studies, "America's Rental Housing: Expanding Options for Diverse and Growing Demand" (Cambridge, MA: Harvard Joint Centers for Housing Studies, 2015); Deidre Schmidt and Sara Proppe, "The Space Between: Realities and Possibilities in Preserving Unsubsidized Affordable Rental Housing" (Minneapolis: Minnesota Preservation Plus Initiative., 2003).

14 HUD, "Comprehensive Housing Affordability Strategy Data, 2012–2016" (Washington, DC.: US Department of Housing and Urban Development, 2017).

15 Wyly and DeFilippis, "Running to Stand Still: Through the Looking Glass with Federally Subsidized Housing in New York City."

16 Desmond and Wilmers, "Do the Poor Pay More for Housing? Exploitation, Profit, and Risk in Rental Markets."

17 Kathryn L. Howell, Elizabeth J. Mueller, and Barbara Brown Wilson, "One Size Fits None: Local Context and Planning for the Preservation of Affordable Housing," *Housing Policy Debate* 29, no. 1 (2019): 148–65, https://doi.org/10.1080/10511482.2018.1476896.

18 Schwartz, *Housing Policy in the United States.*

19 Elizabeth J. Mueller and Alex Schwartz, "Reversing the Tide: Will State and Local Governments House the Poor as Federal Direct Subsidies Decline?," *Journal of the American Planning Association* 74, no. 1 (2008): 122–35; NHT, "The Preservation Catalog," Website (Washington, DC: National Housing Trust, 2016), http://www.prezcat.org/catalog-search; Wyly and DeFilippis, "Running to Stand Still: Through the Looking Glass with Federally Subsidized Housing in New York City."

20 Paul Davidoff, "Advocacy and Pluralism in Planning," *Journal of the American Institute of Planning* 31, no. 4 (1965): 331–38.

21 Xavier Briggs, Susan Popkin, and John Goering, *Moving to Opportunity: The Story of an American Experiment to Fight Ghetto Poverty* (Oxford: Oxford University Press, 2010).

22 Susan Fainstein, *The Just City* (Ithaca, NY: Cornell University Press, 2010).

23 Kathryn S. Quick and Martha S. Feldman, "Distinguishing Participation and Inclusion," *Journal of Planning Education and Research* 31, no. 3 (2011): 272–90;

Judith E. Innes and Judith Gruber, "Planning Styles in Conflict: The Metropolitan Transportation Commission," *Journal of the American Planning Association* 71, no. 2 (2005): 177–188.

24 David Harvey, "The Right to the City," *The New Left Review*, 2008; Don Mitchell, *The Right to the City: Social Justice and the Fight for Public Space* (New York: The Guilford Press, 2003); Kathryn Howell, "Planning for Empowerment: Upending the Traditional Approach to Planning for Affordable Housing in the Face of Gentrification," *Planning Theory & Practice* 17, no. 2 (2016): 210–26.

25 Amanda Huron, *Carving out the Commons: Tenant Organizing and Housing Cooperatives in Washington, D.C*, Diverse Economies and Livable Worlds 2 (Minneapolis: University of Minnesota Press, 2018).

26 R. Allen Hayes, *The Federal Government and Urban Housing: Ideology and Change in Public Policy* (New Yok: State University of New York Press, 1995); Walter I. Trattner, *From Poor Law to Welfare State: A History of Social Welfare in America* (New York: The Free Press, 1994); Helene Slessarev, "Racial Tensions and Institutional Support: Social Programs during a Period of Retrenchment.," in *The Politics of Social Policy in the United States*, ed. Margaret Weir, Ann Shola Orloff, and Theda Skocpol (Princeton: Princeton University Press, 1988), 357–79.

27 Peter Hall, *Cities of Tomorrow* (Maldon, MA: Blackwell Publishing, 2014).

28 Desmond and Wilmers, "Do the Poor Pay More for Housing? Exploitation, Profit, and Risk in Rental Markets."

29 P. Marcuse, *The Myth of the Benevolent State: Towards a Theory of Housing*, Papers in Planning (Columbia University, Graduate School of Architecture and Planning, 1978), https://books.google.com/books?id=kvVnHQAACAAJ; Alexander von Hoffman, "The Lost History of Urban Renewal," *Journal of Urbanism: International Research on Placemaking and Urban Sustainability* 1, no. 3 (2008): 281–301, https://doi.org/10.1080/17549170802532013; Edith Elmer Wood, "Slums and Blighted Areas in the United States" (Washington, DC: Federal Emergency Administration of Public Works, Housing Division, 1935).

30 Lawrence Vale, *Purging the Poorest: Public Housing and the Design Politics of Twice-Cleared Communities* (Chicago: University of Chicago Press, 2013).

31 Hayes, *The Federal Government and Urban Housing: Ideology and Change in Public Policy*; Schwartz, *Housing Policy in the United States*.

32 American Institute of Planners, "Urban Renewal: A Policy Statement of the American Institute of Planners," *Journal of the American Institute of Planners* 25, no. 4 (1959): 217–21.

33 Charles Abrams, "Criteria for Urban Renewal," *Architectural Record*, 1962, 155–58; Cameron Logan, *Historic Capital: Preservation, Race, and Real Estate in Washington, D.C* (Minneapolis: University of Minnesota Press, 2017); Chris Myers Asch and George Derek Musgrove, *Chocolate City: A History of Race and Democracy in the Nation's Capital* (Chapel Hill: The University of North Carolina Press, 2017).

34 Alexander von Hoffman, "Housing and Planning: A Century of Social Reform and Local Power," *Journal of the American Planning Association* 75, no. 2 (2009): 231–44.

35 Vale, *Purging the Poorest: Public Housing and the Design Politics of Twice-Cleared Communities*.

36 David Harvey, *Social Justice and the City* (Athens, GA: University of Georgia Press, 2008); Peter Marcuse, "From Critical Urban Theory to the Right to the City," *City* 13, no. 2–3 (2009): 185–96.

37 Rachel Bratt, Michael Stone, and Chester Hartman, "Why a Right to Housing Is Needed and Makes Sense: Editors' Introduction," in *A Right to Housing: Foundation for a New Social Agenda*, ed. Rachel Bratt, Michael Stone, and Chester Hartman (Philadelphia: Temple University Press, 2006), 1–19; Elizabeth K. Julian and Demetria L. McCain, "Housing Mobility: A Civil Right," in *The Integration Debate:*

Competing Futures for American Cities, ed. Chester Hartman and Gregory D. Squires (New York: Routledge, 2009), 85–98.

38 Heather L. Schwartz et al., "Preservation of Affordable Rental Housing Evaluation of the MacArthur Foundation's Window of Opportunity Initiative" (RAND Corporation, 2016); Kathryn L. Howell, "Housing and the Grassroots: Using Local and Expert Knowledge to Preserve Affordable Housing," *Journal of Planning Education and Research*, May 16, 2017, 0739456X17709500, https://doi.org/10.1177/0739456X17709500.

39 Schwartz, *Housing Policy in the United States*.

40 Hayes, *The Federal Government and Urban Housing: Ideology and Change in Public Policy*; Schwartz et al., "Preservation of Affordable Rental Housing Evaluation of the MacArthur Foundation's Window of Opportunity Initiative."

41 Schwartz, *Housing Policy in the United States*.

42 J. Rosie Tighe, "How Race and Class Stereotyping Shapes Attitudes Toward Affordable Housing," *Housing Studies*, 2012, 1–22; Edward G. Goetz, *The One-Way Street of Integration: Fair Housing and the Pursuit of Racial Justice in American Cities* (Ithaca: Cornell University Press, 2018).

43 Edward G. Goetz, *New Deal in Ruins: Race, Economic Justice, and Public Housing Policy* (Ithaca, NY: Cornell University Press, 2013); Vale, *Purging the Poorest: Public Housing and the Design Politics of Twice-Cleared Communities*; Richard Rothstein, *The Color of Law: A Forgotten History of How Our Government Segregated America*, First edition (New York, London: Liveright Publishing Corporation, a division of W. W. Norton & Company, 2017).

44 Sutherland, J., Village of Euclid v Ambler Realty Company, No. 31 (US Supreme Court November 22, 1926).

45 Elizabeth Mueller and Sarah Dooling, "Sustainability and Vulnerability: Integrating Equity into Plans for Central City Redevelopment," *Journal of Urbanism* 4, no. 3 (2011): 201–22.

46 Goetz, *New Deal in Ruins: Race, Economic Justice, and Public Housing Policy*; Reina and Begley, "Will They Stay or Will They Go: Predicting Subsidized Housing Opt-Outs."

47 Goetz, *New Deal in Ruins: Race, Economic Justice, and Public Housing Policy*; Vale, *Purging the Poorest: Public Housing and the Design Politics of Twice-Cleared Communities*.

48 Vale, *Purging the Poorest: Public Housing and the Design Politics of Twice-Cleared Communities*.

49 Schwartz et al., "Preservation of Affordable Rental Housing Evaluation of the MacArthur Foundation's Window of Opportunity Initiative."

50 Vincent Reina and Ben Winter, "Safety Net? The Utility of Vouchers When a Place-Based Rental Subsidy Ends" (2017), https://papers.ssrn.com/sol3/papers.cfm?abstract_id=2940015.

51 Christopher Klemek, "The Rise and Fall of New Left Urbanism," *Doedalus* 123, no. 2 (2009): 73–82; Ira Katznelson, *City Trenches: Urban Politics and the Patterning of Class in the United States* (Chicago: University of Chicago Press, 1981); Brandi Summers, "H Street, Main Street, and The Neoliberal Aesthetics of Cool," in *Capital Dilemma: Growth and Inequality in Washington, DC*, ed. Derek Hyra and Sabiyha Prince (New York: Routledge, 2015).

52 Kathryn Howell, "Transforming Neighborhoods, Changing Communities: Collective Agency and Rights in a New Era of Urban Redevelopment in Washington, DC" (Dissertation, University of Texas, 2013).

53 Howell, "Transforming Neighborhoods, Changing Communities: Collective Agency and Rights in a New Era of Urban Redevelopment in Washington, DC".

54 Brian Asquith, Evan Mast, and Davin Reed, "Supply Shock Versus Demand Shock: The Local Effects of New Housing in Low-Income Areas," Working Paper

(Kalamazoo, MI: W. E. Upjohn Institute for Employment Research, 2019), https://doi.org/10.17848/wp19-316; Tony Damiano and Chris Frenier, "Housing Submarkets and the Effects of New Construction on Existing Rents," Working Paper (Minneapolis: University of Minnesota: Center for Urban and Regional Affairs, 2020); Xiaodi Li, "Do New Housing Units in Your Backyard Raise Your Rents" (New York: NYU Furman Center, December 16, 2019), https://72187189-93c1-48bc-b596-fc36f4606599.filesusr.com/ugd/7fc2bf_2fc84967cfb945a69a4df7baf8a4c387.pdf.

55 Kathryn Howell, "Preservation from the Bottom Up: Affordable Housing, Redevelopment, and Negotiation in Washington, DC.," *Housing Studies* 31, no. 3 (2016): 305–23.

56 Marcuse, "From Critical Urban Theory to the Right to the City"; Mitchell, *The Right to the City: Social Justice and the Fight for Public Space.*

57 Harvey, *Social Justice and the City.*

58 Bratt, Stone, and Hartman, "Why a Right to Housing Is Needed and Makes Sense: Editors' Introduction"; Julian and McCain, "Housing Mobility: A Civil Right."

59 David Harvey, *Justice, Nature, and the Geography of Difference* (Malden, MA: Blackwell, 1996); Mitchell, *The Right to the City: Social Justice and the Fight for Public Space.*

60 Marcuse, "From Critical Urban Theory to the Right to the City."

61 Huron, *Carving out the Commons.*

62 Andrea R. Roberts, "Performance as Place Preservation: The Role of Storytelling in the Formation of Shankleville Community's Black Counterpublics," *Journal of Community Archaeology & Heritage* 5, no. 3 (2018): 146–65, https://doi.org/10.1080/20518196.2018.1480002; Brandi Thompson Summers, *Black in Place: The Spatial Aesthetics of Race in a Post-Chocolate City* (Chapel Hill: University of North Carolina Press, 2019).

63 Schwartz et al., "Preservation of Affordable Rental Housing Evaluation of the MacArthur Foundation's Window of Opportunity Initiative."

64 Mueller and Schwartz, "Reversing the Tide: Will State and Local Governments House the Poor as Federal Direct Subsidies Decline?"

65 Corianne Payton Scally, "The Past and Future of Housing Policy Innovation: The Case of US State Housing Trust Funds," *Housing Studies* 27, no. 1 (2012): 127–50.

66 Housing Trust Fund Project, "Opening Doors to Homes for All" (Washington DC: Center for Community Change, 2016), http://htfp.wpengine.com/wp-content/uploads/2016/10/HTF_Survey-Report-2016-final.pdf.

67 "Community Land Trusts," Grounded Solutions Network, 2019, https://groundedsolutions.org/strengthening-neighborhoods/community-land-trusts.

68 Richard D. Margerum, "Collaborative Planning: Building Consensus and Building a Distinct Model for Practice," *Journal of Planning Education and Research* 21 (2002): 237–53; Lawrence Susskind, "Complexity Science and Collaborative Decision-Making," *Negotiation Journal* 26, no. 3 (2010): 367–70.

69 Mueller and Schwartz, "Reversing the Tide: Will State and Local Governments House the Poor as Federal Direct Subsidies Decline?"; NHT, "The Preservation Catalog"; Scally, "The Past and Future of Housing Policy Innovation: The Case of US State Housing Trust Funds"; Wyly and DeFilippis, "Running to Stand Still: Through the Looking Glass with Federally Subsidized Housing in New York City"; Schwartz et al., "Preservation of Affordable Rental Housing Evaluation of the MacArthur Foundation's Window of Opportunity Initiative."

70 Howell, "Housing and the Grassroots: Using Local and Expert Knowledge to Preserve Affordable Housing"; Schwartz et al., "Preservation of Affordable Rental Housing Evaluation of the MacArthur Foundation's Window of Opportunity Initiative."

71 Diane Levy, Jennifer Comey, and Sandra Padilla, "In the Face of Gentrification: Case Studies of Local Efforts to Mitigate Displacement," *Journal of Affordable Housing & Community Development Law* 16, no. 3 (2007): 238–315.

72 "Project-Based Housing: The National Low Income Housing Coalition," accessed, April 28, 2016, http://nlihc.org/issues/project-based.

73 Leonie Sandercock, "Out of the Closet: The Importance of Stories and Storytelling in Planning Practice," *Planning Theory and Practice* 4, no. 1 (2003): 12.

74 William Peterman, *Neighborhood Planning and Community-Based Development: The Potential and Limits of Grassroots Action* (Thousand Oaks, CA: Sage, 2000); Alan Twelvetrees, *Organizing for Neighborhood Development* (Brookfield: Avebury, 1989); Mandi Isaacs Jackson, *Model City Blues: Urban Space and Organized Resistance in New Haven* (Philadelphia: Temple University Press, 2008); Slessarev, "Racial Tensions and Institutional Support: Social Programs during a Period of Retrenchment."

75 Kathe Newman and Robert Lake, "Democracy, Bureaucracy and Difference in Community Development Politics Since 1968," in *Progress in Human Geography* 30, no. 1 (2006): 45.

76 Twelvetrees, *Organizing for Neighborhood Development*; Herbert J. Rubin, *Renewing Hope Within Neighborhoods of Despiar: The Community-Based Development Model* (Albany, NY: State University of New York Press, 2000).

77 Ross Gittel and Avis Vidal, *Community Organizing: Building Social Capital as a Development Strategy* (Thousand Oaks, CA: Sage, 1998); Jackson, *Model City Blues: Urban Space and Organized Resistance in New Haven*; Peterman, *Neighborhood Planning and Community-Based Development: The Potential and Limits of Grassroots Action.*

78 Newman and Lake, "Democracy, Bureaucracy and Difference in Community Development Politics Since 1968."

79 Deborah Martin and Joseph Pierce, "Reconceptualizing Resistance: Residuals of the State and Democratic Radical Pluralism," *Antipode* 45, no. 1 (2013): 61–79.

80 Randy Stoecker, "Understanding the Development-Organizing Dialectic," *Journal of Urban Affairs* 25, no. 4 (2003): 493–513; Gittel and Vidal, *Community Organizing: Building Social Capital as a Development Strategy.*

81 Levy, Comey, and Padilla, "In the Face of Gentrification: Case Studies of Local Efforts to Mitigate Displacement."

82 Stoecker, "Understanding the Development-Organizing Dialectic."

83 Peterman, *Neighborhood Planning and Community-Based Development: The Potential and Limits of Grassroots Action.*

84 Levy, Comey, and Padilla, "In the Face of Gentrification: Case Studies of Local Efforts to Mitigate Displacement."

85 Janice L. Bockmeyer, "Devolution and the Transformation of Community Housing Activism," *The Social Science Journal* 40 (2003): 175–88; Rubin, *Renewing Hope Within Neighborhoods of Despiar: The Community-Based Development Model.*

86 The Urban Institute, "Federal Funds, Local Choices: An Evaluation of the Community Development Block Grant Program, vol. 1" (Washington, DC: US Department of Housing and Urban Development, 1995).

87 Levy, Comey, and Padilla, "In the Face of Gentrification: Case Studies of Local Efforts to Mitigate Displacement."

88 Leonie Sandercock, "The Democratization of Planning: Elusive or Illusory," *Planning Theory & Practice* 6, no. 4 (2005): 437–41.

89 Quick and Feldman, "Distinguishing Participation and Inclusion," 272.

90 Lucie Laurian, "Trust in Planning: Theoretical and Practical Considerations for Participatory and Deliberative Planning.," *Theory and Practice* 10, no. 3 (2009): 373.

91 Sherry R. Arnstein, "A Ladder of Citizen Participation," *Journal of the American Institute of Planners* 35, no. 4 (1969): 216–24.

92 Reina and Winter, "Safety Net? The Utility of Vouchers When a Place-Based Rental Subsidy Ends."

93 Lynne C. Manzo et al., "'Moving Three Times Is Like Having Your House on Fire Once': The Experience of Place and Impending Displacement among Public

Housing Residents," *Urban Studies* 45, no. 9 (2008): 1855–1878; Aime Thurber and James Fraser, "Disrupting the Order of Things: Public Housing Tenant Organizing for Material, Political and Epistemological Justice," *Cities* 57 (2016): 55–61; Robert J. Chaskin, Florian Schilling, and Mark L. Joseph, "Youth In Mixed-Income Communities Replacing Public Housing Complexes: Context, Dynamics and Response," *Cities* 35 (2013): 423–31.

94 Benjamin F Teresa, "Managing Fictitious Capital: The Legal Geography of Investment and Political Struggle in Rental Housing in New York City," *Environment and Planning A* 48, no. 3 (2016): 465–84, https://doi.org/10.1177/0308518X15598322; Desiree Fields, "Unwilling Subjects of Financialization," *International Journal of Urban and Regional Research* 41, no. 4 (2017): 588–603, https://doi.org/10.1111/1468-2427.12519.

95 Judith E. Innes, "Collaborative Rationality for Planning Practice," *Town Planning Review* 87, no. 1 (2016): 1–4.

96 John Friedman, *Planning in the Public Domain: From Knowledge to Action* (Princeton, NJ: Princeton University Press, 1987); Johnna Flood et al., "The Collective Impact Model and Its Potential for Health Promotion Overview and Case Study of a Healthy Retail Initiative in San Francisco," *Health Education & Behavior* 42, no. 5 (2015): 654–68; Oren Yiftachel and Margo Huxley, "Debating Dominance and Relevance: Notes on the 'Communicative Turn' in Planning Theory," *International Journal of Urban and Regional Research* 24, no. 4 (2000): 907–13.

97 Susskind, "Complexity Science and Collaborative Decision-Making"; Quick and Feldman, "Distinguishing Participation and Inclusion."

98 Kathryn Howell and Barbara Brown Wilson, "Preserving Community Through Radical Collaboration: Affordable Housing Preservation Networks in Chicago, Washington, DC, and Denver," *Housing, Theory and Society* (2018): 1–19, https://doi.org/10.1080/14036096.2018.1490812.

99 Ashok Kumar and Ronan Paddison, "Trust and Collaborative Planning Theory: The Case of the Scottish Planning System," *International Planning Studies* 5, no. 2 (2000): 205–23.

100 Quick and Feldman, "Distinguishing Participation and Inclusion," 284.

101 John Forester, *Planning in the Face of Power* (Berkeley: University of California Press, 1989); Bent Flyvberg, "Bringing Power to Planning Research: One Researcher's Praxis Story," *Journal of Planning Education and Research* 21, no. 4 (2002): 353–66.

102 Lawrence Susskind, Alejandro E. Comacho, and Todd Schenk, "A Critical Assessment of Collaborative Adaptive Management in Practice," *Journal of Applied Ecology* 49 (2012): 47–51; Innes, "Collaborative Rationality for Planning Practice."

103 Innes and Gruber, "Planning Styles in Conflict: The Metropolitan Transportation Commission"; Margerum, "Collaborative Planning: Building Consensus and Building a Distinct Model for Practice."

104 Kumar and Paddison, "Trust and Collaborative Planning Theory: The Case of the Scottish Planning System."

105 Since starting my work in 2011, Boston and San Francisco have introduced rights of first refusal. Other jurisdictions, including Minneapolis, New York City, New York State and Oakland are currently considering their own laws.

106 Kathryn Howell et al., "Creating and Sustaining Limited Equity Cooperatives in the District of Columbia" (Washington, DC: Coalition for Nonprofit Housing and Economic Development, 2020).

107 Market-affordable housing is housing that is affordable to low- and moderate-income households without subsidy. Also called Naturally Occurring Affordable Housing, it is the largest source of affordable housing in the US.

2 Preservation and Its Permutations

Welcome to the show Reeves-Shaw (What's Up-What's Up?)
Welcome to the show, 58 (What's Up-What's Up?)
Welcome to the show Stanton Road (What's Up-What's Up?)
Welcome to the Show Stanton Terrace (What's Up-What's Up?)
Welcome to the show, now, welcome to the show
Welcome to the show Wheeler Road (What's Up-What's Up?)
Welcome to the show Geraldine (What's Up-What's Up?)
Welcome to the show Savannah Terrace (What's Up-What's Up?)
Welcome to the show, now, welcome to the show

Rare Essence, 1996

Go-Go shows in Washington, DC are not events for passive spectators. Rather, you are part of the show through the call and response songs from bands like Chuck Brown or the Vibe Band and through roll calls such as in Rare Essence's *Welcome to the Show*. Go-Go is a music and culture that has been a baseline of the District since it started in the early 1970s, playing in venues and community centers across the District every night[1]. As he explained at the funeral of well-known local graffiti artist "Cool Disco Dan" at the 9:30 Club in 2018, through a combination of papers passed to the stage by attendees and the acknowledgement of regulars that the band sees in the audience, Rare Essence's lead singer keeps the beat while welcoming attendees. The names called in the song are a mix of individuals; numbers, such as 58 for the Northeast DC zip code 20258; neighborhoods, such as Trinidad or Shaw; and multifamily buildings, such as Savannah Terrace, Sursum Corda, Stanton Terrace or the Geraldine – almost all of which are buildings subsidized through federal housing programs such as Section 8 or other legacy programs from HUD. Decades after Rare Essence welcomed the first community to the show, the recordings act as an oral history of affordable housing, neighborhood change and community identity in DC.

As a result of the gentrification of DC that results in the displacement of low- and moderate-income households of color, many of the communities that are called out in *Welcome to the Show* have been discussed in the collaborative, cross-sector DC Preservation Network (DCPN) over the past 12 years. Some of the buildings called out have been preserved for or by the residents, while others have faced ongoing instability or loss as their subsidies expire or owners allow the buildings to deteriorate. But these buildings, like affordable housing across the country, are more than just a place to live for millions of US households. These buildings house and facilitate community and identity for those who can stay. They represent a broad range of experiences in DC's changing neighborhoods – but each has a story that contributes to a broader conversation about affordable housing preservation in the District and, ultimately, across the country.

The Geraldine, a 42-unit apartment building in Southeast DC, was built in 1949 when the surrounding neighborhood was 92% white, adjacent to the Maryland state line. The building was all-white and housed working class households. Over the next two decades, white residents fled to the suburbs to purchase homes using federally-insured loans and escape DC's newly desegregated schools in the 1950s and 1960s. Meanwhile, African American residents moved in, following affordable housing and new neighborhoods, which were steadily opening up east of the Anacostia, beginning during the Southwest Urban Renewal. By 1970, the neighborhood was 98% African American, and construction of new subsidized housing had grown apace. In 1969, the US Department of Housing and Urban Development (HUD) granted the owner a Federal Housing Administration (FHA)-insured mortgage to preserve and repair the building. As a result, the Geraldine was restricted to low- and moderate-income households. Less than 20 years later, DC Housing Finance Agency (DCHFA) supported a rehabilitation with bonds and added a Section 8 contract to keep rents affordable.

Over the next 30 years, the Geraldine would be cited for poor conditions many times. In 1994, the building was in such poor condition that District building inspectors deemed it unfit several times. *The Washington Post* reported chronic conditions issues and threats of eviction by the landlord[2]. The District government intervened several times to require improvements through code enforcement and placed liens on the property. The District made critical repairs, and organizers who visited the building found it in terrible condition 15 years later. However, the Section 8 contract was ultimately terminated in 2010 due to a failed Real Estate Assessment Center (REAC) score, resulting in a bankruptcy after two prolonged appearances on the DCPN agenda in 2008 and 2010.

The Geraldine is now categorized as a lost property in the DC Preservation Network catalog of buildings. As an early loss in the District's effort to track affordable housing, the Geraldine was lost almost without notice. The residents and the DC Housing Authority received the notice from HUD, and without a sale that would have enabled Tenant Opportunity to Purchase Act (TOPA) rights, the building was lost from the affordable stock. While residents could remain with Tenant Protection Vouchers (TPV), the owner told residents they had to leave, in violation of the law. Further, the covenants that protected the building's affordability were erased, and the owner continued to be cited for poor conditions. The Geraldine also represents one of the ways that buildings are lost from the stock. Though the common story is of buildings being lost through gentrification and redevelopment or sale to a private developer, a common pathway to losing buildings in DC and other places across the country was through poor conditions that resulted in multiple failed REAC scores – and ultimately a termination of the Section 8 contract by HUD. Though HUD has made this a last resort in recent years, DC and other cities lost many buildings this way, particularly in disinvested neighborhoods. It follows a pattern of property "milking" by owners that occurs commonly in unsubsidized housing, leading to higher profit margins than in higher-income neighborhoods.

In other properties, the pathway to preservation or loss was different and, at times, more complex. Preservation looks different based on the existing conditions of the building, power of the residents and tools available. But what is clear is that preservation or loss of a subsidy is typically a long process and displays a pattern. The Geraldine, like many that were lost, went through a long process of poor conditions and threats of opt-outs by the owner. Yet this information, based in tenant experiences, often goes unnoticed where there is limited support for tenant organizing. In other buildings in DC that faced similar challenges, organizing and advocacy, along with local government partnerships helped to preserve the building. The critical point here is that there is often time, if the data, advocacy and funding is available, to engage effectively, regardless of how one defines preservation.

Through this chapter I will expose the quantitative data on the neighborhood, building and historical context of buildings that were preserved and lost during that time. I use this to get a better sense of the long-range process and build on the governance, tools and policy that are the focus of this book to better understand the way that these tools have been effectively (or not) employed to keep buildings affordable. Here I explore the ways practitioners, residents and academics define preservation, the paths buildings take to get there and the patterns that contribute to the loss of affordable housing. I take a deep dive beyond the national datasets to follow the 161 properties flagged by the DC Preservation Network over the eight-year period from 2008 to 2015. I start by looking at citywide data about the buildings preserved or lost – including maps and charts indicating neighborhood type, subsidy and building characteristics. I then use neighborhood case studies to uncover nuances in particular buildings, including opportunities to intervene, points of success and failure, the tools employed and the outcomes. I coded the monthly meeting agendas of the DC Preservation Network to create coherent seven-year building narratives. I built on these narratives by researching the pre-2008 history of the buildings through land records, historic newspaper articles, government documents, interviews, casual conversations and observations from my time working in DC Government. I followed buildings that were on the agenda between 2008 and 2015 until 2018, but did not add new buildings to the analysis after December, 2015[3].

I identified lost properties as those that have been entirely lost from the means-tested, subsidized stock[4]. As will be discussed in depth in the next section, this definition is loaded. It was necessary to draw a line in the sand,

and this is a clear line for the quantitative element of this project. However, as the qualitative data will demonstrate, understanding how buildings are preserved or lost is as important as *if they are preserved at all.* These qualitative data allow us to also unpack *for whom* buildings are preserved.

Defining Preservation

Like its more commonly known counterpart "Historic Preservation", affordable housing preservation can be contested on form, substance and perhaps even period of significance. Affordable housing preservation – like affordable housing more generally – also has some often strange bedfellows in practice. Depending on the context and form that it takes, preservation can be an awkward and ongoing first date of organizers, tenants, banks, city officials, developers and landlords who may not agree on what constitutes preservation, how it should be done, or, indeed *if* it should be done. Although much of the preservation in the past decade in Washington, DC has been in the context of gentrification or speculation leading up to gentrification to prevent displacement, preservation of affordable housing has been the focus of policy and practice in Chicago and other cities as a way of addressing vacancy and poor housing conditions. The form and goals of preservation are ultimately driven by context.

Unlike new construction of affordable housing, which requires a site, funding and developer, preservation needs a broad range of information, tools and networks to be effective and systematic. The jurisdiction and community context of existing housing stock, resident engagement, advocacy networks and funding sources are the base for preservation. First, preservation requires access to the market to enable the acquisition and rehabilitation of the property. Second, assuming the building is occupied, there must be a knowledge and acknowledgement of existing tenants, including rent rolls, special needs, income, family structure and culture, among many things. Next, preserving existing housing must involve flexible funding sources to accommodate those disparate household needs, and additional funding to address the rehabilitation needs stemming from decades of deferred maintenance of the aging building stock. As a result, preservation can be defined and understood in many ways by the various stakeholders. Preservation can be about the land, the subsidy, the building or the people and can happen in subsidized, rent controlled and unsubsidized "market-affordable" buildings in hot markets and down markets.

First, preservation can be focused on preserving the land for affordable housing. For example, the redevelopment of public housing has been a contested form of preservation[5]. The subsidy (public housing) is typically not preserved specifically, but land is preserved for affordable housing, and frequently Low Income Housing Tax Credits (LIHTC) or another source might be used to build affordable units in a mixed-income format. While, nominally, former residents of public housing properties have a right of return, the timing of the redevelopment, unit sizes and screening requirements can stymie the efforts of residents from moving back. For example, the Capper-Carrollsburg public housing development in Southeast

Washington, DC was a low-rise development near Capitol Hill and the Nationals Park baseball stadium. It was demolished starting in 2002, but the development has only recently been completed. The development planned a one-for-one replacement, which means that for each subsidized unit that has been lost, a subsidized unit replaces it. However, the new units are not all subsidized as public housing, the rent for which is 30 percent of an individual household's income. Instead, the financing of the project was mixed, meaning that they have diverse funding sources, specifically the Low Income Housing Tax Credit, the rent for which is affordable for households earning 60% of the Area Median Income (AMI), or $75,600 for a four-person household. Because most of the families living in DC's public housing earn less than 30% of AMI ($37,000), low-income tenants need a Housing Choice Voucher to make the rents affordable. This approach has been typical in public housing due to the compounding limitations on funding for capital repairs, the multi-billion-dollar national backlog of repair needs and the inability to leverage private financing in the project. Over the past several years, the Rental Assistance Demonstration Project (RAD) has been a tool used to preserve the units in existing public housing by facilitating a shift to a project-based Section 8 contract and potentially changing ownership to a nonprofit or maintaining ownership while adding other funding sources to support rehabilitation of the project. The program has been critiqued because it puts buildings at risk of opt-out over time and privatizes a public resource[6].

Second, preservation can also be viewed as the retention of the existing subsidy. In this case, the physical building may or may not be preserved, but the existing subsidy – Section 8, 202 or other subsidy – is moved to a new building. This may be on the same site – as is the case of Portner Place near the corner of 14th Street NW and U Street NW, a gentrified and high-density corridor of Washington, DC. Portner Place was a 48-unit development built in the Shaw School Urban Renewal Area in the early 1970s with a HUD mortgage and a Section 8 contract. Portner Flats reopened in 2018 after a redevelopment in which the residents assigned their right of first refusal through the Tenant Opportunity to Purchase Act (TOPA) to a mission-driven affordable housing developer and, because of TOPA, the tenants were able to negotiate the terms on which they would stay. The residents allowed the new owners to demolish the existing garden-style apartment buildings. The residents also demanded a separate five-story building for the existing residents retaining the Section 8 contract. The developers proposed new buildings with more than 300 new units, including 288 market rate units and 48 new affordable units using the Low Income Housing Tax Credit at 60% of the Area Median Income. While the building form changed, the affordability and, ultimately, most of the existing tenants remained. This type of preservation can be effective in buildings that are not feasible in a changing market, were poorly maintained or, like Portner, are located in areas like U Street, where surface parking lots and low-rise buildings no longer fit in the urban fabric. In this case, redevelopment increased the total number of both affordable and market rate units in the project and improved the feasibility of this otherwise expensive project. At the same time, it balanced the rights of tenants to remain in their community.

Subsidies can also move to new buildings entirely. In 2015, the 549-unit Ft. Chaplin Park Apartments was coming to the end of the first 15 years of Low Income Housing Tax Credit affordability. The owners offered the building for sale, and the residents selected Standard Communities as the new owner who re-syndicated the tax credits and was awarded tax-exempt bonds to make repairs. To support some existing tenants who were rent-burdened, the developer was able to take on a Section 8 contract from Richmond, Virginia through a Section 8(bb) transfer, which allows a new owner to take on a contract from an owner who is opting out. This facilitated the retention of a deep subsidy that otherwise would have been lost, but also allowed a group of residents to remain in place. However, it also meant that Richmond lost one of the few deeply subsidized affordable buildings it had, leaving the residents with Tenant Protection Vouchers, but no fixed building asset. This put residents in the precarious position of having to use their vouchers on the open market and protections in the case of a future redevelopment. Typically, this approach is used within the same region because it ensures that the region as a whole does not lose deep subsidies when individual owners opt out.

Third, preservation can support the retention of the existing building, tenants and subsidy. In this case, ownership might change or new subsidies might be added to finance needed renovations. Wah Luck House, discussed in the previous chapter, is an example of this focus. While the building has retained its Section 8 contract, in 2018, the building was also awarded 4% Low Income Housing Tax Credits and tax-exempt bonds to fund much-needed renovations to the building. The result was that the residents could retain stable networks, location and affordability without having to relocate for multiple years or risk not being able to return. This approach was a return to the approach of the late 20th century when buildings constructed in the pre-war period were recapitalized and subsidized to keep residents in place.

Finally, while I have focused less on this for the purposes of this introduction, preservation is applicable to buildings that have never been subsidized. For example, the Norwood was an apartment building near Dupont Circle in Washington, DC. One of the gentrifying neighborhoods originally cited in the 1980 legislation creating TOPA, Dupont Circle retained market-affordable buildings like the Norwood into the early 2000s. The Norwood was home to a large population of largely central American immigrants, but it was unsubsidized. The residents fought poor conditions and threats to sell to developers for seven years, creating public awareness campaigns about fire safety and bed bugs and holding protest actions in the small lobby of the building to put pressure on the owner. Finally, the owner agreed to sell to the residents who received funding from DC's Housing Production Trust Fund (HPTF) to buy and convert it into a Limited Equity Cooperative. The HPTF funding allowed the residents to purchase and renovate, keeping monthly costs affordable while maintaining their community networks and identity within the neighborhood. They have subsequently partnered with a local church to develop community organizations and a childcare cooperative.

Throughout the book, there will be stories of all of these types of preservation in DC. I choose not to define preservation narrowly for several reasons. First, because preservation is dependent on time, funding, existing stock, need and access to the market for buildings. Keeping a building that is dilapidated or was poorly constructed in the first place may not be the best course of preservation, for example. But jumping to a mixed-income model may also be ill-advised. Second, I do not define it because residents have a critical role in defining what preservation means to them. For some residents, preservation is owning the building themselves, while others are happy to keep the affordability and their neighbors the same, and still others are happy to keep their affordability, regardless of the structure of the neighbors who live in their building. In short, it's not up to me to decide if residents are happy with the structure of their preservation. Finally, I leave it open because, ultimately, preservation is rarely perfect due to the strange networks that have to at least talk – if not collaborate – to make preservation possible. And, like any repair of an existing building, surprises always come up behind the walls – both real and proverbial – when the process starts.

Pathways to Preservation

As the definitions of preservation differ so do the ways buildings are preserved. More importantly, the issues of preservation have changed in response to the historic changes to the federal affordable housing finance landscape, local development conditions and the implementation of federal and local policy. Though certainly not comprehensive of all cases, the DC Preservation Network offers a window into these often-disparate routes to preservation or loss. Between 2008 and 2015, there were 161 buildings on the DCPN agenda, representing 21,480 units, or about half of all subsidized buildings in the District. The network, particularly in the early years, focused exclusively on subsidized buildings, and so this chapter does not measure the number of unsubsidized buildings that were converted to luxury housing over this period. During this time, 20 buildings, or 2,775 units, were lost to opt-outs and redevelopments. Buildings came to the DCPN agenda for two primary reasons: the subsidy was to expire within six months, or a participant – organizer, developer, lender or government staff – learned about an issue with the building – including building conditions complaints or tenants' rights violations; a financing or management issue; or rumors of a building sale. The network primarily focuses on buildings that were subsidized, but, increasingly, they discuss solutions to preserve any buildings that serve low- and moderate-income households. Buildings are discussed specifically, rather than on a policy level, and that information is recorded in the agenda and the database. Many of the buildings were on the agenda multiple discrete times, separated by at least one month, meaning that there were 243 individual events on the agenda over the seven-year period. I tracked each distinct time the buildings were on the agenda to understand links between incidents and start to see patterns.

Figure 2.1 shows the outcomes of buildings that were on the agenda from 2008 to 2015. To simplify the analysis, I evaluated four broad categories of outcomes: Lost, Preserved, Ongoing (or still on the agenda) and Short-Term Renewal (a subsidy renewal of five years or fewer). Preservation typically occurred through a standard contract renewal of more than five years (in the case of a Section 8 building) or through a refinance and rehabilitation, followed by long term renewal or, in the case of tax credits, re-syndication of the credits. The notable exceptions are buildings on the agenda due to a single failing REAC score. Preservation in that case is most often passing a new inspection that often requires small repairs, rather than a redevelopment, as REAC inspections can address both small and large issues with a similar broad brush. For example, Gibson Plaza, a 217-unit building opened on 7th Street NW in 1973, failed a REAC inspection shortly after its renovation in 2014. The inspection found issues such as a broken door, a malfunctioning smoke detector and other small items that were quickly resolved by the owner. However, other buildings failed multiple REAC scores, as in Museum Square 1, indicating deeper issues.

The majority of the buildings that came up on the agenda were preserved, and those that were preserved were on the agenda for fewer months than the other categories, indicating a less complicated process overall. This suggests that most preservation successes are not due to protracted fights. Figure 2.1 gives an overview of the data on the agenda. More than 40% (51 buildings) of all properties on the agenda were on the agenda for more than a year, and half of all lost buildings were on the agenda for more than a year in the study period. Almost 80% of the buildings that became at risk due to a termination or foreclosure remained on the agenda for longer than a year, and 60% of the buildings that were part of a redevelopment or had a tenant rights violation remained on the agenda for more than a year.

As illustrated in Figure 2.2, the majority of the buildings on the agenda were located in the gentrifying neighborhoods in the north and east of the District. More than 60% of these units were located in low-poverty neighborhoods in Wards 1, 2 and 6. The remaining 36% were located in Wards 7 and 8. This reflects the overall

Total Events	243
Total Buildings	161
Repeat Appearances	63 Buildings
Long Term Appearance	51 Buildings
Total Subsidized Units	21,480
Total Lost Buildings	20
Total Lost Units	2,775

Figure 2.1 Snapshot of DCPN Buildings, 2008–2015

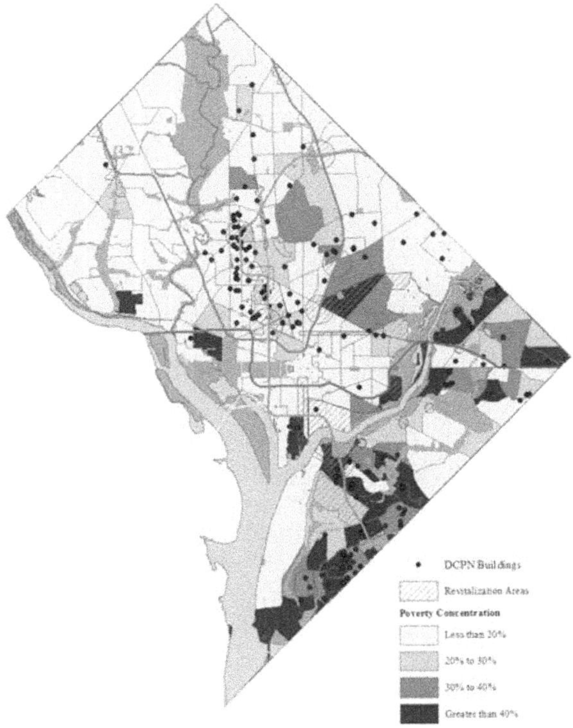

Figure 2.2 Map of Buildings on the DCPN Agenda, 2008–2015

location of subsidized buildings in the District and the patterns of redevelopment. From 2008 to 2015, the primary locus of development was in the neighborhoods closest to Downtown, meaning that those were the most at risk of an opt-out[7]. The bulk of the buildings on the agenda at this time were constructed or made affordable using legacy program subsidies such as Section 8, HUD 202 Mortgages or HUD 236 Mortgages for buildings subsidized and built before 1983 like the Geraldine. This is consistent with similar research by the National Low Income Housing Coalition and others about the risk to existing subsidized housing. While a handful of buildings had Low Income Housing Tax Credits entering their second 15 years of affordability, the relative newness of these buildings suggests that, over time, the tax credit properties at risk of loss will increase. In most cases in DC, coming to the end of the first compliance period led to a re-syndication and preservation. However, it also created confusion for those leading meetings in the early years. A recent article in Affordable Housing Finance Magazine developed a list of risk factors for LIHTC buildings including the end of the first 15 years of affordability, suggesting this is an increasingly pervasive issue in the industry[8]. DCPN addressed the risks by keeping the buildings at the end of the first compliance period on the agenda until they were certain of the outcome.

Figure 2.3 illustrates all DCPN events by the reason for their appearance on the agenda and the outcome. While all buildings with subsidies that expire within six months are added to the agenda, many of their subsidies are automatically renewed for greater than five years. Although almost half the buildings were on the agenda due to an expiring subsidy, only three of the buildings lost during this period were added to the agenda due to an expiring subsidy. In interviews and observation, an expiring use alone was rarely a concern among participants. Lost buildings came on the agenda primarily due to forced terminations due to failed REAC scores (6 buildings, 1,185 units), notice of sale (3 buildings, 594 units) and missing data (3 buildings, 262 Units). While the first two categories are clear, missing data is a little less clear. Often buildings came in because a participant would hear something about a building – they may have received a call or found it in asset management, but could not find information about the subsidy, ownership or status, which could trigger a longer conversation. Many of the buildings that were on the agenda for reasons other than expiring subsidies often came with more than one issue. Often a secondary issue arose when the building was discussed at the meeting.

Variable Preservation Outcomes

What was clear from the data – and as I discussed in the first section – was that preservation had multiple definitions, and one person's preservation was another's loss. There were many successes that were struggles in and out of

Reason for Building Appearance on the Agenda	**All Buildings**	**Lost**
Bankruptcy/ Foreclosure/ Termination	7.9%	42.7%
Conditions	6.0%	0.0%
Condo Conversion	1.2%	10.8%
Expiring Use	45.5%	9.2%
Failing REAC	9.5%	0.0%
Missing Data	8.7%	9.4%
Notice of Sale	6.9%	21.4%
Opt-Out Notice	0.6%	6.5%
Prepayment	0.4%	0.0%
Redevelopment	8.7%	0.0%
Tenant Rights Violation	2.7%	0.0%
Total Buildings	161	20

Figure 2.3 Reasons for Appearance on the Agenda for DCPN, 2008–2015

court and failures that happened with little fanfare. But the reality was that there were many paths to preservation and loss. While it is easy to dwell on the losses – as this is a common story in the unsubsidized affordable housing stock in DC, as elsewhere - there was as much variation in the wins, which were by far the bulk of the outcomes for DC's subsidized stock. Many had automatic renewals with intentional preservation by owners interested in maintaining quality affordable housing. For others, the preservation required significant tenant organizing in the midst of poor conditions.

An example of a preservation that did not require a lengthy fight by the tenants – though the process took most of a decade – is Delta Towers. Delta Towers is located at the Starburst Intersection of H Street NE, 15th Street, Maryland Avenue, Benning Road and Bladensburg Road. Now a busy entertainment and restaurant corridor in Northeast DC on the edge of Capitol Hill, H Street was one of the three corridors impacted by the uprisings following the assassination of Dr. Martin Luther King, Jr. in 1968 and subsequently became one of DC's 11 Urban Renewal Areas. Opened in 1980 and sponsored by the Delta Sigma Theta Sorority, Delta Towers is a 149-unit senior building supported by a HUD-202 loan on land acquired by the District during Urban Renewal. Across the street from the building is the 250,000 square foot Hechinger Mall, opened the same year as Delta Towers, which is home to a Safeway grocery store and several other retail shops that have changed over time.

Delta has undergone several automatic long-term renewals. In 2012, Delta Towers was added to the agenda because the contract was to expire at the end of the year. However, in 2013, HUD reported that the owners made a request to divide the property in order to build more than 100 new units on the parking lot of the building. This was the second time this proposal had been discussed. Over the next five years, the H Street corridor where the building is located changed dramatically. In 2009, when the sisters of Delta Sigma Theta first proposed an expansion, the corridor was largely two-story rowhouse businesses, including check cashing, barber shops and other businesses geared toward the largely African American clientele.

Since then, the built environment on the corridor has undergone massive redevelopment with a new streetcar line, an entertainment district, a Whole Foods and new luxury apartments[9]. As a result, the demographics of the corridor have shifted from majority Black to majority white. On the east end of the corridor where Delta Towers is located, the demographics remain mixed, largely due to the presence of the Pentacle Apartments, Capitol Hill Towers, Carver Terrace, Azeeze Bates, and several other smaller affordable housing developments within five blocks of Delta Towers. In 2018, Delta Sigma Theta worked with the DC Department of Housing and Community Development (HUD), the DC Housing Finance Agency and the DC Housing Authority to plan and finance 179 new units in a new building for senior households earning less than 30% of Area Median Income on the former surface parking lot for Delta Towers. The new building opened in the fall of 2020, and includes 18 permanent supportive housing units for those experiencing homelessness. The old Delta Towers building will be rehabilitated or redeveloped as affordable housing.

Delta Towers represents a preservation of community and subsidy. The new building retains its existing Section 8 contract, keeping rents deeply affordable. However, by building first, the current residents of Delta Towers also will be able to move directly from the old building to the new one without having to find temporary housing. This is particularly critical for seniors in the gentrified neighborhood in which the residents live. Finding temporary housing nearby – even with a voucher – is difficult, and yet critical for households dependent on transportation and access to shopping and healthcare. In the long-term, this also means that the community that exists at Delta Towers can be preserved.

At another building, the outcome of its preservation was different – as was its start. 1919 Calvert Street NW was one of the last remaining single-room occupancy rooming houses in the Adams Morgan neighborhood just east of Rock Creek Park. While not subsidized, 1919 Calvert was subdivided in 1964, like many buildings in the area, due to the high demand for housing in segregated Black neighborhoods east of the park. By 2013 it was market-affordable, housing 14 individuals with shared bathroom facilities. In 2013, the residents received a notice that the building would be sold, and that they had the right to buy it under TOPA. The building was in poor condition and housed residents for less than $175 per week in a neighborhood of 100-year-old homes selling for more than $750,000. The tenants had already been managing the building on their own because the aging owner did not have the capacity to manage it, making their capacity to organize and rally resources smoother.

The building came to the DCPN agenda by a community-based organization in an effort to brainstorm solutions. While it was clear that the building was subject to TOPA, what was less clear was whether it could continue to be a rooming house, if they could obtain funding and if the process would work into the TOPA timeline. Participants discussed potential solutions and partners in the process, engaging District government partners. Ultimately, they worked with a Georgetown University law clinic, a local bank supported them with the earnest money deposit needed to start the process and the tenants assigned their right to purchase to Mi Casa, a local affordable housing developer. Mi Casa then bought the building to preserve it as an affordable rental building. The Department of Housing and Community Development lent them $1,400,000 for acquisition and rehabilitation from the Housing Production Trust Fund, which ensured a 40-year affordability covenant. The rehabilitation was completed in 2015, keeping the tenants in place in a gentrified neighborhood.

In both cases, the residents were the primary focus on the preservation, yet in form, size, subsidy and resident population, they differed dramatically. Preservation can be done on many scales with different populations, reflecting the disparate needs across the housing continuum. Because preservation typically begins with the residents that are in place, rather than starting with an available subsidy and working backward, each deal and path to preservation will be a little different and require flexibility, creativity and, in some cases, a little luck. Different incomes, special needs and a range of family sizes have to be addressed in real time.

However, at both Calvert Street and Delta Towers, the preservation kept residents in place in neighborhoods that had undergone dramatic changes in affordability and from a policy perspective, facilitated affordability in neighborhoods where the acquisition of land for a new development would have presented significant cost and feasibility barriers. The preservation of market-affordable housing in DC and across the country has become a necessary response as city and county leaders and developers propose large-scale redevelopments and new transit lines that result in ongoing displacement at the neighborhood level. Only a quarter of those who need housing assistance receive it, meaning that reductions in the market-affordable stock represent the loss of one of the largest sources of affordable housing in American communities[10]. As a result, market-affordable housing is a critical frontier for preservation while communities also maintain their limited subsidized resources.

In 2019, the residents of 3218 Wisconsin Avenue NW received notification that their building was to be sold. The 20-unit building is located north of Georgetown in Ward 3, two blocks from the National Cathedral. Working with two community-based organizations, the residents organized and exercised their TOPA rights, deciding to purchase the building to become a limited equity cooperative. They received a loan from the DC Affordable Housing Preservation Fund and closed in the Fall of 2019. The residents have a mix of incomes, and, while some of the residents considered becoming a market-rate condominium, they realized this would have displaced many of their neighbors. The residents will now complete their conversion to a limited equity cooperative structure, make critical repairs and apply for permanent financing and rehabilitation funding from the District's Housing Production Trust Fund. Wisconsin Avenue is located in the wealthiest ward of the District where there are currently just three small subsidized affordable buildings. This building's pathway highlights the need to support affordable housing preservation in a neighborhood with few existing resources – and even fewer opportunities to create those resources due to the lack of existing market-affordable buildings.

These three pathways to preservation are but a few that are possible. Not all preservation efforts are successful or straightforward due to the challenge of amassing the resources, timing and people needed to make it happen. However, as the next section will discuss, these projects, like the Geraldine or Museum Square One, have long histories that can create opportunities for proactive advocates, government agencies and tenants.

Multiple Opportunities to Intervene

When buildings were lost from the subsidized stock in DC, there were multiple opportunities in which to intervene over the years. While not all lost buildings on the agenda appeared more than once, this was in part because DCPN did not first convene until the end of 2007. Of the 161 buildings that were on the agenda between 2008 and 2015, 40.4% were on the agenda more than once, 31.1% were on the agenda twice and 8.7% were on the agenda three times.

Repeat appearances were most common among buildings that experienced short-term renewals, or those of fewer than five years. More than 85% of buildings that experienced a short-term renewal were on the agenda more than once and a third were on the agenda more than twice. It is notable that 16 of these buildings had additional short-term renewals, and of those, 12 still were on the agenda in 2018 with compounding threats such as poor conditions or a failing REAC inspection, notices of sale, conflicts in ownership or a new subsidy expiration, meaning that residents in these buildings face ongoing housing instability. Fewer than half of buildings that have had a short renewal have been actively preserved, meaning they had a new long-term contract, a refinance or rehabilitation. Eight of these were preserved through a rehabilitation or refinance. For those, a short-term renewal was used while waiting for additional local or federal financing so that the new contract could start at the same time as – and be part of the financing for – another funding source such as the Low Income Housing Tax Credit.

Buildings lost after 2010 were lost after at least two distinct appearances on the agenda or under discussion for longer than a year. Although many of the nine buildings lost before 2010 did not have repeat or long-term appearances on the agenda, they, like the Geraldine, had long histories with tenant organizers, city and HUD staff, and legal services providers in the preceding five to ten years before the network started meeting. It is likely that, had DCPN existed, these buildings would have been on the agenda several times.

Another example, Lincoln Westmoreland II, was lost after threats of opt-outs from 2009 to 2013. Located in the Shaw neighborhood, Lincoln Westmoreland II was a 122-unit building opened in 1980 funded through the project-based Section 8 Program and constructed on property acquired and disposed of by the DC Redevelopment Land Agency. It was the second phase of a two-phase project that filled an entire city block between 7th, 8th, R and S Streets NW, which now faces the Shaw/Howard University Metro station. The first phase, Lincoln Westmoreland I was completed shortly after the uprisings of 1968 on the 7th Street NW corridor, along with several other buildings constructed with HUD funds.

In 2009, Lincoln Westmoreland II appeared on the DCPN agenda when the owner threatened to opt out of the Section 8 contract. In 2009, the Shaw neighborhood was already in the throes of a gentrification process that would change DC's Black Broadway – the U Street Corridor – into a high-cost neighborhood of million-dollar condominiums, high-end restaurants and class conflict. Though many of the subsidized buildings were preserved, the redevelopment or rehabilitation of the market-affordable housing in the neighborhood displaced the majority Black population. Yet the slow-down of the economy starting in 2009 reduced outside interest in the property. The owner also made no repairs during the recession, and in 2012, the owner issued the opt-out notice that took effect in 2013. Residents received enhanced vouchers that allowed them to stay, but over time, the population changed and those residents who remained reported feeling unwelcome. Conversely, in neighboring Lincoln Westmoreland I, all 110 units and the rental subsidy were preserved using a combination of bonds and 4% Low Income Housing Tax Credits for rehabilitation. In 2018, the owners then added 51 new units in an extension using a parking lot facing 7th Street NW. Like Delta Towers, this project occurred with no advocacy – but as part of an automatic renewal and redevelopment instigated by the building owners.

As was discussed in Chapter 1, starting in 2008, Museum Square One made five separate appearances on the agenda, and it had long history with organizers and city agencies in the six years before that. It was on the agenda for conditions complaints, threats to opt out of the contract, failing REAC scores and subsequent refusal to upgrade the building, resulting in 13 years of opportunities for proactive engagement. Among city government agencies, Museum Square One represents a missed opportunity. When the mayor introduced her Preservation Strike Force, a task force of high-level stakeholders in affordable housing preservation, in the spring of 2015, she cited the failure of Museum Square One as a driver for proactive policy. It acted as a public catalyst for citywide discussion of preservation.

Anne, a long-time tenant organizer, explained that expiring subsidies get the most attention:

> The big thing we would hear about at those early meetings [of DCPN] was like the universe of expiring – like the universe is huge and so people were kind of flipping out, but really what we should've been looking at and what we later started to look at was, "well, what are the real running threats and what are the real threats?" Failed REAC inspections, pre-payment of a mortgage is a sign that they want to get out of the contract ... An owner who's talking about re-developing and a lot of times they talk to HUD about that pretty early [...] the whole expiration date didn't mean anything because you have to have a year before expiration.

As a result, she argues, advocates have to be aware of more than just the subsidy expiration date, but also conditions at the building, conversations with HUD and financial stability of the building. Melissa, who has had several jobs in affordable housing development finance while participating in the network, argued that ownership is another key factor at play because "if you've got profit-motivated owners, with an expiring use property in a hot market, they would be stupid not to want to maximize their profit, and part of that is getting rid of your affordability restrictions." These additional warning signs offer practitioners multiple opportunities to intervene before owners opt out of their subsidies months or – most often – years later.

This was the case with the Sayles Place Cooperative. Constructed with an HUD mortgage in 1970, the building is located in Southeast DC near the Anacostia Metro Station and the historic Barry Farms Public Housing Development. Over time, the building fell into disrepair and failed multiple REAC inspections before local agencies were involved. The combination of HUD policy of cancelling contracts in buildings that repeatedly failed REAC inspections and Sayles Place's location in a high-poverty neighborhood meant that there was little that would be done to assist the residents. After its subsidy was lost, the building was sold at auction to investor Sanford Capital in 2013, which allowed the building to fall deeper into disrepair. Four years later, the building was part of a portfolio put into receivership due to the poor practices of the investor by DC's Office of the Attorney General, triggering a change. The Section 8 contract, which was under threat of termination due to poor conditions, was extended, and the building was purchased by a developer who made it part of the final elements of a 2007 HOPE VI project to replace Sheridan Terrace, a former public housing community next door. Unfortunately, the decades of poor conditions and bad management took its toll, leaving few long-term residents in the building, making it a questionable preservation from a resident perspective. The preservation of the building met affordable housing goals from a citywide perspective, but it did little to support the tenants' right to the city.

Missing Data

Multi-sector data collection and dissemination was critical to understanding the history and capitalizing on opportunities to intervene and disrupt the process of subsidy loss in Washington, DC. When the NLIHC developed the housing preservation database and convened the network, they identified a lack of information about where buildings were located, how – and if – they were subsidized, who lived there and the building conditions. By developing a consolidated database of federally-funded affordable housing, NLIHC helped to equalize the access to information. Inviting those most engaged in affordable housing to bring community-level data expanded the depth and breadth of the data available by adding on-the-ground data.

Building and subsidy expiration data collected through publicly available federal and local sources provided a base from which to begin when there was an expiring subsidy. Participants then provided both clarifications and additional points of departure for preservation threats. HUD participants often provided early REAC scores which tenant organizers used to determine which buildings they should proactively visit. Publicly reported REAC and renewal data often lagged the actual inspections and renewals, meaning HUD's information reduced redundancies and facilitated early action. Meanwhile, organizers shared information about conditions or tenant rights violations with the group that could provide a point for city agencies to intervene. As a result, over the past decade, the network has added buildings to the database as they learn about them, specifically, locally funded affordable buildings.

The network also enabled participants to differentiate the threats of the loss of a subsidy from misinformation or missing information. While fewer than 9% of DCPN events were due to missing data, data clarifications resolved almost 17% of all events on the agenda. Data clarifications might take the form of determining that an owner had already applied to a local housing agency for funding for a building and would not sell the building, or to explain the history of a building such as an ongoing redevelopment, existing land lease or other factor. This enabled the DCPN database to become a common source of data for government agencies, nonprofits and lenders to understand the background on buildings, the location of subsidized housing in the city and the buildings that are at risk of being lost. As Elizabeth, a government agency staff member explained, "I'm always thinking 'I hope it's up to date' because then I can make sure I use it for fact basing, so I think that's the other key part about the catalogue ... it made sure the facts were all the same."

In January of 2015, 1107 11th Street NW was put on the agenda because of missing information of an expired subsidy. There was a use agreement, but no one knew when it expired or what it included. The building was built in the early 20th century, and a 1933 classified ad for a one-room apartment with a Murphy bed and dining alcove advertised rent for $37.50 per month. By 1971, the building was vacant, and it was renovated using the federal Project Rehab, a program that used federal funding to support the rehabilitation and preservation of buildings housing low- and moderate-income households.

Over the next few decades, it would become home to a community of Ethiopian immigrants, but it also fell into disrepair due to a lack of investment by the owner. After several failed REAC inspections, HUD planned to terminate the Section 8 contract in 2006. The residents hoped to assert their TOPA rights to select a nonprofit developer and remain rental housing. However, the owner declared bankruptcy, which overrides the tenants' TOPA rights. The building remained in limbo with the city due to the poor conditions and bankruptcy until it went to auction and was purchased by a for-profit developer. The District worked with the developer to create a master lease of the building to support housing for homeless women as part of the District's effort to provide permanent supportive housing. However, this displaced the existing community of Ethiopian immigrants.

When the building came up on the agenda in 2015, most of the DCPN attendees had changed due to turnover in jobs, and few of those who had attended from the beginning of 1107's story remembered the history. But having the DCPN database and agendas allowed the network to clarify the length of the use agreement and follow up to make sure the building was still affordable. Having a common dataset also facilitated ongoing institutional knowledge about the state of affordable buildings in the District and an opportunity to learn from what was, ultimately, a mixed outcome for preservation; displacing the tenants, yet continuing to provide affordable housing.

More than just clarifying questions, preservation of affordable buildings depends on a multi-sector approach to data, involving a broad range of players to provide data. In 2013, tenant organizers in Congress Heights reported significant conditions issues, including a lack of heat and security in the collection of five buildings that were recently purchased by an investment company with a history of similar behavior in multiple buildings on the agenda since 2010. The buildings are located across the street from the Congress Heights Metro Station and the large-scale redevelopment of the former St. Elizabeth's psychiatric hospital campus that now includes a new arena for the Washington Mystics Women's Basketball team, the US Department of Homeland Security and new housing. With the assistance of organizers, the five buildings created a tenant association and prepared to exercise their TOPA rights when the owner applied for a raze permit to redevelop the property under a Planned Unit Development (PUD) application in 2015. Because the zoning board had not notified the DC Department of Housing and Community Development (DHCD), the agency was unaware that the property had a pending PUD application, in spite of the fact that they had an affordability covenant on one of the five parcels. When they learned about it through the network, they wrote a response to the zoning application, and continue to leverage their covenant on the property to prevent the displacement of the extremely low-income and disabled population who live in 48 units.

Since 2017, the owner has been cited, sued and had several of his properties put into receivership by the city's Office of the Attorney General (OAG). The successful lawsuit by the OAG prohibited the owner from doing business in the District, required him to divest of his properties and pay rent back to the tenants at several of his properties, including Congress Heights, due to the poor conditions in which the buildings were kept[11]. At the same time the DC Council has been working to improve the protections for tenants living in poor conditions. In 2018, it appeared a nonprofit housing developer would be able to work with the tenants to purchase one of the buildings for $3 million. However, the negotiation was underway while the owner was working with another buyer to transfer the properties through a foreclosure sale. OAG and the tenants dispute the process through which the new owner acquired the property. While this preservation effort is ongoing, its continuation is largely due to the information shared during network meetings.

DCPN participants relied on data from multiple sources, including published subsidized housing databases, funding information from agency staff, funders and nonprofit developers; hearsay from the development community; and conditions information from tenant organizers and leaders. In addition to clarifying potential threats to affordable housing, the data helped participants create a triangulated picture of the issues at the subsidized properties and the opportunities to intervene from multiple levels before the buildings could be lost.

Flexible Tools to Facilitate the Diverse Pathways of Preservation

As has been argued many times, preservation is about the building that you have, rather than the one that might be built. These communities often come with a broad range of household incomes, household types and sizes and building conditions. As such, preserving affordable buildings does not conform easily to a one-size engagement, financing, or technical assistance framework. The only standard approach is to engage with residents and understand the existing needs and vision for the community.

Many of the buildings on the DCPN agenda were built in the context of Urban Renewal Plans in the wake of the riots after the assassination of Dr. Martin Luther King, Jr. Notably, while Wards 1 and 5 were over-represented in the percentage of buildings on the agenda, they lost far fewer buildings than would be expected, given the percentage on the agenda. This was largely due to the use of the flexible tools such as TOPA, city-funded tenant organizing and legal services, and the District's Housing Production Trust Fund (HPTF). In the period between 2008 and 2015, more than a quarter of the buildings that had been on the agenda were either rehabilitated with local housing funds or the tenants exercised their rights to purchase through the Tenant Opportunity to Purchase Act, or a combination of both. Because the tenant associations have the right to decide to whom they sign their rights in the event of a sale, they have significant negotiation power in the transaction. However, as cases like Delta Towers and Lincoln Westmoreland I demonstrate, often, preservation of existing subsidies is a part of an owner's mission and happens without tenants exercising their rights. Figure 2.4 illustrates the tools used to preserve buildings by the reason for their appearance on the agenda. Long term renewals, refinance and rehabilitations, data clarifications, and passing a subsequent REAC inspection represented 85% of the preservation that occurred.

In 2010, five properties, an entire portfolio of Low Income Housing Tax Credit properties, were put up for sale by their owner 10 years into the first 15-year compliance period. The buildings were located in neighborhoods across the city. While four were located in neighborhoods that were still relatively affordable, one building, Mass Place Apartments, was located in Downtown DC, seven blocks from both Dupont Circle and the White House. When a buyer offered to keep the building affordable, the tenant association used their bargaining power through TOPA to push the buyer to purchase the entire portfolio to maintain the affordability. One board member explained, "We, because of our building being where it is and [...] as many units as it is, was what he wanted. He didn't want to buy the other four buildings ... we forced him to do that." The organizer at Mass Place, who was a participant in DCPN, explained:

> We wanted somebody who had LIHTC experience to buy them and people to invest in the long term, and so [...] at the network, I was just like, "anybody interested?" I had sent out emails – actually I had sent emails to some of the people in that room. At that meeting [I could say] "here's what's going on with these buildings and here's why you should come take a look at them." That, then was a real discussion.

She was also able to connect with organizers at other buildings and use their networks to create a common platform.

While the buyer did not upgrade the other four buildings after buying the buildings, the purchase enabled the tenants to remain in their buildings and to keep their subsidies. In 2015, the buyer put the buildings up for sale again, and

	Affordable Conversion		5+ Year Renewal		Data Clarification		Refinance and Rehabilitate		Passed New REAC		Secondary Subsidy		TOPA Assigned Rights		Other		All Preserved
	Units	%	Units	%	Units	%	Units	%	Units	%	Units	%	Units	%	Units	%	Units
Bankruptcy/ Foreclosure/ Termination	9	0.5	0	0.0	569	34.5	1,019	61.7	0	0.0	23	1.4	0	0.0	31	2	1,651
Expiring Use	0	0.0	4,466	50.9	1,581	18.0	2,372	27.0	0	0.0	179	2.0	171	2.0	0	0	8,769
Missing Data	0	0.0	0	0.0	1,775	93.2	130	6.8	0	0.0	0	0.0	0	0.0	0	0	1,905
Notice of Sale	0	0.0	48	4.8	0	0.0	64	6.5	0	0.0	0	0.0	569	57.4	310	31	991
Failing REAC	0	0.0	274	7.1	0	0.0	366	9.4	3,242	83.5	0	0.0	0	0.0	0	0	3,882
Condo Conversion	39	100	0	0.0	0	0.0	0	0.0	0	0.0	0	0.0	0	0.0	0	0	39
Conditions	0	0.0	187	20.5	371	40.7	353	38.7	0	0.0	0	0.0	0	0.0	0	0	911
Redevelopment	0	0.0	0	0.0	235	10.7	181	8.3	0	0.0	250	11.4	0	0.0	1525	70	2,191
Opt-Out Notice	0	0.0	0	0.0	0	0.0	0	0.0	0	0.0	0	0.0	0	0.0	0	0	-
Tenant Rights Violation	0	0.0	0	0.0	246	100	0	0.0	0	0.0	0	0.0	0	0.0	0	0	246
Prepayment	0	0.0	0	0.0	0	0.0	129	100.0	0	0.0	0	0.0	0	0.0	0	0	129
All Reasons	48	0.2	4,975	24.0	4,777	23.1	4,614	22.3	3,242	15.7	452	2.2	740	3.6	1,866	9	20,714

Figure 2.4 Preservation Tools by Reasons for Appearance on the Agenda

the tenants from all the buildings, now better organized and resourced – and in a far different housing market – had more opportunities to use their TOPA rights. Most selected developers to keep the buildings as rental properties, and one became a limited equity cooperative. The board president for one of the buildings that remained a rental property explained, "we talked to three developers I think, but there was one in particular that was very ... hands on in the neighborhood and in the building and the tenants before they even considered." She explained that the new buyer immediately addressed security concerns, created a redevelopment plan that kept the tenants in the building while they worked and have promised community services and spaces. The new owners will also use local housing trust fund support to rehabilitate the buildings, including security, deferred maintenance and updates to individual units for energy efficiency.

Conclusion

That affordable housing is viewed concurrently as a commodified asset, individual necessity, citywide resource and collective power means that its preservation – both the process and outcomes – is contested. Preservation can be defined as keeping the building, the subsidy, the community and any combination of those things. Yet goals for preservation can have significant implications for the power, community networks and stability of tenants – as well as the current and future needs for affordable housing at the neighborhood, city and regional levels.

In DC, the ways that buildings were preserved or lost – both in the macro sense and at the individual level are key to understanding the broad landscape of preservation. Exploring the "what" of preservation, this chapter helps to understand risk factors for the loss of affordable housing or the opportunities for preservation. But preservation in a jurisdiction does not happen without a deeper understanding of the mechanics of preservation. Looking back at these pathways also clearly highlights the efforts that residents have to make to be recognized partners in their own futures.

Buildings come in with a broad range of contexts – building conditions, community networks, financing, ownership, incomes, neighborhood conditions and histories – that create unique challenges for preservation. Many of the buildings that have been preserved in DC are in their second or even third preservation process. They were created by a mix of policies and funding sources, including federal Urban Renewal, FHA lending, local zoning and tenant protection. In the District, the large number of Section 8 properties is a critical asset for deeply affordable housing. But the lack of multifamily housing in other parts of the city has created a divided city where preservation is challenging. The impact of such a broad range of tenants, subsidies, building structures and tenant organizations is that quantitative and qualitative data are critical to making preservation more than a modified Urban Renewal process.

The governance structure also helped to make preservation possible in DC. District actors have a stable, long-term space that include the odd bedfellow stakeholders of affordable housing preservation – lenders, organizers, developers, government agencies and advocates - to collaboratively create and share data that can be used for action. The DC Preservation Network created data – and more importantly, knowledge – built trust, made connections between sectors and build knowledge among participants. At the same time, data-sharing was only one piece of the preservation landscape. The existing governance ecosystem for housing in DC has been developed over decades to advocate, challenge decisions and propose new ideas, while also continuing to build affordable housing, provide services, organize residents and engage in technical assistance about challenging processes.

Determining how to preserve buildings is more than acting one building at a time. Preservation demands a citywide and context-dependent policy approach that addresses coordination among housing agencies and between housing agencies and planning and enforcement agencies and the prioritization of the preservation of existing subsidized buildings. The broad range of pathways to preservation in DC show the roots, opportunities and challenges of preservation. On paper, the process for opting out of a subsidy is standard – a notification to the tenants and HUD. Preserving the building technically requires the renewal of a subsidy, re-syndication of tax credits or adding a subsidy. But what is clear about preservation when we look deeper into the process is that it is neither linear, nor simple. The successes in preservation in DC were not the result of a one-time intervention that was part of a short-term strategy – but rather decades of failures and successes in policy and practice that facilitated or inhibited an infrastructure for affordable housing.

All jurisdictions come with a similar overlay of federal policy that has driven much of the housing policy in the last century. The retreat of federal funding for affordable housing in the past 40 years has turned attention to the state and local efforts. More importantly, housing is inherently dependent on local and state policy around land use, code enforcement, tenants' rights, physical infrastructure and economic development investments. As I will explore through the following chapters, the ways buildings were preserved or lost demonstrate the evolution of the usage and limitations of the building, policy and governance infrastructures.

Notes

1 Natalie Hopkinson, *Go-Go Live: The Musical Life and Death of a Chocolate City* (Durham: Duke University Press, 2012).

2 Hamil Harris, "Complaints Put Roof Over DC Tenants' Heads," *Washington Post*, January 29, 1994, https://www.washingtonpost.com/archive/local/1994/01/29/complaints-put-a-roof-over-dc-tenants-heads/4e673d74-d002-41df-b3de-a141ea3ac6d9/.

3 I then coded the narratives for: the reason for appearing on the agenda, the actors involved, the actions of the DCPN, the date the building came on and off the agenda for each preservation event and how the buildings were preserved or lost. These data were entered into a spreadsheet to quantify the movement of buildings through time and subsidy.

4 This includes buildings that lost their subsidies and have subsequently reverted to rent control because they are no longer means-tested, and buildings where residents remained with individual Housing Choice Vouchers after the subsidy was lost.

5 Lynne C. Manzo et al., "'Moving Three Times Is Like Having Your House on Fire Once': The Experience of Place and Impending Displacement among Public Housing Residents," *Urban Studies* 45, no. 9 (2008): 1855–1878; Aime Thurber and James Fraser, "Disrupting the Order of Things: Public Housing Tenant Organizing for Material, Political and Epistemological Justice," *Cities* 57 (2016): 55–61; Robert J. Chaskin and Mark L. Joseph, "Contested Space: Design Principals and Regulatory Regimes in Mixed-Income Communities in Chicago," *The Annals of the American Academy of Political and Social Sciences* 660 (2015): 136–54; Lawrence Vale, *Purging the Poorest: Public Housing and the Design Politics of Twice-Cleared Communities* (Chicago: University of Chicago Press, 2013).

6 Alex Schwartz, "Future Prospects for Public Housing in the United States: Lessons From the Rental Assistance Demonstration Program," *Housing Policy Debate* 27, no. 5 (2017): 789–806, https://doi.org/10.1080/10511482.2017.1287113.

7 Vincent Reina and Jaclene Begley, "Will They Stay or Will They Go: Predicting Subsidized Housing Opt-Outs," *Journal of Housing Economics* 14 (2014): 1–16.

8 David Davenport, "Your Project May Be Headed for a Dispute as It Nears the End of Its Compliance Period" (Affordable Housing Finance, January 27, 2020), https://www.housingfinance.com/management-operations/10-red-flags-for-year-15-deals_o.

9 Brandi Thompson Summers, *Black in Place: The Spatial Aesthetics of Race in a Post-Chocolate City* (Chapel Hill: University of North Carolina Press, 2019).

10 National Low Income Housing Coalition, "State and City Funded Rental Housing Programs" (NLIHC, 2020), https://nlihc.org/state-and-city-funded-rental-housing-programs.

11 OAG, "Attorney General Racine Sues Sanford Capital for Violating District's Housing Laws at Second Complex in Ward 8" (DC Office of the Attorney General, October 26, 2016), https://oag.dc.gov/release/attorney-general-racine-sues-sanford-capital; Andrew Giambrone, "Notorious Landlord Sanford Capital Agrees to Exit D. C.," *Washington City Paper*, April 28, 2018, https://www.washingtoncitypaper.com/news/loose-lips/blog/21002590/notorious-landlord-sanford-capital-agrees-to-exit-dc.

3 Building Bridges and Digging Moats

The Infrastructure for Affordable Housing Preservation

> In addition to the economic limitations of many Negro households, social and psychological barriers exist which impede the movement of Negroes into predominantly white communities. Although some progress has been made in several jurisdictions, the prospects for a substantive change of this basic situation in the near future is very dim. All indications are that the largest part of the low-income nonwhite housing problem will continue to by concentrated in the District over the next decade. If the District of Columbia is not to become the residence of only two classes of people – the high income white and the low-income Negro – then every conceivable and concerted effort has to be made to break the economic, psychological, and social barriers that restrict the Negro to the central city.
>
> DC Redevelopment Land Agency Office of Community Renewal, August 1968[1]

Hubbard Place is an apartment building located in the Northwest Washington, DC neighborhood of Columbia Heights, part of what was the 14th Street Urban Renewal Area. When it was opened in 1927, the 214-unit apartment building, originally called Hilltop Manor, was under a cooperative structure, offering "high-speed elevators;"and a "luxuriously furnished" lobby with office and telephone service – for "continuous twenty-four hour service" as well as "Select Neighbors" who require business and social references to purchase[2] (Figure 3.1). In a neighborhood where restrictive covenants were part of regular home sales and the 1904 advertisement for the new street-car neighborhood of Columbia Heights promoted it as "free from the objectionable classes," African Americans and other people of color were excluded from the building[3]. Interest in the cooperative ownership was lackluster, and the building was rebranded "The Cavalier" and advertised for investors as a luxury apartment building that "occupies a unique location in the upper 14th Street district of Washington, DC, one of the most thickly populated residential sections of the city, which is a community within itself[4]."

In spite of a lawsuit after the stock market crash in October of 1928, classified ads suggest the building remained an all-white luxury building throughout the 1950s in the context of a neighborhood whose racially restrictive covenants governed the structure of housing until they were no longer enforceable in 1948. However, the neighborhood had faced significant housing challenges as continued

Figure 3.1 Hilltop Manor Classified Advertisement

redlining and direct legal discrimination in the suburbs limited the ability of the growing population of African Americans to move around or out of the city to the growing suburbs of Maryland and Virginia. DC schools were desegregated in 1954, and white residents in Columbia Heights began moving rapidly with federally-insured mortgages in segregated neighborhoods. A 1965 report on the challenges facing the neighborhood explained that African Americans in Columbia Heights paid more in rent than their white suburban counterparts for housing that was in poor condition[5]. In the late 1960s, rents at The Cavalier dropped noticeably, and, by late 1972, building conditions had declined significantly. Tenants reported "no heat or hot water, creeping roaches, unjustified summonses, bottomless sinks, broken refrigerators, falling plaster in the building, and the landlord reported that half of the tenants were rent delinquent due to a rent strike[6]."

Located in the 14th Street Urban Renewal Area, The Cavalier was in the middle of the slow neighborhood rebuilding process of Columbia Heights after the uprisings in 1968 following the assassination of Dr. Martin Luther King, Jr. The eight days of unrest resulted in significant property damage on 14th Street, as well as 7th Street NW and H Street NE. The President of the United States called in the Army to cordon off federal and white sections of the District. But when the dust settled, the National Capital Planning Commission and Redevelopment Land Agency kicked off an Urban Renewal process that engaged radical groups in the neighborhood.

The tenants of The Cavalier appealed to the District's Redevelopment Land Agency (RLA) for assistance, and The Cavalier, like several buildings in the Upper 14th Street Urban Renewal Area, was eventually rehabilitated and subsidized using the federal Project Rehab and the Section 8 program. This building joined 18 other buildings that were renovated or built for low- and moderate-income households within the 14th Street Urban Renewal Area to house residents displaced inside and outside of the neighborhood.

In spite of the construction, the pattern of decline and disinvestment repeated over the next three decades. By the early 2000s, The Cavalier had all the hallmarks of a distressed project-based Section 8 property, including significant code violations, failing REAC scores, significant drug activity, violence inside and outside of the building, and general neglect by the owners. In an interview, Jean, an African American woman and tenant leader who lived in the building for more than 20 years, discussed the state of the building when she moved in:

INTERVIEWER: So, what was going on?
INTERVIEWEE: The drugs.
INTERVIEWER: The drugs.
INTERVIEWEE: Maybe the prostitution for the drugs. We had seniors in here that were being held hostage if you don't sell drugs. It was really bad you know? They were scared. If you go up on the elevator, I lived on the first floor, you may get jacked. That's how it was. But there were a lot of good people here. There were a lot of good people. They outweighed the bad.

She also explained that security was lax or non-existent, the building was overcrowded and poorly managed, and had significant maintenance issues. At the same time, the neighborhood around the building, Columbia Heights, was undergoing a massive change. After the uprisings in 1968, the Redevelopment Land Agency (RLA) acquired 13 acres in the heart of the neighborhood, which were left mostly vacant for almost 40 years with few improvements. In 1998, a new Metro stop opened, and the neighborhood held a three-day charrette to plan for the neighborhood. The process continued for a year and resulted in plan principles for maintaining community diversity and accepting additional density on the 14th Street corridor to accommodate growth. In 2002, the District disposed of the land to developers to implement a neighborhood-based plan for dense, transit-oriented development. Between 2000 and 2010, the neighborhood added thousands of housing units, a mixed-use retail building with big box anchors, and improvements and development of five public spaces across the neighborhood. At the same time, the neighborhood demographics visibly changed. White population increased by 326%, African American population declined by 26% and the Latinx population declined by 11%.

New residents of Columbia Heights outside The Cavalier complained about the building due to violence and drug activity in the building, yet the building reflected the larger trends of landlord disinvestment and surrounding neighborhood neglect and vacancy. When The Cavalier was put up for sale again in 2005, the tenants exercised their rights using the District's Tenant Opportunity to Purchase Act (TOPA), which gives tenants the right of first refusal when their building is for sale, and selected a mission-driven developer to purchase it, retain the Section 8 subsidy and rehabilitate it using Low Income Housing Tax Credits and Historic Tax Credits. The building's for-profit, mission-driven developer-owner explained:

> We worked on it for about three or four years before we finally got control of it working with the tenants, had a lot of tenant meetings ... and now it is just a complete – total transformation. Beautiful physically, socially, there have been vibrant resident services programs that became actively part of – involved in – school programs, summer camp, computer training, programs for adults, just all kinds of stuff – just wonderful, wonderful. And all very low-income, federally assisted Section 8 [...] people who wouldn't have lived there had the market forces accelerated the market conversion situation that they [the previous owners] were intentionally trying [to intentionally fail HUD inspections] to get the Section 8 contract canceled.

Similarly, the tenants expressed appreciation of the building, including the community activities, improved safety and security, and the ongoing sense of community they have maintained before and after the preservation. The building now has a long-term covenant and contributes to the supply of more than 2,500 income-restricted units in the neighborhood.

Hubbard Place is an example of the long-term infrastructure of affordable housing in Washington, DC. Hubbard, like many now-subsidized buildings, was created as part of a high-density zoning regime implemented in much of the core starting in 1920 and was maintained as the neighborhood changed with a variety of funding sources and programs. Yet the affordable infrastructure has not been evenly implemented across the city. While neighborhoods of later Urban Renewal processes are home to a mix of rental housing and limited equity cooperative communities targeted at a broad range of incomes below

80% of the region's median, other areas of the city implemented a different type of housing infrastructure that precluded affordability, and still others missed opportunities to use government programs to invest in long term equitable infrastructure. Over the past decades, neighborhoods with Urban Renewal designations have experienced significant speculation, displacement and subsequent neighborhood change. Yet even with sporadic focus on housing policy and attention by the District in the intervening years, DC's Urban Renewal neighborhoods retained affordable housing that continues to house low- and moderate-income households.

Unfortunately, affordable housing is typically viewed as a social service or social engineering for individual households – access to neighborhoods, upward mobility, schools or jobs – rather than a critical long-term investment in community and citywide and neighborhood success that must undergird both new development and redevelopment. Subsidized housing is easier to track and ultimately recapitalize as the city gentrifies, the property ages or the subsidy expires, but the need for affordable housing is also difficult to address ex post facto as part of a social service regime. The costs for hard units become prohibitive, land is unavailable and vouchers – a typical "market" solution – are often not accepted in tight markets because of the competition for units and payment standards that do not reflect rising rents. As a result, there is a critical need to investigate the way the cities can develop comprehensive long-term approaches to affordable housing development that address direct and collective displacement from communities as they change. The rapid growth, rising home costs and increase in the share of upper middle-class white residents in cities like Washington, DC makes understanding the physical infrastructure that facilitates or prevents displacement and inclusion critical. Other forms of infrastructure – roads, bridges and bike lanes – that facilitate mobility in growing cities have been well-explored, but affordable housing is most often a social policy problem, responding to needs, rather than anticipating them.

Since 2000, Washington, DC has added more than 100,000 new residents, led largely by a 48% increase in white population. While the number of low- and moderate-income households has remained steady, the number of units affordable to them has decreased by 50%, and rents citywide have doubled. However, the District also has a significant stock of subsidized affordable housing across the city, including more than 32,000 federally and locally funded units across the city. Importantly, just over 3% of the District's housing units are subsidized using Section 8 and other place-based subsidies that were put into place during and immediately after Urban Renewal. The remaining affordable housing is funded through the Housing Authority, the Low Income Housing Tax Credits and the local Affordable Housing Trust Fund.

This chapter investigates how the patterns of affordable housing construction developed as they did across the Washington, DC in the early 21st century. I analyze historic affordable housing and archival data on subsidized buildings in these Urban Renewal areas over the past 60 years to better understand the importance of this type of infrastructure to communities over time, as well as the policies, networks and relationships that maintain these buildings as a critical infrastructural asset for the District. I also look at more recent zoning patterns that have concentrated or prohibited affordable housing in neighborhoods across the city. I investigate the ways in which housing created in the later era of Urban Renewal has served as the base for much of the deeply affordable housing.

The Groundwork for Urban Renewal in Washington

In the late 19th century, Washington, like many American cities experienced significant population growth from international immigration, post-Civil War Black migration from the south, as well as white rural migration for employment and opportunity. The result was crowding into all available spaces – particularly for African Americans with the lowest incomes and highest barriers to housing – including the alley dwellings, subdivided single-family homes and poorly constructed housing in the Southwest quadrant of the District[7]. In 1873, the city prohibited the construction of frame housing – except in Southwest and Southeast near the present-day National Park – where it was encouraged because speculative builders of poor quality housing would start development that would create demand for higher quality buildings. In other words, the local government encouraged speculation and justified the future redevelopment of the area[8].

At the same time, elite social reformers were trying to expose the poor conditions in Southwest similar to Jacob Riis and other group efforts around the world[9]. In Washington, this led to the creation of the Washington Sanitary Improvement Company (WSIC) in 1897, and the Washington Sanitary Housing Commission (WSHC) in 1904, which were rooted in elite organizations focused on trade and civic engagement[10]. The WSIC and WSHC focused on the demolition of poor quality housing, and rebuilding housing – though rarely, it is argued – for those who were displaced. Two of the last projects done by the WSHC were Sternberg Court (1937) and Kober Court (1939), named after the first president and first secretary of WSHC, respectively[11]. Initially housing all-white residents, these buildings were low-rise garden style surrounded by green space, reflecting Garden City principles of the time.

A decade later, the area surrounding Sternberg and Kober was designated the District's first Urban Renewal Area, and in 1955, the WSHC sold the properties to the developer selected for the Southwest Urban Renewal[12]. Four years later, the Redevelopment Land Agency (RLA), the agency that managed Urban Renewal, bought the properties to satisfy its mandate for site control in Urban Renewal projects – with plans to sell it back to the master developer. But by 1962, the property had significant code violations[13], and the RLA was facing vocal criticism from Congress and local activists about the lack of affordable housing built and the number of African American households displaced in Southwest[14].

In 1963, seeing an opportunity, RLA announced that Sternberg and Kober would be joined and sold for $500,000 to the Foundation for Cooperative Housing (FHC), which would later become the National Association of Cooperative Housing (NACH)[15]. FCH had recently also developed a neighboring market rate cooperative in Southwest[16] and 46 others across the country in 1967 alone[17]. They would use the relatively new HUD 221 (d)(3) insured mortgage program for new construction and substantial rehabilitation that made the building affordable for moderate-income households and give the existing tenants the right to buy[18]. The 107-unit building was rebranded "St. James Mutual Home Cooperative" (Figure 3.2). Later the residents added a Section 8 contract to keep monthly costs affordable and stabilize the building[19].

St. James Mutual Home remains one of the District's affordable cooperatives and was nominated for the National Registry of Historic Sites in 2015 by the residents of the building[20]. Yet the neighborhood has changed around it, from the Southwest of alley dwellings and frame houses – a haven for African

Figure 3.2 St. James Mutual Home

Americans fleeing the Deep South – to a modernist Urban Renewal project of high-cost buildings for white households. Now the building is at the heart of change in the District, two blocks from the newly-developed Audi Field where DC's Major League Soccer team plays, three blocks from Nationals Park and three blocks from The Wharf, a luxury residential and restaurant redevelopment of the Southwest Waterfront. Yet it remains affordable and resident-owned. St. James is part of the infrastructure to support multiple periods of redevelopment and displacement in Washington, but its roots as a backstop to the Urban Renewal provide a critical landscape to examine that period.

Urban Renewal in Washington, DC

The case of the Southwest Urban Renewal Area typifies the worst critiques of Urban Renewal: lack of community control, race-based decision-making about neighborhood destruction, wholesale displacement of African American communities and a lack of equitable redevelopment. The Southwest Urban Renewal Area spurred community-based protest movements, mobilization and public critique both by low- and moderate-income African American communities and white historic preservationists across the city. However, the District had 11 Urban Renewal Areas (URA) with different stories varying by time, location and political and social context of the time. Each iteration reflected the critiques of the previous era. Washington was also shaped by the tradition of mobilized communities, as well as its location in the backyards of the US Department of Housing and Urban Development and Congress. Figure 3.3 illustrates the URAs with the year of their designation starting with the Southwest Urban Renewal Area in 1949 and ending in the Ft. Lincoln area in 1972.

I argue the District's Urban Renewal can be broken down into three eras. The first, Urban Renewal before 1960 (Southwest, Northeast One and Columbia Plaza) was a traditional story of the program in which demolition, displacement, top-down planning and inequitable development were hallmarks across the country. Between 1960 and 1968 (Northwest One, Downtown, Adams Morgan and Shaw), the program shifted to focus on affordable housing provision for existing residents and to preserve existing buildings, reflecting a move toward putting Davidoff's theory of advocacy planning – which argues that planners should be working to reduce the impacts on those most marginalized in society – in practice. Finally, after the 1968 uprisings in Columbia Heights, Shaw and the H Street corridor following the assassination of Dr. Martin Luther King, Jr, the program changed again to focus on community participation, as well as affordable housing, homeownership and the preservation of existing structures for the Downtown, H Street, Shaw School, and 14th Street Urban Renewal Areas. These disparate approaches illustrate key differences in the opportunities for the preservation and creation of affordable housing in Washington.

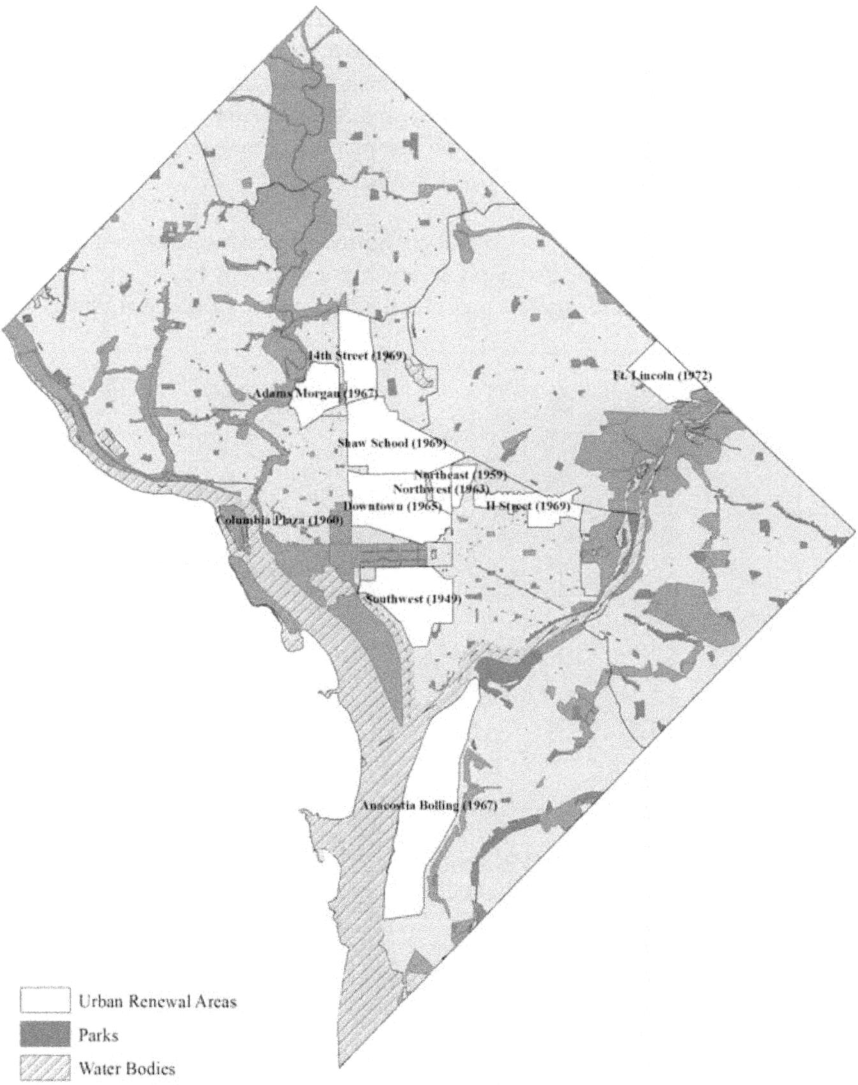

Figure 3.3 Urban Renewal Areas in Washington, DC

Southwest Urban Renewal

In 2017, Mayor Muriel Bowser cut the ribbon for the District's newest large-scale development: The Wharf. What had been part of the notorious Southwest Urban Renewal Area was now a tourist destination with a new boat marina, 27-acres of waterfront, two music venues, dozens of restaurants and hundreds of units of housing – 15% of which are affordable for households earning under 60% of Area

Median Income, and 15% are affordable for households earning less than 30% of Area Median Income. The materials advertise access to Downtown, monuments and other amenities of the city to encourage lease-up of space. As part of one of the two piers, the Wharf includes plaques commemorating the history of the neighbourhood. While acknowledging the thriving African American community in Southwest since the early 19th century on one plaque on the pier (Figure 3.4a), the plaque for Urban Renewal (Figure 3.4b), reads:

> At the beginning of the 20th century, Southwest was considered a decaying neighborhood suffering from poor housing and urban blight. In 1945, the Redevelopment Land Agency was created and its urban renewal efforts saw

Figure 3.4 Southwest Wharf Historical Markers

Figure 3.4 (Cont.)

> the displacement of approximately 1,500 businesses and 23,000 residents, ultimately leading to the construction of the Southwest Freeway, the relocation of Maine Avenue, a waterfront promenade, and parks.

Notably missing from the presentation of history was that the strong African American community discussed in the previous pillars was destroyed and scattered – and, more importantly, that the land on which the new Wharf development was built had been taken decades before with little or no provision of housing for those displaced, many of whom found new housing with limited access to the core of the city where they worked and miles from the neighborhoods where they had built businesses and communities.

In 1949, the National Capital Housing Authority and the Redevelopment Land Agency designated the thriving African American community in Southwest Washington as one of the first Urban Renewal Areas in the United States. In the analysis of the benefits of the area, planners document the proximity for current residents to Downtown for jobs, shopping and other amenities. In spite of the benefits of the location, the plan focused on "maximum opportunity for private enterprise to undertake large-scale development and demonstrate the contribution it can make in the redevelopment program" rather than facilitating ongoing use by the mostly African American residents[21]. There were two primary proposals for the plan for Southwest DC, but the only specific item that did not change was the location of the affordable housing – at the far southeast corner of the neighborhood adjacent to industrial areas of the city and the Anacostia River. Approximately 99% of the buildings located in Southwest were razed and replaced, thousands of families were displaced and there was relatively little affordable housing developed to replace those units[22]. A block away from the new subsidized housing, the Frederick Douglass Memorial Bridge on South Capitol Street, which opened in 1950, provided a fourth crossing to alleviate traffic from the "large developing area of Maryland" and the growing population of the DC neighborhoods east of the Anacostia River where hundreds of units of public housing and post war single-family homes were under construction[23].

In August of 1960, *The Washington Post* published an article about an NAACP rally at which Rev. Walter Fauntroy offered scathing critique of the program, calling it "urban removal," echoing James Baldwin's "Negro Removal" epithet about the program[24]. District officials would deny ever having heard it critiqued that way when Representative Frank Thompson, Jr. demanded an explanation in a letter a few days later. Instead an official touted the 1,000 new units and the successful relocation of "hundreds of families to safe and sanitary housing" in spite of having displaced more than 25,000 people from the area[25]. These families were relocated to growing neighborhoods east of the Anacostia River and two miles north and east of Capitol Hill. At best, this response illustrated a lack of understanding of the needs of low- and moderate-income households in the District. Southwest was decried by African American activists throughout DC's Black neighborhoods and white historic preservationists in neighborhoods like Capitol Hill and Georgetown who were part of the nascent preservation movement[26]. By September, the federally appointed DC Council began the process of documenting the impact of the Southwest Urban Renewal on minorities[27]. By that time, fewer than 300 affordable units had been created in Southwest[28].

Urban Renewal in Northwest Washington

At the end of 1960, the Washington, DC Redevelopment Land Agency (RLA) issued a report on Urban Renewal. In it, they announced that Adams-Morgan, a neighborhood adjacent to Rock Creek Park in Northwest DC, would be "the first urban renewal project in the District of Columbia in which conservation and rehabilitation of existing properties will be emphasized"[29]. This would mark a turning point in the way that Urban Renewal in Washington was undertaken and a tacit acknowledgement of three primary critiques of Urban Renewal in Washington: the lack of housing for low- and moderate-income households; the indiscriminate tear-down of historic structures; and the lack of community engagement in the process.

In 1962, a year before the Northwest One area was designated, one official sent memos to several other agency staff members throughout RLA and the National Capital Planning Commission (NCPC) that included Charles Abrams' "Criteria for Urban Renewal" from the May edition of Architectural Review[30]. In it, Abrams argued that planning, a relatively young discipline, failed to understand the larger ramifications of the Urban Renewal projects. In four pages, he argued for better criteria for development because "the costly and permanent projects erected today and in the future will remain as monuments either to urban health or to urban paralysis"[31]. While Abrams' critique does not include a call for community voice or power, his prescriptions make a strong argument toward preservation of existing buildings, the need for the community to have a space to grow into the area and find space for expression, and that planners continue what exists at the outset of a redevelopment process. The memo and subsequent Urban Renewal plans suggest that this approach would be part of the larger goals of agency actors moving forward.

That same year, the DC Board of Commissioners proposed a residential anti-discrimination ordinance for the city. The 1963 report that emerged from hearings on the ordinance acknowledged ongoing discrimination based on race, the housing available to Black households was in poorer condition for higher costs and that "discrimination in housing results in, or is likely to result in, danger to the lives, limbs, health, comfort, quiet and property of the inhabitants of the District of Columbia"[32].

While this ordinance was not passed, the growing acknowledgement of the need to change both the process and outcomes of the District's housing approach is notable and previews elements of the Kerner Commission report of five years later.

In 1963, the Northwest One URA, located adjacent to Downtown, the Capitol and Union Station, was the first plan to demand specific targets for affordability within the area, essentially setting up goals for a mixed-income community. The plan required 30% to serve low- and moderate-income households and remain affordable for at least 30 years after the last modification to the plan. The plan's stated goals were to provide "sound and attractive housing for families of low and moderate-income," as well as to replace existing community facilities, "rehabilitation of existing structures wherever feasible; clearance of structures which cannot be rehabilitated" and more than 800 affordable units to support low- and moderate-income households displaced by Urban Renewal[33]. In fact, in 1966, in their report to Congress, the Redevelopment Land Agency reported that "the Agency became active, for the first time, in the urgent problem of providing new low- and moderate-income housing for District residents"[34]. The plan, while separate from the sunken "center leg" (I-395) highway construction underway in the neighborhood, interacted with those plans, proposing the development of affordable housing atop the freeway and further use of the air rights over the highway to connect the two neighborhoods across the highway. While the latter plan to build over much of the highway would not be completed until 2020, Carmel Plaza Apartments were built on air rights over the highway near its end on K Street NE, and it continues to serve 133 households[35].

By 1965, Adams-Morgan residents had joined together to fight Urban Renewal plans for their community, demanding a different approach than the one employed in Southwest[36]. Across the city resistance to massive redevelopment of Urban Renewal and highway projects grew through neighborhood organizations, nonprofits like the NAACP and through new organizations like the Emergency Committee on the Transportation Crisis[37]. The mobilization, including tactics like picketing the home of then transportation secretary Brock Adam, sit-ins and participation in community meetings led to a shift in the goals and outcomes for Urban Renewal[38]. By the time the National Capital Planning Commission started the Shaw School Plan, these protests had brought home the critical importance of working with the community. In 1967, internal written comments on the draft plans for the Shaw URA's process expressed a shift in thinking:

> I am in full agreement with Mr. Griffith's remarks on community participation and suggest that language to be added emphasize the close working relationship with MICCO (Model Inner Cities Community Organization). In fact, I don't see how this project can be successfully executed without it.

The archives on the Shaw Urban Renewal Area reveal letters of support from MICCO and other organizations for the program, the selection of contractor and an ongoing process of discussion with community groups. While this does mean blanket support from all residents, the focus on pluralism and advocacy planning in practice at the time suggests an evolution that is often not reflected in Urban Renewal plans.

The Shaw School Plan was not yet complete in April, 1968 when Dr. Martin Luther King, Jr. was assassinated, changing the game once again to focus on community participation, as well as affordable housing, homeownership and the preservation of existing structures for the Downtown, H Street, Shaw School, and 14th Street Urban Renewal Areas. These areas experienced significant destruction and burning of properties, highlighting the impacts of existing disinvestment and segregation on these communities. On 14th Street, the plan included the following priorities: "preserve historic buildings and areas as important reminders of past national and local achievements, events, and notable personalities. Retain buildings of architectural interest as examples of earlier styles and times as community focal points." It also included specific housing objectives to argue for focus on low- and moderate-income housing, specifically, "families and individuals within the Project Area should be afforded priority in acquiring new and rehabilitated housing"[39].

Community groups, including MICCO, various churches and the New Inner City Community Organization (NICCO) demanded greater community control of land. Interviews with participants in the process – as well as news reports and plans from that time – demonstrated a change in the type of public participation. One former NCPC staff member engaged in the process argued that the agency was predisposed to support community will in the process in the 14th Street and H Street URAs. He argued, "The community organization [...] really drove the process that resulted in writing of the Urban Renewal plan controls as they ultimately were approved and all that was built. Thinking back at the time in terms of the bureaucratic response, there was a lot of concession – acquiescence if you will – to the community preferences." However, in a 1972 public hearing to amend the Urban Renewal Plan adopted in 1969, a resident and member of the local organization Change, Inc., expressed frustration with the long process and poor timing of community engagement which was, from her perspective, "a clear violation of the spirit of community consultation and participation we are entitled to." However, more importantly, while the residents had a voice in some of the elements of the plan, they did not have ultimate control over the larger principles of planning in the areas, specifically land ownership or control.

The community organizations – particularly on Shaw and 14th Street – wanted a larger mix of housing and community control of land and rejected public housing development in the community. The plans were created to include retail centers, housing and community spaces (Figure 3.5). However, larger structural issues slowed and ultimately ended the work of the Redevelopment Land Agency. RLA executive director Melvin Mister pointed to the challenge of working "with more than forty major Federal, local and regional entities in carrying out its program. Frequently these various entities have conflicting, overlapping, and contradictory plans and policies"[40]. Moreover, continued racism in lending – along with a slow pace of development and ultimate demise by 1974 of the Urban Renewal Program – meant that redevelopment through private investment was virtually nonexistent. The primary investor was HUD, which funded affordable housing developments along the impacted corridors. The disposition of properties for homeownership, a priority in the some of the plans, was not implemented seriously until the 1980s with the DC Homestead Housing Program. Instead, the plans, which called for intensive retail and outside investment, would be shelved until the late 1990s.

A critical turning point for housing policy across the US came in 1973 when President Nixon put a moratorium on all new affordable housing construction. Notably, however, Washington, DC was exempted from the moratorium and received funding to sharpen the focus on rehabilitation of structures and rebuilding in the riot-impacted areas[41]. Thus, as other cities shut down new production of affordable housing, Washington increased production, creating or rehabilitating almost 1,100 units in 1973 and 1974 – and a total of 2,200 by 1976. The pace remained steady throughout the 1970s – with approximately 9,700 units being produced in that decade alone. Figure 3.6 illustrates the total production of subsidized affordable units committed by the time HUD no

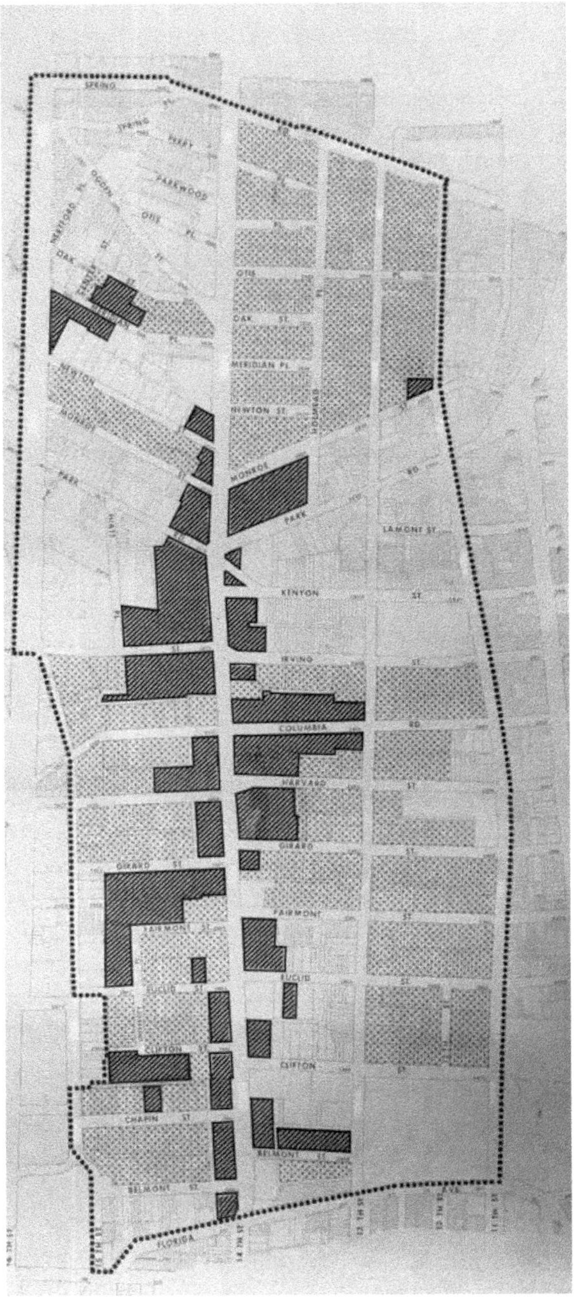

Figure 3.5 14th Street Urban Renewal Area Map

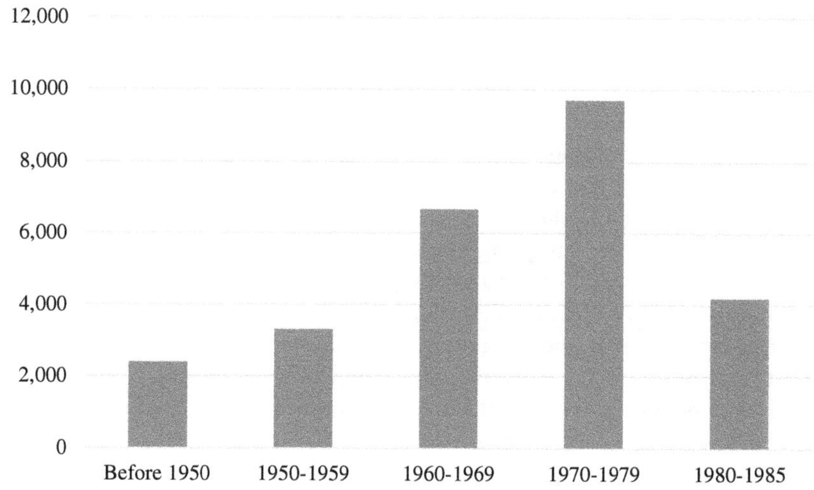

Figure 3.6 Total Subsidized Units Produced by Decade

longer awarded new Section 8 contracts for new construction or renovation. While rehabilitation and preservation of existing structures had been part of all of the Urban Renewal plans starting with the Downtown plans, little had been done to actualize the goal on a large scale until the 1970s. While the RLA built new affordable housing, they also subsidized existing buildings such as Hubbard Place Apartments in the 14th Street URA, kicking off the first of many preservations of existing units across the District.

Digging the Moat Versus Burning the Gates: Zoning Across the District

In 2018, the George Washington University Center for Washington Area Studies hosted "A 10 Year Reflection on the Williams Administration's Development Legacy," a panel including former Mayor Anthony Williams (1999–2007) to discuss the long-ranging impact of his time in office. Mayor Williams famously set what was an ambitious goal in 2003: increase the DC population by 100,000 new residents in ten years[42]. While the population was already on an upswing that started in 2000, no one anticipated that 15 years later, the District would add almost 1,000 net new residents monthly. This growth was uneven geographically, with some areas seeing growth of more than 100% and others staying stable or falling, and a comment of former Mayor Williams illustrated what numbers would show. He said he told his staff never to send him an up-zoning proposal for Ward 3 because "those people get me elected." This ultimately shut the door for new multi-family, much less affordable, housing.

Ward 3, the setting for books such as Gore Vidal's *Washington*, is the least densely populated ward of the city. It is also the wealthiest, whitest and most conservative in the city. The neighborhood is 82% white, compared to 42% in the District as a whole, with a median household income of almost $150,000. Bounded by the Potomac River to the west, wealthy Maryland suburbs to the north and Rock Creek Park to the east and south, Ward 3 has been protected through natural barriers, zoning and politics. In 2016, Mayor Muriel Bowser announced a plan to deconcentrate the city's shelter system and place temporary family housing in all eight wards of the city. Ward 3 residents unsuccessfully sued to prevent the shelter from coming to the ward, arguing that adding 50 families would disrupt the neighborhood. The court disagreed and supported the city's decision to build the 50-unit shelter.

Two years later, the DC Fiscal Policy Institute, a local thinktank, released an interactive map, to great outrage among advocates, that visualized the pipeline for the District's annual $100 million Housing Production Trust Fund[43]. The headlines across blogs and local papers decried the lack of units planned for Ward 3. Yet, as of this writing, there are only three affordable housing developments in the ward – a fourth was lost in the decades since its construction – meaning that this was not a new problem – but one that was part of a longer pattern of land use, neighborhood resistance and policy-making. While Mayor Williams limited the possibility for growth in population – as well as in affordable housing – in Ward 3, his efforts were merely a modern effort in an area that had been protected for decades.

In the late 19th century, the area that is now Ward 3 – as well as the western section of Ward 2 – of the District had two primary areas of African American settlement – Southern Georgetown and Fort Reno, adjacent to Tenleytown near the border with Maryland. Both areas – much like Southwest DC and areas such as Uniontown and Barry Farm in Southeast DC – served as havens for formerly enslaved people during and immediately after the Civil War. Georgetown faced an early form of gentrification as new federal employees moved to the neighborhood in the early 20th century. The combination of increased demand and a focused and intentional historic preservation movement in the neighborhood made the housing prices out of reach for the working-class African Americans living in the neighborhood[44]. Meanwhile, Fort Reno's African American population faced a more direct assault through the use of eminent domain. Originally far outside the city, demand for housing near Tenleytown grew in the early 20th century with the advent of streetcars and widespread car ownership. The African American community had built a school, churches, businesses and housing, and the area was majority African American. However, in the 1930s, the Federal Government authorized the taking of African American property to build Alice Deal, an all-white middle school and, eventually, Woodrow Wilson, an all-white high school[45]. This effectively removed African Americans from the community.

In a 1934 report, *Experiences with Zoning in Washington, DC, 1920–1934*, the zoning commission documented the changes in zoning since the District's first ordinance in 1920. The report stated:

> No distinction was made originally between apartment houses and other residences. In the building boom following the war, the apartment house became very important, and a strong agitation among home owners was

> started to exclude it from restricted residential sections ... As a response to this agitation, the Zoning Commission created in 1923 a new zoning district called "A" restricted, from which apartment houses were excluded. In 1926 further restrictions were added, so that only wholly detached single-family dwellings with two side yards, churches and school buildings were to be permitted ... This preponderance of the "A" restricted areas reflects both the popularity of the restrictions and the bias of the Zoning Commission in favor of those home sections[46].

The focus of this new zoning was Ward 3. By the time a map was created in 1937 to grade DC neighborhood for safe investment, Ward 3 was wealthy and white enough to be rated an A or B – both considered protected from negative outside influences[47].

In 1940, a proposed rezoning to build an apartment house with first floor parking on the portion of a Georgetown estate – one city block – brought out a fury of protest from well-heeled neighbors. The property was located at R Street NW and Wisconsin Avenue NW, now the site of a row of large, detached single-family homes. A *Washington Post* article covering the zoning commission hearing described the event:

> Cheers and applause by the socially prominent who gathered to protest the petition, greeted the remarks by Fontaine Bradley, counsel for the protestants, when he said: 'Attractive Georgetown would stick out like a sore thumb if the petition for rezoning is granted[48].'

Highlighting the elite power in the area, this protest of the change in zoning in Georgetown was ultimately successful. While race is a clear factor in the segregation of DC's neighborhoods through redlining and restrictive covenants, the ability to fight multifamily housing development in the District had an overlay of class-based power that maintained the elite, single-family estate communities west of Rock Creek Park.

Because African Americans had largely been removed from neighborhoods west of Rock Creek Park by the time Urban Renewal was in full effect in Washington, by design, there was no blight – racially defined – to justify the adoption of an Urban Renewal Area. The notable exception was the Columbia Plaza URA, located in nearby Ward 2. Adopted in 1960, Columbia Plaza is located across from what are now the Watergate Hotel and the Kennedy Center and three blocks from George Washington University, which experienced rapid growth through the first half of the 20th century. This URA facilitated the acquisition and subsequent destruction of industrial buildings and the creation of new luxury apartments and State Department Office Buildings, as well as interchanges for I-66 connecting the District to Arlington, Virginia. However, it included no affordable housing.

Ward 3 continues to maintain relatively large lot single-family zoning with exceptions for Metro stations along the city's Red Line and apartments created before zoning became widespread in the early 20th century. This protectionist zoning, combined with a lack of affordable housing construction and a banishment of African Americans early in the 20th century, supported by discriminatory housing practices through the mid-century, have pushed prices and, with the help of ongoing single-family zoning, have created an unassailable space in Washington, DC. More importantly, it means there is little affordable housing to preserve.

Impacts of Affordable Housing Infrastructure

The result of these policies, illustrated in zoning and Urban Renewal planning, was that more that 40% of all affordable housing created in the District before 1983 was located in an Urban Renewal area. Almost 60% was located either inside of or within a half mile of a URA. Those that were built outside of an Urban Renewal Area were typically built to rehouse those displaced as a result of the Southwest project, far from Downtown and city amenities. Of the 185 buildings constructed by 1983 across the city, 133 buildings used Section 8/221/202/236 programs for creation; 39 became public housing; the remainder were turnkey projects acquired through public housing programs, but largely sold to private owners for rental or for sale affordable housing. The public housing developments had largely been completed by the early 1960s, reflecting both the national trend away from public housing, the local preferences for privately-constructed housing and new federal rules preventing public housing from being placed in minority concentrated areas.

In some cases, subsidies were used to recapitalize existing buildings such as Hubbard Place and in the Upper 14th, Shaw and Adams Morgan Urban Renewal Areas, where there was a significant supply of historic multifamily housing that was augmented with new construction. However, in the post-1968 uprising corridors of the Shaw School, 14th Street and H Street Urban Renewal Areas, there also were several buildings of 100 units or more constructed in the 1960s that remain critical resources for affordable housing. A former planner with RLA who coordinated the Urban Renewal plans in both Shaw and 14th Street explained:

> It was an interesting period and of course we acquired the properties, cleared the land, and over time the RLA disposed of the sites. The early dispositions were for HUD-assisted housing – and that was to provide the affordable housing for the existing residents. Well, one of the consequences of all of that was that 14th Street – the 14th Street Urban Renewal Area – became designated as an over-impacted neighborhood in respect to HUD assisted housing.

This meant that they had higher percentages of affordable housing. As the Urban Renewal Areas – all located near Downtown except the Anacostia-Bolling area, which was to support the housing and redevelopment Bolling Air Force Base, the housing in these areas became targets for redevelopment as well as resources for preservation when the District started to gentrify in the 1990s.

As discussed in Chapter 1, Portner Place, a 48-unit garden apartment complex located near 14th and U Street NW, was part of a larger plan for acquisition that included much of the block starting in 1967. Supported by MICCO and other organizations in the neighborhood, the buildings replaced dilapidated and abandoned single-family homes on the block to make way for a new government building and two affordable housing developments – Portner Place and Paul Lawrence Dunbar (formerly Campbell Heights). While both buildings have faced potential loss and demolition due to the high redevelopment pressure of the now high-cost area of U Street NW, they have been preserved such that Paul Lawrence Dunbar has retained the same building and subsidy structure, and Portner Place was recently redeveloped, keeping the existing residents and Section 8 subsidy and adding 48 new Low Income Housing Tax Credit units and 288 market rate units to the formerly low-density development. Figure 3.7 shows the dispersal of housing constructed by 1983 in the District. 154 Buildings (or 84.2%) of the buildings constructed before 1983 are still known to be still active[49]. Within the URAs, 77% of the buildings constructed before 1983 are still active and 74% of the buildings in the half mile buffer of the URAs are still active.

Although the creation of affordable housing in these neighborhoods was critical to rehousing those displaced by Urban Renewal and riot destruction, the buildings were economically segregated for 20 years or more, aided by redlining and restrictive zoning in DC's white and wealthy neighborhoods. Figure 3.8 shows the neighborhood poverty rates for affordable housing constructed before 1983 in 1980 and 2015. In 1983, only 16 of the 148 buildings still operating today were located in low poverty neighborhoods[50]. By 2015, that number rose to 58. Meanwhile the number located in high poverty neighborhoods fell from 131 buildings in 1980 to 89 by 2015. The bulk of the 24 buildings located in neighborhoods with poverty rates between 20 and 29.9% are in the midst of gentrified neighborhoods in which the subsidized housing itself is a primary factor in the poverty rate. For example, those located along the 7th Street NW, 14th Street NW and H Street NE corridors play an outsized role in the tract-level poverty rate because the surrounding market rate housing is largely single-family homes or small apartment buildings.

While the number of buildings located in neighborhoods with poverty rates above 40% remained high (38 buildings), it is worth noting that five of those buildings are in one census tract that is bordered by three large-scale mixed-use redevelopments on all sides that has gentrified the neighborhood outside the affordable buildings – specifically the affordable housing created in the Southwest Urban Renewal plan – which are bounded by redevelopments surrounding Nationals Park and Audi Field, where DC United, the District's Major League Soccer team play. Meanwhile eight additional buildings are located adjacent to the 356-acre St. Elizabeth's hospital redevelopment, where the US Department of Homeland Security has created a new headquarters and the District has invested significant funding for mixed-use development. In other words, the concentration of the affordable housing within the tracts itself results in the high poverty rate, demonstrating both the historic decisions to concentrate affordable housing and the vulnerability of these buildings to redevelopment in

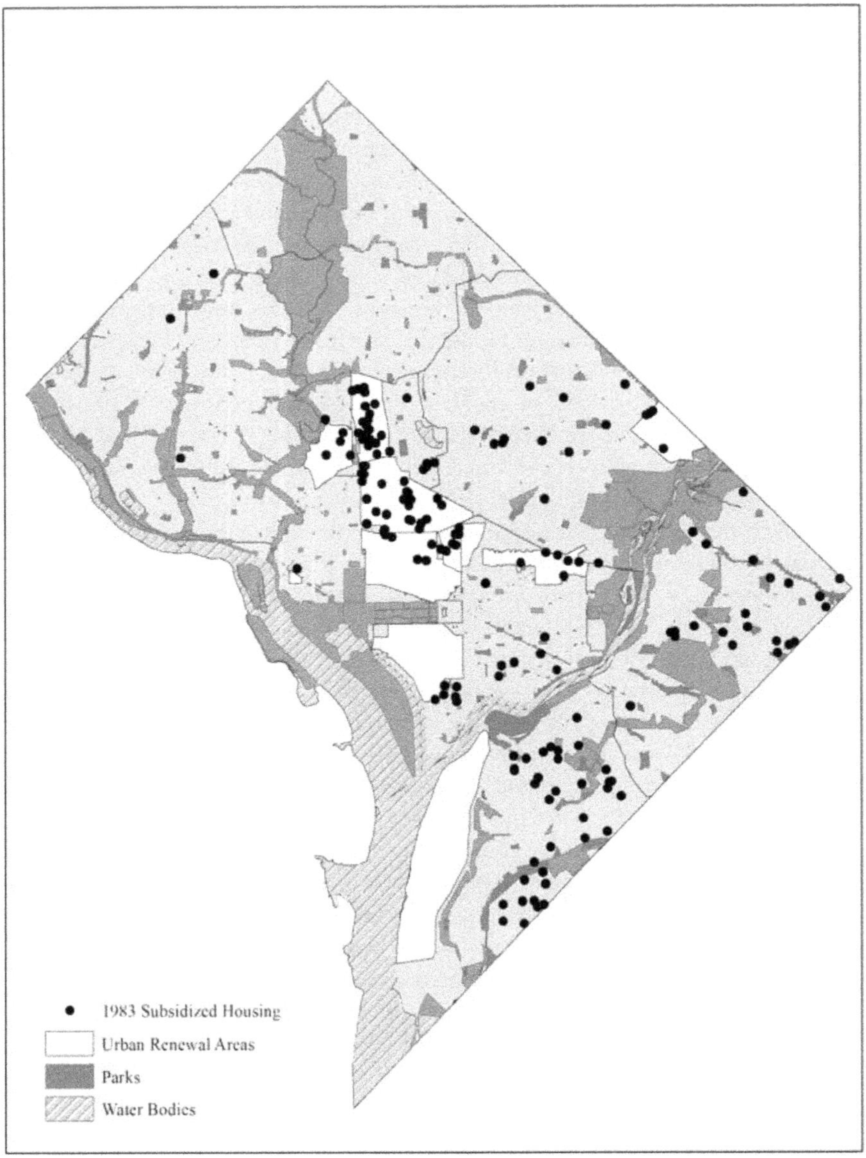

Figure 3.7 Urban Renewal Areas with Subsidized Housing Built by 1983

the present. It seems likely that these neighborhoods also will change dramatically over the next five years, putting pressure on the market-affordable rental housing, as is evidenced by the speculation and redevelopment in the area[51].

By the mid-2000s, the city's Urban Renewal Areas were booming due to investments in transportation, infrastructure and buildings along with concurrent

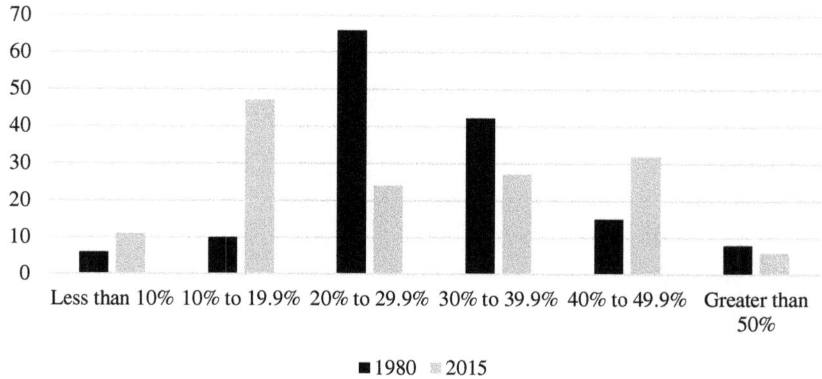

Figure 3.8 Poverty Rates for Neighborhoods of Buildings Constructed Before 1983 in 1980 and 2015

national trends of aggressive promotion of homeownership, widespread delays in family formation and migration to cities by young affluent and educated – largely white – residents. At the same time, the city government invested in affordable housing across the city using federal sources such as the Federal Low Income Housing Tax Credit (starting in 1986), HOME Investment Partnership (HOME) and Community Development Block Grant (CDBG) and local funding through the Housing Production Trust Fund (HPTF) starting in 2002. The HPTF has a dedicated funding source from 15% of transfer taxes on all real estate transactions, meaning that as the housing market moves faster, there are more funds available for affordable housing. This created greater capacity to preserve housing, albeit at higher prices than a steadier funding source would allow. Figure 3.9 illustrates the change in the number of affordable units inside of URAs in 1983 and 2015. More than three quarters of the buildings constructed before 1983 inside of Urban Renewal Areas have been preserved. On top of that, the number of units inside of URAs has increased or remained stable in all URAs except Northwest, suggesting that the patterns created in the early and mid-20th century have continued.

Figure 3.10 highlights the change in the number of units within a half mile radius of an Urban Renewal Area. What is clear citywide is that the number of subsidized units near Urban Renewal Areas has increased, following a citywide trend of both retention and increases in units. However, what is most notable is the 210% increase in units adjacent to the Anacostia-Bolling URA. The neighborhoods surrounding Anacostia-Bolling have been one of the areas where those displaced by Urban Renewal in Southwest moved. In the wake of white flight, driven by policy and individual decisions about redlining, the end of restrictive covenants and school desegregation, this area, and Ward 8 more broadly, has been highly segregated and disinvested. Thus, the affordable

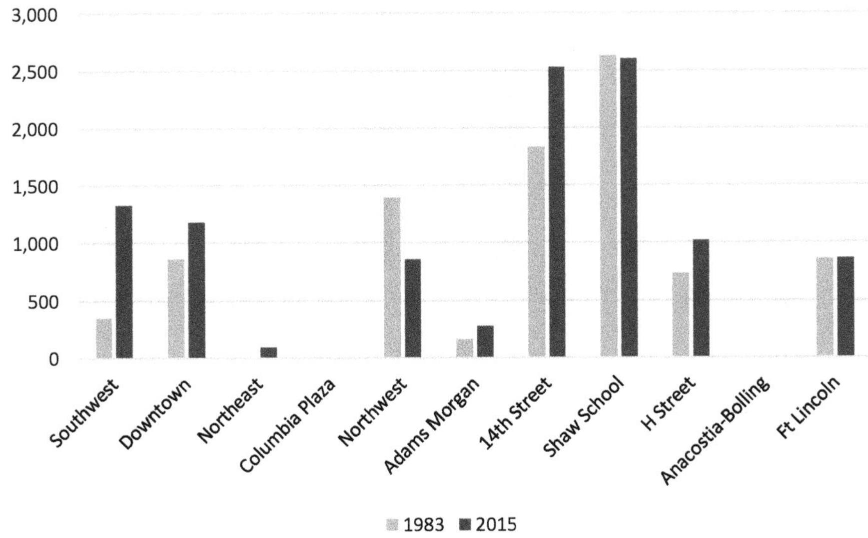

Figure 3.9 Affordable Housing Units Inside of Urban Renewal Areas, 1983 and 2015

	1983		2015		Change	
	Buildings	Units	Buildings	Units	Buildings	Units
Southwest	8	905	12	2,210	50.0%	144.2%
Downtown	5	861	7	1,177	40.0%	36.7%
Northeast	0	0	1	93		
Columbia Plaza	1	140	1	140	0.0%	0.0%
Northwest One	8	1,434	7	1,014	-12.5%	-29.3%
Adams Morgan	5	354	6	358	20.0%	1.1%
14th Street	23	2,287	38	3,414	65.2%	49.3%
Shaw School	32	2,969	33	3,032	3.1%	2.1%
H Street	9	1,132	12	1,714	33.3%	51.4%
Anacostia-Bolling	3	627	13	1,944	333.3%	210.0%
Ft Lincoln	7	1,003	8	980	14.3%	-2.3%
All Urban Renewal Areas	101	11,712	139	16,766	36.6%	37.3%

Figure 3.10 Change in Buildings and Units Within a Half-Mile Radius of Urban Renewal Areas, 1983–2015

housing functions to concentrate poverty and to perpetuate racial segregation using the natural boundary of the Anacostia River. Like the other Urban Renewal Areas across the city, the neighborhoods adjacent to Anacostia-Bolling are seeing increased speculation and redevelopment due to the large number of disinvested and low-cost properties nearby.

Notably, the Northwest One URA saw a decrease in affordable housing. This was primarily due to the demolition of Temple Courts in 2007 and Sursum Corda in 2017 as part of the District's New Communities Program. Though the District has promised to replace the units, they have not yet broken ground on Temple Court as the DC Housing Authority and the Deputy Mayor for Planning and Economic Development continue to disagree on the form and uses for land in the Northwest One area. The primary land use in these areas has been multifamily subsidized housing, but Temple Courts remains a parking lot, while Sursum Corda is in pre-development. In late 2020, ground was broken on the first phase of a three-phase project to replace the housing lost from Temple Courts.

Conversely, the increases in the number of units in the H Street and 14th Street Urban Renewal Areas suggest that the affordable housing has been a lifeline in the neighborhood. Both areas have experienced dramatic growth since 2005, including increases in building permits and economic activity, as well as demographic change, shifting increasingly wealthier and whiter. They experienced similar levels of speculation and redevelopment before 2010, including the wholesale redevelopment of Columbia Heights (the 14th Street URA) from 2002 to 2008[52]. As Figure 3.10 shows, the 14th Street URA not only retained much of the affordable housing created in Urban Renewal, that number increased by almost 50% by 2015 through new development and the use of the Tenant Opportunity to Purchase Act.

Buildings constructed before 1983 have played an outsized role in keeping low- and moderate-income households in gentrifying neighborhoods in Washington, DC. More than 80% of the buildings constructed before 1983 are still operating as subsidized housing. Of those, more than 90% are operating under similar funding structures. Those that have changed were largely the result of HOPE VI or through other large-scale redevelopment efforts by non-profit developers. In the latter case, they retained their Section 8 contracts, but redeveloped the properties, typically adding additional subsidies such as the Low Income Housing Tax Credit. Where they did not retain their covenants – but added tax credits – the affordability changed from 30% of the tenant's income, regardless of income, to being affordable for households earning 60% of the Area Median Income.

As a percentage of total units, Urban Renewal Areas continue to play a critical role. Figure 3.11 illustrates the percentage of total affordable housing in the city by their proximity to URAs in 1983 and 2015. While the overall percentage

	1983		**2015**	
	Buildings	Units	Buildings	Units
Within URA	43.4%	33.2%	35.7%	33.2%
1/4 Mile Radius	50.5%	39.0%	42.5%	39.2%
1/2 Mile Radius	56.6%	44.8%	47.6%	48.4%

Figure 3.11 Percentage of All Subsidized Units by Proximity to Urban Renewal Areas in 1983 and 2015

has decreased, the total number of buildings and units has increased. Almost 36% of DC's current affordable housing development are located inside a URA, while almost 48% are within a half mile of one, meaning that these neighborhoods continue to be critical receiving areas for subsidized affordable housing because zoning allows for multifamily housing in order to build affordable housing, making neighborhood resistance more difficult. While developers can apply for a Planned Unit Development (PUD) or a zoning variance to allow a new multifamily building, this requires a public process that often results in a denial of the application.

Perhaps what is most notable is that, although most of the URAs have gentrified over the past two decades, there are large parts of the city with few, if any, affordable housing developments in 1983 and 2015. Figure 3.12 illustrates the location of subsidized affordable housing across the city in 2017. While Urban Renewal played a critical role in creating affordable housing infrastructure, areas in the city with historically higher incomes and white populations have few resources for affordable housing, specifically Ward 3.

Conclusion

This chapter investigates the ways the use of government tools, including funding and regulation, in Washington, DC can create or prevent the conditions for future affordability. This chapter suggests that affordable housing, like bridges, sewers or other large capital projects, should be understood as a piece of infrastructure necessitating long-range thinking. It is important to remember that, though affordable housing works in a space of physical, financial or social interaction, ultimately, the intersection of planning and housing is often built with concrete and has a level of permanence. Thus, we have to evaluate the ways that policy and planning impact this affordable housing infrastructure. In DC, the exclusionary zoning of Ward 3 not only crystalized the structure of that area – but, perhaps more importantly – that of the rest of the city. Second, process, while not a certain means to equitable outcomes alone, has the potential to address particular outcomes related to the needs and political power of the neighborhood. There is little about the historic practices discussed in this chapter that rise to the acknowledgement of the rights of low- and moderate-income Black households to remain as a basis for affordable housing. Yet, the shift in the role of participation in redevelopment processes build upon and laid a further groundwork for future engagement and power. While this is a different type of infrastructure, it must be part of the long-range thinking for affordable housing.

While the District continues to face losses of market-affordable housing, the existence of affordable housing created using deep subsidies before 1983 has provided a critical base necessary to the prevention of displacement as the city has changed. The goal of this chapter is not to defend Urban Renewal as a policy, but to understand the complicated role it – and other redevelopment efforts – play in the current affordable housing landscape and think about the long-term implications of where and how opportunities for affordable housing are created or constrained.

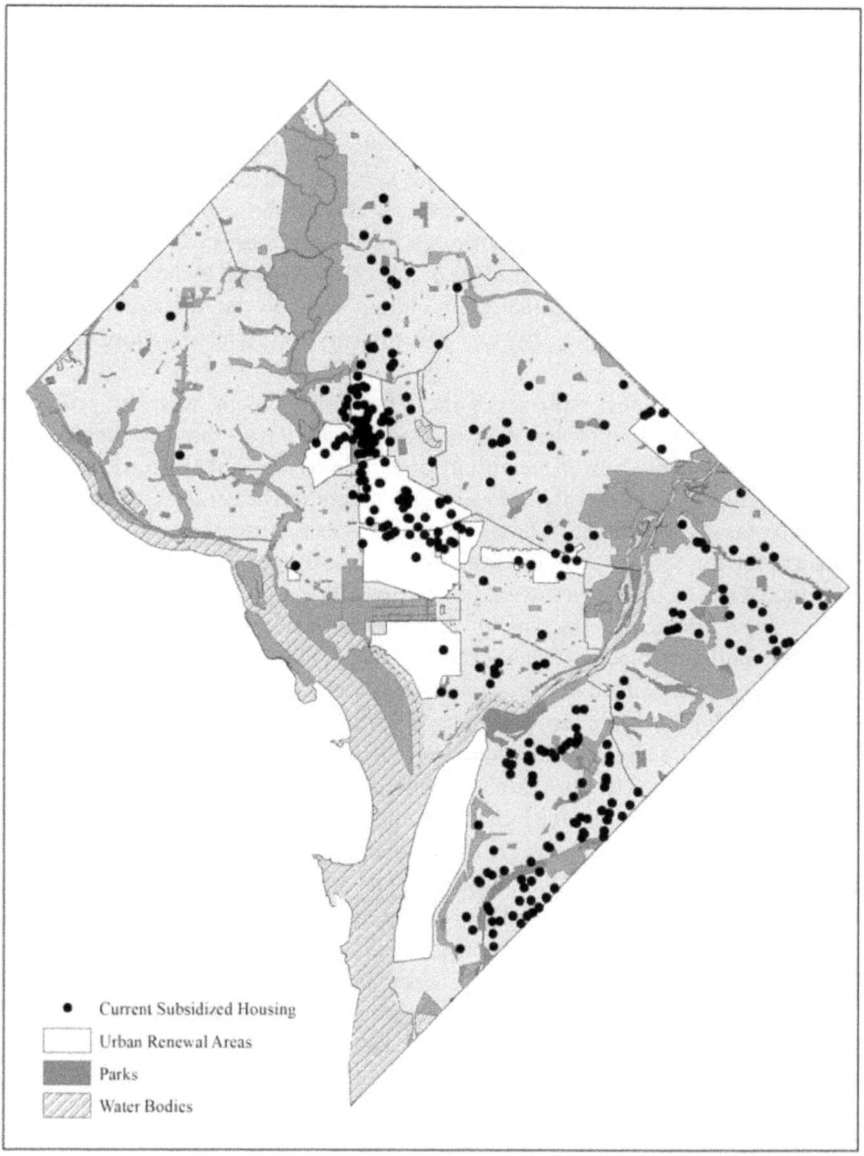

Figure 3.12 Urban Renewal Areas and Subsidized Housing, 2017

The placement of affordable housing into Urban Renewal Areas may have engendered the overcoming of three critical barriers to affordable housing. First, while neighborhood residents frequently complained about the existence of the affordable housing, as was illustrated by the case of The Cavalier, the building required no community process to determine its future beyond that of the existing residents who voted to assign their rights to a mission-driven developer. Thus, the building could prevent Not In My Backyard (NIMBY) resistance to its placement and continue an existing pattern of affordable housing. Second, while most buildings required subsidy to recapitalize and rehabilitate, that could be done through Low Income Housing Tax Credits and other layers of subsidy because the operating subsidy remained in place through Section 8. However, given the differentials in income targeting between pre-1983 programs and the Low Income Housing Tax Credit – currently the primary source for affordable housing production[53] – this base subsidy enabled the preservation of communities for households earning less than 50% of the Area Median Income. Finally, the existence of a subsidy ensured that the buildings were on the radar for advocates, affordable housing developers and city government, and enabled a more proactive approach[54].

At the same time, the existence of these buildings – along with the protective zoning created and maintained west of Rock Creek Park – has facilitated speculation and gentrification in neighborhoods where affordable housing already exists. Having the zoning in place reduces barriers to the creation of new, high-end multi-family buildings. While this supply is critical to accommodating new residents, the unevenness of multifamily zoning means that, rather than developing areas like Ward 3, they have focused on areas with relatively few regulatory barriers or the need for processes of up-zoning. The resulting pressure on formerly low- and moderate-income neighborhoods like Columbia Heights pits the preservation of market-affordable and subsidized housing developments against new, high-cost development in a fast-paced market with rapidly increasingly land values. This sets up a false choice where low- and moderate-income residents themselves are framed as barriers to affordability while high-income and white communities continue to argue for community character through low-density corridors[55].

Taken together, this suggests that preservation of affordable housing requires significant long-range thinking about tools and resources available, including control of land, existing buildings and knowledge about the community. Washington, DC was one of several cities in the early 2000s to use the MacArthur Foundation's Windows of Opportunity to develop data about subsidized properties as an opportunity for cohesive action[56] that is far more difficult to track in unsubsidized properties. While many cities have used Inclusionary Zoning as a tool to insert affordable housing into redevelopments, the income targets are often higher and the number of units created are far lower than what can be maintained or created through preservation and new creation[57]. The District's further development of additional tools such as TOPA and the Housing Production Trust Fund – as well as community-run collaborations like the DC Preservation Network – have enabled stakeholders to take advantage of the existing housing to preserve affordability.

Another critical element that this case demonstrates is the need for long-range thinking and community collaboration in redevelopment processes. It is difficult to create a "but-for" analysis of Urban Renewal due to the changes in the market, other policies that encourage or discourage urban redevelopment, and individual decision-making. But what is clear is that if there had been no investment in affordable housing through the mid- to-late 20th century, it is difficult to imagine that the District would have housing affordable to extremely low-income households in its gentrified neighborhoods today. This may be most closely evaluated through the examination of the multiple reports of lost market-affordable (or unsubsidized affordable) housing across the District and across the country[58]. Affordable housing covenants, created through the mid-20th century have been critical supports for the preservation of affordable housing in Washington, DC.

While it is unclear the degree to which the National Capital Planning Commission and Redevelopment Land Agency intended to provide this base in perpetuity, what is clear is that the planning process and goals shifted in the 1960s to include more affordable housing targeted to contemporary neighborhood residents and others displaced by Urban Renewal. The first change in direction demonstrates a concurrent shift in thinking on planning practice at the time, which was enshrined in federal policies such as Model Cities and Community Action planning from the Office of Economic Opportunity. In 1962, Charles Abrams' explicit critique of planning practice and Urban Renewal and Davidoff's implicit critique and call to change in 1963[59] signaled a shift in the role of planners. While neither questioned the expertise of the planner – or his (as he was typically male) role as a decision-maker – they both suggested that planners had to consider what went before and the needs of the existing community. Thus, planners, Davidoff argued, should be advocates for and acknowledge the needs of marginalized people. In Washington, this was done through public housing and early Section 221 projects before 1968.

The shift toward listening to community voice occurred as decision-makers began to acknowledge the frustrations leading to the uprisings of the late 1960s[60]. Unfortunately, this engagement ultimately came too late for meaningful implementation, and these efforts suffered from larger macro problems of discriminatory lending, declines in federal funding and a trend toward white and middle class flight that had accelerated since DC's school desegregation in 1954. The demise of Urban Renewal funding also may have played a role in the degree of community control possible in the riot corridors. Community control was never fully realized in terms of business ownership and land. However, the role of participation and community empowerment was ultimately adopted in DC law through TOPA, the city's strong human rights law and continued support for community groups. This focus on control ultimately meant that residents of the buildings constructed during Urban Renewal had the power to determine the terms under which they lived as the neighborhood changed[61]. Just as importantly, the infrastructure built through the housing in corridors always intended to gentrify create a base from which advocates could begin to preserve – not once, but over and over again in cases like Hubbard Place and others throughout this book. The existence – or not – of not only subsidized but multifamily housing foreshadowed the land use of the current period.

While the bulk of this chapter has been to understand where affordable housing was actually placed, it is equally important to examine where it was not placed – namely in the high-cost and long-standing white neighborhoods west of Rock Creek Park. Not only does this highlight the structural limits of affordable housing policies such as the requirement of blight, but the persistence of this pattern into the modern era shows the missed opportunities for affordable housing creation in high-cost neighborhoods. Given the initial structural constraints, as well as the legal segregation of housing and neighborhoods until 1968 (and its continuation due to lack of enforcement into the 1980s), this was the only pattern likely. But it also means that, because of the weakness of ongoing federal tools for affordable housing and local zoning, it is unlikely that new affordable housing in high-opportunity neighborhoods will ever be more than one-off developments. Rather, this type of infrastructure requires deep, long-term investment.

As a whole, the ability for Washington, DC to create a deep affordable housing infrastructure on which to build was predicated on early and sustained development of subsidized housing created at redevelopment points, specifically, Urban Renewal and later policies that enabled access to land and political opportunity. While this chapter does not seek to paint a definitive picture of what might have happened without this development of affordable housing, it does suggest that, without its development, Washington would have fewer affordable housing resources in high-cost neighborhoods. Just as importantly, the difficulty of using vouchers in high-cost neighborhoods suggests that few low- and moderate-income Washingtonians would have access to the neighborhoods where they've lived and worked for generations in the absence of stable affordable housing resources.

Examining this period suggests that housing should be framed, not as an ancillary social service to be provided as time and funding are available, but rather, as a priority in all development over time. It is also critical that tools must be put in place to take advantage of the existing housing resources – particularly in high-cost areas. In Washington, this meant tenant protections like TOPA and resources like the well-funded Housing Trust Fund. Finally, this research suggests that we need to continue to refine our preservation and redevelopment processes to include the voice, need and priorities of existing low- and moderate-income households if we are to address long-term housing needs.

Notes

1 Office of Community Renewal, "Community Renewal in the District of Columbia: A Program of Total Action for Solving the Problems" (Washington, DC: Redevelopment Land Agency, 1968).
2 "Hilltop Manor Advertisement," *Evening Star*, October 2, 1926, sec. Advertisements.
3 Columbia Heights Citizens' Association, "A Statement of Some of the Advantages of Beautiful Columbia Heights: A Neighborhood of Homes" (Washington, DC: Columbia Heights Citizens' Association, 1904).
4 "Advertisement for F. H. Smith Company," *Evening Star*, June 10, 1929, sec. Classified.

5 Dagmar Horna Perman, *The Girard Street Project. All Souls Church Unitarian* (Washington, DC: All Souls Church Unitarian, 1965).
6 Clarence Johnson, "Adult-Only Rule Fought by Apartment Tenants," *Evening Star*, December 8, 1972.
7 James Borchert, *Alley Life in Washington: Family, Community, Religion, and Folklife in the City, 1850–1970* (Urbana University of Illinois Press, 1982).
8 "The Building of Houses: What Has Been Done during the Last Week – Improvements Contemplated," *Washington Post*, June 22, 1884.
9 Peter Hall, *Cities of Tomorrow* (Maldon, MA: Blackwell Publishing, 2014); Jacob Riis, *How the Other Half Lives: Studies Among the Tenements of New York* (Boston: St Martin's Press, 1890).
10 "Homes for the Poor: Sanitary Housing Company Prepares for Work," *Washington Post*, April 30, 1904.
11 "Model Housing Project to Open: Housing-Warming Is Slated on Friday Afternoon at Sternberg Court," *Washington Post*, November 19, 1937.
12 "D.C. Housing Firm Sold, Fred Smith Elected Head," *Washington Post*, October 5, 1954.
13 "Violations Laid to RLA Apartments: 21 Code Infractions at Old SW Project," *Washington Post*, September 9, 1962.
14 W.E. Finley, "Correspondence from W.E. Finley to Hon Frank Thompson, Jr.," September 20, 1960, National Archives; "Urban Renewal Gets Hit at NAACP Rally," *Washington Post*, August 19, 1960, sec. B, ProQuest Historical Newspapers: The Washington Post.
15 NAHC, "History of NAHC" (National Association of Cooperative Housing), accessed December 18, 2019, https://coophousing.org/about-nahc/history-of-nahc/.
16 "RLA Acts on Renewal Housing," *Washington Post*, November 7, 1963.
17 "Cooperative Housing Group Changes Name," *Washington Post*, May 27, 1967, Times Herald edition.
18 "Apartments Rehabilitated for Low-Income Families," *Washington Post*, August 5, 1967.
19 "Housing Insights Tool," Housing Insights, 2019, http://housinginsights.org.
20 DC Historic Sites, "Saint James Mutual Homes," accessed December 18, 2019, http s://historicsites.dcpreservation.org/items/show/888.
21 NCPC, "Redevelopment Plan, Southwest Redevelopment Project Area B: A Report of Existing Conditions and A Plan for Redevelopment", National Capital Planning Commission, October 24, 1952).
22 Chris Myers Asch and George Derek Musgrove, "'We Are Headed for Some Bad Trouble': Gentrification and Displacement in Washington, DC, 1920–2014," in *Capital Dilemma: Growth and Inequality in Washington, DC*, ed. Derek Hyra and Sabiyha Prince (New York: Routledge, 2016), 107–135.
23 "New Bridge Relieves Traffic on Anacostia Benning, Sousa Spans," *Evening Star*, January 22, 1950, sec. A.
24 "Urban Renewal Gets Hit at NAACP Rally."
25 W.E. Finley, "Correspondence from W.E. Finley to Hon Frank Thompson, Jr."
26 Cameron Logan, *Historic Capital: Preservation, Race, and Real Estate in Washington, D.C* (Minneapolis: University of Minnesota Press, 2017).
27 DC RLA, "Urban Renewal – 1966 Annual Report D.C. Redevelopment Land Agency," September 30, 1966.
28 Washington Council of Governments, "Subsidized Housing Information File," Housing Technical Report (WCOG, March 1983), Washington DC Public Library.
29 DC RLA, "1960 DC Redevelopment Land Agency Annual Report," 1960, 7.
30 Charles Abrams, "Criteria for Urban Renewal," *Architectural Record* 5 (1962): 155–58.
31 Abrams, "Criteria for Urban Renewal,"156.

32 Board of Commissioners, Government of the District of Columbia, "A Proposed Anti-Discrimination Housing Ordinance For the District of Columbia" (March 1963).

33 DC RLA, "Urban Renewal - 1966 Annual Report D.C. Redevelopment Land Agency"; Washington Council of Governments, "Subsidized Housing Information File."

34 Washington Council of Governments, "Subsidized Housing Information File."

35 Washington Council of Governments, "Subsidized Housing Information File"; D.C., "DC Preservation Network Database" (Washington DC: NeighborhoodInfo, 2015).

36 Robert Asher, "D.C. Asked to Hold Off on Renewal," *Washington Post*, January 13, 1965, sec. B.

37 Bob Levey and Jane Freundel-Levey, "END OF THE ROADS; In the Interstate Era, Congress Ruled Washington like a Fiefdom. Then a Fight over Some Freeways Inspired a Biracial, Neighborhood-Level Movement to Fight the Federal Power," *Washington Post*, November 26, 2000, sec. Magazine.

38 Douglas Feaver, "No New Freeways Within the District," *Washington Post*, October 30, 1978.

39 NCPC, "Urban Renewal Plan for the 14th Street Urban Renewal Area" (National Capital Planning Commission, September 1, 1969), Box 51 A1 13 NN3–328–94–011, National Archives: RG 328 Records of the National Capital Planning Commission Records Relating to Urban Renewal, 1952–1986.

40 DC City Council, "Testimony of Melvin Mister, Executive Director of the DC Redevelopment Land Authority before the DC City Council," February 20, 1973, Box 51 A1 13 NN3–328–94–011, National Archives: RG 328 Records of the National Capital Planning Commission Records Relating to Urban Renewal, 1952–1986.

41 Kirk Scharfenberg, "D.C. to Get $30 Million For Renewal: City to Get Funds for Renewal," *Washington Post*, March 6, 1973.

42 Alice Rivlin, "Testimony of Alice M. Rivlin On the Recommendations and Final Report of the DC Comprehensive Housing Strategy Task Force," June 13, 2006, https://www.brookings.edu/wp-content/uploads/2016/06/20060613_Rivlin-1.pdf; Craig Timberg, "Williams Aims To Be Mayor of A Bigger D.C.; Attracting Residents Is Goal As 2nd Term Begins Today," *Washington Post*, January 2, 2003.

43 Claire Zippel, "Where Is Affordable Housing Being Developed in DC? Explore DCFPI's New Interactive Map" (Washington, DC: DC Fiscal Policy Institute, September 11, 2018), https://www.dcfpi.org/all/affordable-housing-pipeline-interactive-map/.

44 Logan, *Historic Capital.*

45 David Kathan, Amy Rispin, and L. Paige Whiteley, "Tracing a Bethesda, Maryland, African American Community and Its Contested Cemetery," *Washington History* 29, no. 2 (2017): 24–41; Neil Flanagan, "The Battle of Fort Reno," *Washington City Paper*, November 2, 2017, https://www.washingtoncitypaper.com/news/article/20981322/the-battle-of-fort-reno.

46 S.G. Lindholm, "Experiences with Zoning in Washington, DC 1920–1934" (Washington, DC: District of Columbia Zoning Commission, 1935), 9.

47 Prologue DC, "Mapping Segregation: Residential Sub-Areas, Federal Housing Administration (1937)" (Washington, DC: Prologue DC, 2019), http://mappingsegregationdc.org.

48 "Apartment Proposal Stirs Georgetown: Social and Citizen Leaders Fight Zone Change Asked by Kirk," *Washington Post*, October 3, 1940.

49 Seven additional buildings have an unknown status because they were scattered sites without addresses or did not have data that could be matched with an address or current affordable housing data.

50 Low Poverty is defined as a neighborhood with a poverty rate of less than 20%.

51 Abigail Hauslohner and Jonathan O'Connell, "Poorer Tenants Fear Being Pushed out by Planned Congress Heights Complex; In a Neglected Corner of the Nation's Capital, the Mayor's Commitment to Affordability Is Being Put to the Test," *Washington Post*, October 15, 2015.

52 Kathryn Howell, "Preservation from the Bottom Up: Affordable Housing, Redevelopment, and Negotiation in Washington, DC.," *Housing Studies* 31, no. 3 (2016): 305–23.
53 Alex F. Schwartz, *Housing Policy in the United States* (New York: Routledge, 2015).
54 Kathryn L. Howell, "Housing and the Grassroots: Using Local and Expert Knowledge to Preserve Affordable Housing," *Journal of Planning Education and Research*, May 16, 2017, 0739456X17709500, https://doi.org/10.1177/0739456X17709500.
55 Marcia Rosen and Wendy Sullivan, "From Urban Renewal and Displacement to Economic Inclusion: San Francisco Affordable Housing Policy, 1978–2012" (Washington: Poverty & Race Research Action Council, December 2012), 1223387787, Ethnic NewsWatch, http://proxy.library.vcu.edu/login?url=https://search.proquest.com/docview/1223387787?accountid=14780; Filip Stabrowski, "Inclusionary Zoning and Exclusionary Development: The Politics of 'Affordable Housing' in North Brooklyn: INCLUSIONARY ZONING AND EXCLUSIONARY DEVELOPMENT," *International Journal of Urban and Regional Research* 39, no. 6 (2015): 1120–1136, https://doi.org/10.1111/1468-2427.12297.
56 Heather L. Schwartz et al., "Preservation of Affordable Rental Housing Evaluation of the MacArthur Foundation's Window of Opportunity Initiative" (RAND Corporation, 2016).
57 Howell, "Preservation from the Bottom Up: Affordable Housing, Redevelopment, and Negotiation in Washington, DC."
58 Jenny Reed, "Disappearing Act: Affordable Housing in DC Is Vanishing Amid Sharply Rising Housing Costs" (DC Fiscal Policy Institute, May 7, 2012), https://www.dcfpi.org/wp-content/uploads/2012/05/5-7-12-Housing-and-Income-Trends-FINAL.pdf; Freddie Mac, "Rental Affordability Is Worsening" (Freddie Mac Multifamily, October 23, 2017), http://www.freddiemac.com/multifamily/pdf/rental_affordability_worsening.pdf.
59 Paul Davidoff, "Advocacy and Pluralism in Planning," *Journal of the American Institute of Planning* 31, no. 4 (1965): 331–38.
60 United States, ed., *The Kerner Report*, 2016 edition, James Madison Library in American Politics (Princeton: Princeton University Press, 2016).
61 Kathryn Howell, "Planning for Empowerment: Upending the Traditional Approach to Planning for Affordable Housing in the Face of Gentrification," *Planning Theory & Practice* 17, no. 2 (2016): 210–26.

4 Policy and Practice Foundations for Preservation

> When market forces create a conflict between the goals that would offer increased tax revenue, but yet would cause substantial displacement of the poor, the elderly and the handicapped then this government will act on behalf of those needing maximum protection. To do less would sacrifice the poor, the elderly and handicapped on the altars of increased tax revenue. I do not believe that we are at a point where consideration of revenues over people's lives is up for discussion.
>
> Mayor Marion Barry, testimony before the Housing Committee on the District of Columbia (1980)[1]

In Washington, DC, a DC Department of Housing and Community Development (DHCD) colleague argued, there are "three DCs." First there is the international DC, folks who don't bother with District government (if they're even aware of it). If they have an issue, they go to their consulate or to the federal government. Then there's the federal DC. In this group, are the federal workers who moved to the District for their careers. They may be aware of DC government, they may not. But they are short timers, not committed to the city. Then there's Black DC – "the rest of us." One of his points was that DC residents differ in terms of their commitment, or attachment, to the city as residents and public servants, and these lines have historically fallen along race and class lines, particularly in the way different residents see the role of government policies and planning interventions. While interviewing a long-term resident and community activist during my dissertation research, she argued that there are those who are in the "City in the Clouds" and the "City on the Hill" – they come and go and use the District as a stepping stone for other things. Then there are the people on the ground – those who are "largely invisible," living, working, and "making their lives here."

DC is, in many ways, a contested discourse as much as a physical space. Asch and Musgrove argue that one of those contests is between DC's historic Black and community-focused government agencies, illustrated by the quote from former Mayor Marion Barry at the start of this chapter, and the era after the District's 1995 financial collapse and subsequent Congressional take-over[2]. The shift, seen in cities across the country, can be seen in the "colorblind," business-centered approach to development in the District[3].

My colleague was a long-term resident and public servant of the District. He remembered the city before Home Rule when, as he told me, the District was used as a slush fund by Congress, and African Americans were excluded from local government. He remembered the uprisings following the assassination of Dr. Martin Luther King, Jr. in 1968, as well as the cadre of Civil Rights leaders who arrived in the District determined to make meaningful change in Black Power, Civil Rights, Women's movements and others of the time and ultimately, build the new District government. And he remembered the growth of the African American middle class as a result of government hiring practices and minority contracting rules. I was part of the newest wave of newcomers, a Mayor Fenty[4] hire. He was a Mayor Barry[5] hire. But as I reflected on this cultural difference, it was clear, as others have argued, that DC's culture is changing from one rooted in the District's deep history of organizing and organizers focused on rights, racial equity and neighborhoods[6] to one where development, modernity and progress are all parts of the dominant paradigm[7]. Progressive on many fronts, this view starts with a need to develop and grow – population, tax base, jobs and national prominence. This neoliberal narrative centers economic growth as the first step to modernity. These histories – contested and powerful – have overlapped temporally and geographically in ways that have impacted both the opportunities for preservation and the reality of power for residents in the District.

Framing Preservation

These contested narratives in DC mirror the debates within particularly affordable housing preservation across the country. What is preservation? Is it a building, a subsidy, a community? What are the goals of preservation? How is it prioritized? Who decides how we preserve? These questions lie in larger questions about how we understand the power of renters and low- and moderate-income households – particularly African American and Latinx households. They are based in the ways we prioritize these households, economic efficiency and community-based power in the midst of changing cities – but more importantly the larger ways affordable housing is framed – rights, needs or economy.

A rights approach to housing policy frames housing as a universal right and a platform for political power. The right to housing focuses less on housing as a need, but rather as a platform for full citizenship[8]. For many cities, this change in approach happened with the decline of federal funds for community-based programs like model cities and supports for organizing. Much of DC's policy infrastructure is rooted in a rights-based approach, while newer approaches shift to needs and economy as the driving focus of affordable housing. In DC, this way of addressing housing needs often overlaps geographically with other ways of seeing affordable housing due to the policy infrastructure created in the wake of Home Rule.

A second approach examines housing in a need-based frame, as was seen in the second wave of Urban Renewal in DC with Northwest One. Housing as a need, places housing in a charity framework with those in power determining who needs or deserves housing and what that entails. Typically, this is how affordable housing development is done through federal programs that require little to no engagement with residents about the future of their housing. It can also be seen in programs such as inclusionary zoning that addresses housing as part of a negotiated policy.

Finally, housing is framed as a financial necessity where the issue of downstream costs is prioritized as a reason to support affordable housing[9]. For example, the costs of concentrated poverty and the cost of repairing public housing were cited as driving forces in the redevelopment of public housing through programs like HOPE VI. These frames create a further conflict in housing policy – between process and outcome as well as between co-production of knowledge and top-down experts[10]. If economic benefits trump social concerns and that expertise is held by those underwriting a project, determining the subsidy or redeveloping the project, there is little space for residents who have a use-value interest in the property to challenge the method or outcome of the project. These conflicts play out in DC as well as in other cities in affordable housing policy development and housing governance.

This chapter explores how the unique local policy and practices that developed ultimately came to influence the ways local jurisdictions approach preservation and where these are situated in the larger context of US housing policy. This chapter relies on analysis of archival data from legislation, public testimony and interagency memos. However, I also use both direct and participant observation of meetings with and among advocates, government agencies and the public, legislative hearings, and other public and private events from my experience as both a researcher and practitioner in local government. This chapter helps to set the stage for the ways that advocacy, residents and city government agencies understood the needs, opportunity and resident power in the preservation of affordable housing. These policies are rooted in larger histories of activism in the District. I will also discuss the current push and pull of community-based preservation and the focus on development, property rights and the concept of modernity in Washington. Bringing this analysis forward, I will examine the changing perception as it plays out in new debates in Washington about both whether and how we preserve affordable housing.

The Roots of DC Policy: The City and the Federal Government

Before digging into the debates in the District, it's important to lay the groundwork for the relationship between the federal government and the District government. Much is written about the role of the federal government in Washington[11], but depending on where in the District you work, the federal government's role in daily life is a big shrug since Home Rule was granted in 1974, as a way of asserting independence in a fundamentally unequal system[12]. Yet in the bigger picture, Washington has limited control over its own fate. Like many cities, the state – in this case the federal government – can preempt legislation made by the District. But, unlike other cities, District residents have no vote in the body that preempts the legislation. Those representatives who serve on the Committee for the District of Columbia have a 30-day review of all legislation, including the budget, passed by the DC Council. While they often pass on the opportunity to review or veto legislation, issues of national importance – needle exchanges, marijuana legalization, abortion, for example – create opportunities for legislators assigned to this committee that otherwise offers little to deliver to their constituents the chance to prove their credentials to their voters. At the same time, being in the backyard of the federal government creates both risks and rewards. As Chapter 2 suggests, having Congress and the US Department of Housing and Urban Development (HUD) nearby meant that the District avoided the moratorium on new HUD contracts and that Congress was watching Urban Renewal's implementation and the neighborhood reaction to it.

Being in Washington, DC creates another challenge and opportunity. As a central spot for political power and organizing, DC attracts new residents as government, nonprofits, lobbying or other issue related to government shifts. In the 1960s and 1970s, this meant the District welcomed activists from the Civil Rights Movement, voter mobilization drives, women's rights activism, legal activism and community organizing who saw the possibility for a more equitable city. These activists became the base of the District's first elected council in 1975. This trend has been critical since the District's founding and has resulted in a broad range of native Washingtonians over time – both those focused on emancipation and Black and community-based power and those focused on the bureaucracy and political functions of the District. However, as times change, so have new residents coming to the District. The national trend that has fueled the growth of cities more broadly – including investment, demographic shifts in family formation and household preferences – has meant that the growth in population in Washington, like many coastal cities, has come from white, upwardly mobile households with little connection to the ideals of Black and low-income empowerment or collective, rights-based policy.

Outside of the federal influence, Washington, DC sits in a unique spot of having the functions of both the state and a local government. This is particularly important in housing and community development policy and land use. The District, acting as a state, manages the Low Income Housing Tax Credit, as well as all other housing funds, creating opportunities for a coordinated approach to local housing. It also controls all land use decisions, including taxation, growth management, title and enforcement. While, in other contexts, this is not insurmountable, at a minimum, DC's relatively independent status removes the need to negotiate with state agencies to engage in land use or coordinated housing finance.

Tenant Organizing and Community-Based Power

Washington, DC has a deep history of tenant mobilization leading to significant policy change. The Tenant Opportunity to Purchase Act (TOPA), and the creation of Limited Equity Cooperatives (LEC), was but one result of the work of tenants, organizers and advocates. DC's tradition of Black organizing tracks back to a critical history of activism before the Civil War and the local struggle for voice and power in the changing city as Jim Crow segregation took hold. The segregated District, like many cities across the south, was a critical site in the fight for a voice in housing, voting and access. A watershed event was the notorious Southwest Urban Renewal Plan, discussed in Chapter 2, that displaced approximately 25,000 residents, primarily African Americans. More than 90% of the buildings were destroyed and only 500 units of affordable housing were built to replace them[13]. This redevelopment shined a light on the ongoing displacement of DC's Black residents and helped to mobilize a broad range of activists.

At the same time, racially restrictive covenants were enforceable by law until 1948, meaning that through the courts, the state could enforce deed restrictions prohibiting the sale or rental of property by race. Developed with the new suburbs in the early 20th century, restrictive covenants were a tool to maintain all-white communities. As an advertisement for the newly developed streetcar neighborhood of Columbia Heights in Washington, DC, "Nowhere in the District of Columbia can be found a community freer from the objectionable classes than that on the 'Heights'; and there is every assurance that present conditions in this regard will continue in the future development and building up of the section. All are alive to the importance of co-operating to that end"[14]. Restrictive covenants were challenged in the Dupont Circle neighborhood of Washington in 1926 and upheld by Corrigan v Buckley[15].

Two decades later, with the St. Louis Shelley v Kraemer case in 1948, as well Hurd v Hodge in DC, covenants were deemed unenforceable by the courts. However, the continued legal discrimination through redlining in mortgage lending and direct discrimination through refusal to rent or sell to nonwhite residents prevented Black households from moving to new developments in and outside the District, including neighborhoods in Northwest DC. Many African Americans moved into parts of Columbia Heights, Bloomingdale and other white neighborhoods adjacent to Black neighborhoods initially. While there were notable examples of buildings for "professional" African American families, many working-class residents continued to be excluded and displaced from white areas. Increasingly, African Americans lived in crowded and poor quality conditions, paying more for these accommodations than their white counterparts. This mass displacement, ongoing discrimination and deteriorating conditions led to organizing at the neighborhood level across the city to resist Urban Renewal efforts and poor conditions[16]. In 1958, as displacement and dispossession were underway in DC's Southwest Urban Renewal Area, the local housing agency launched an intensive – but ultimately unsuccessful – pilot project to address massive code violations in neighborhoods undergoing racial change in the District, specifically Columbia Heights[17].

By this time, white households had already started moving to the DC suburbs or to new communities in upper Northwest Washington with low-cost mortgages protected from desegregation by legal discrimination. This pattern was exaggerated in neighborhoods east of Rock Creek Park due to the desegregation of schools in 1954. The white children of neighborhoods like Columbia Heights, Bloomingdale and Ledroit Park would have been sent to desegregated schools, which accelerated white resident departures from the eastern half of the city. By 1960, these neighborhoods would be majority African American due to a combination of in-migration from African Americans and an out-migration of whites. At the same time, the all-white upper northwest neighborhoods west of the park grew through post-war construction of housing and access to federally funded mortgages. African Americans, locked out of much of the region, were forced to remain in small areas with higher costs and aging and poor-quality housing relative to white households in the region[18].

In the 1960s and 1970s, conditions continued to deteriorate in Black neighborhoods across the District. Tenants in several buildings in the Columbia Heights neighborhood conducted rent strikes to protest the horrible conditions in their buildings. One of the first rent strikes of this time in the city was at 1415 Girard Street, currently a limited equity cooperative, in 1964, supported by the Student Nonviolent Coordinating Committee (SNCC) and the All Souls Unitarian Universalist Church in the neighborhood. Tenants at Clifton Terrace, a few blocks away, went on rent strike due to more than 1,200 code violations on the property. As Paige and Reuss explain:

> [B]y the late 1960s, rent strikes had become a widely used weapon to force landlords to maintain their properties. Tenants became increasingly militant, striking at the landlord where damage could be more severe – the cash flow of the building.
>
> 1983, p. 42

The Columbia, located at 14th and Girard Street NW, was one of the most notorious buildings in the neighborhood. After the uprisings following the 1968 assassination of Dr. Martin Luther King, Jr., code violations and a subsequent rent strike, the management company abandoned the building, leaving it with no security and a rat infestation. It subsequently suffered repeated arson attempts. The city's efforts to evict the tenants and condemn the building were thwarted by a lawsuit brought by the Neighborhood Legal Services Program on behalf of the tenants. The building was put in receivership under city control and the city was required to pay utility costs until they could relocate the residents to units with similar rents. Yet the pattern of abandonment by landlords persisted in DC's Black neighborhoods.

Starting in the late 1960s, a series of cases made the use of retaliatory evictions, particularly those stemming from reports of poor housing conditions, illegal[19]. While the 1968 Fair Housing Act made housing discrimination illegal, there were few enforcement mechanisms, and Black residents continued to be forced into poor conditions across the city. In 1973 an inter-racial coalition of tenants formed in response to a wave of mass evictions, condominium conversions, rapid gentrification in neighborhoods like Adams Morgan, Capitol Hill and Dupont Circle and conditions complaints in neighborhoods like Columbia Heights[20]. The tenants, representing all parts of the District, protested and demanded stronger rent control laws and enforcement of building codes.

Congress voted to grant the District Home Rule officially in 1975, enabling the city to manage itself in day-to-day activities. What it actually meant was that DC would have a non-voting member of the House of Representatives and a "shadow" Senator and thus no say in national decisions, including taxation. All legislation passed by the DC Council goes through a 30-day review period in Congress. At that time, they can veto the legislation or let it pass. This review period includes the local budget. DC's new self-governance was based on ideals of Civil Rights and Black empowerment in 1975. Jaffe and Sherwood argue that power for downtown development remained in the hands of white elites through the Federal City Council, a group of business elites in Washington[21]. In the wake of the election of the first Home Rule council, the ongoing tenant rights movement asserting a right to remain in their neighborhoods pressured the City Council to pass legislation to keep residents in place[22].

Between 1975 and 1980, lawmakers passed a series of laws, which were intended to prevent displacement and increase tenants' rights. The first, rent control, straddled the pre and post-Home Rule period. In the hearings on the law, "of more than seventy witnesses, few were landlords. Those landlords who did appear did not deny there might be a need for controls. They pleaded for a higher percentage ceiling [for rent increases] and a relaxation of the burden of paperwork"[23]. The legislative report also cited a vacancy rate of 2.7% and a sharply decreasing stock of affordable housing, echoing previous reports dating back more than 25 years. In the current version of rent control, buildings constructed after 1976 are exempt, originally to encourage new construction due to the low vacancy rate in the District.

In addition to rent control, the District included the original form of a right of first refusal when their rental housing was sold in the updated Rental Housing Act of 1977. This first right to purchase increased the creation of housing cooperatives in the District. However, the law did not provide a process by which tenants could claim their right or the conditions necessary to do so. The Department of Housing and Community Development (DHCD) secured a grant from the US Department of Housing and Community Development (HUD) in 1978 to support those individuals and tenant organizations that wanted to purchase their units. Eighteen lawsuits were filed between 1977 and 1980 to purchase buildings representing approximately 1,200 units[24]. The District Council passed the Condominium and Cooperative Conversion Stabilization Act of 1979 and paused the onslaught of condo conversions with a 90-day moratorium, which was extended by the Council for another 90 days in response to the wave of condominium conversions underway in the late 1970s. In 1975, according to *The Washington Post*, 468 units were converted to condominiums, but by 1978, more than 10,000 units had been converted. Another 8,000 were in some process of conversion[25]. These conversions were in the context of ongoing abandonment, evictions and poor conditions in Black neighborhoods that exacerbated the shrinking supply for low- and moderate-income households – particularly in the Dupont and Adams Morgan neighborhoods in Northwest DC[26].

These efforts spurred a series of permanent housing laws that brought together rent control, condominium conversion regulations and the right of first refusal, culminating in the 1980 Rental Housing Conversion and Sale Act, which included the Tenant Opportunity to Purchase Act (TOPA). TOPA gave renters the right of first refusal when their buildings were for sale. Tenants of single-family and multifamily homes had this right when it was initially passed, meaning that if a landlord wanted to sell the building or unit, he or she first had to offer it to the resident or residents. In the case of a multi-unit building, this right is collective, meaning that 50% of the tenants had to collectively exercise the right. The residents have three options: first, they can opt not to do anything and allow the building to be sold with no protections; second, they can purchase and turn the building into an owner-occupied structure, including condominium, cooperative or limited equity cooperative in the case of a multi-unit building; or they could negotiate with and select a developer who would keep the building as a rental building.

The law specifically cited the displacement of low-income and senior households, a need to preserve affordable rental housing and the formation of tenant associations as policy goals. In his testimony before the House Committee on the District of Columbia, then Mayor Marion Barry argued that the supply of housing for low- and moderate-income households was shrinking and that families were being displaced by high-income households. He specifically made an argument that filtering, or the idea that housing filters down to lower-income households as newer housing comes on the market, was going the other direction. Thus, as homeowners and developers renovated old buildings, the units filtered upward to higher-income households, displacing low- and moderate-income residents. The legislation states, "These controls are necessary to more effectively assure that housing will be preserved at a cost which can be afforded by current tenants who would otherwise be involuntarily displaced and forced into overcrowded or otherwise substandard housing conditions"[27]. Congress ultimately declined to veto the legislation, but this decision was based on a deference to local power in the quasi-independent District, rather than an agreement with the legislation.

This policy was, and continues to be highly controversial with developers and brokers complaining that it slows down the process for building owners, while the proponents argue the slow-down allows access to those who would, otherwise, be locked out of the process, unable to control their tenure[28]. However, it was passed in the context of a government and city focused on the development of cooperatives of many kinds, including food, worker and housing, led by a council rooted in organizing and activism. The Barry administration continued this tradition in the post-Home Rule era, explicitly using cooperatives, and TOPA more broadly, to promote collective, rather than individual, rights. Bockman argues that cooperatives in Washington, DC were a form of resistance in the pre-Home Rule period. The lack of political power – particularly for African Americans who were excluded from many forms of power locally and nationally – facilitated the creation of independently controlled cooperative institutions, including food, worker and housing cooperatives[29]. More importantly, as the case of St. James Mutual Home suggests, housing cooperatives were already moving ahead in Washington with the help of organizations of the Foundation for Cooperative Housing, a predecessor of the National Association of Housing Cooperatives.

Another critical piece of legislation passed during this period was the Human Rights Act of 1977, which protects DC residents from discrimination based on many factors, including source of income, effectively prohibiting landlords from refusing housing vouchers and refusal based on sexual orientation and identity. Though only partially related to housing, this law, like all of these created during the early Home Rule period, became critical in later years as the city experienced significant changes to the built, social and policy environments. Additionally, the District's policy of minority business participation in all levels of contracting helped to support and grow a Black middle class across the country – but particularly in the DC region. This requirement extended from local construction contracts to national searches for fund managers, extending the District's support for a broad range of professional activities. These approaches were part of creating a more inclusive city for African Americans and other marginalized groups, consistent with the new activist council.

The Impact and Ongoing Efforts for Housing Stability

In the early 1980s, newspaper articles featured stories about what the new Rental Housing Act meant for landlords. Brokers and building owners argued that the law gave tenants too much leverage and delayed the sale of buildings – particularly in the case of single-family homes – through TOPA. But the council repeatedly argued that the law was meant to stabilize neighborhoods facing gentrification pressure and acknowledge that renters had a right to remain in their communities[30]. Though the law is now primarily viewed as a benefit primarily to low-income households, the original law often was used to create market-rate cooperatives that facilitated affordability for middle-class households in DC's wealthy and white northwest neighborhoods.[31].

One of the challenges facing tenant associations and residents that wanted to exercise their rights through TOPA was that of negotiating with the owner, amassing the funding necessary, developing a new governance structure and, when necessary, making repairs to the building. In response, consultants and organizers already active in housing issues provided a link between tenants and owners. As one consultant explained in a 1979 *Washington Post* article, "Most groups are accidental organizations with no specific purpose in mind…You're working with a group of people with a variety of interests, and it's often difficult to get a sense of purpose beyond 'Let's buy the building'"[32]. The reactive nature of TOPA means that few tenant associations were prepared for the reality of the purchase.

To support purchases for low- and moderate-income tenants, the District funded pro bono attorneys to support these residents in their purchase. Initially this was done through the 1978 HUD grant, but this was extended as the law expanded. Several organizations, previously part of the push for tenant rights, including working with tenants facing poor conditions, laid a foundation for this community-based power. The Southern Columbia Heights Tenants Association (SCHTA), Southeast Vicariate Cluster Tenant Association (SVCTA), Washington Intercity Self Help (WISH) and Ministries United to Support Community Life Endeavors (MUSCLE) formed the base of organizations that helped tenants actualize their rights under TOPA. Over time, additional organizations, primarily located in Ward 1, a central space for central American immigrants and where change has been swift, have become critical players in organizing tenants as they exercise their rights.

The District also provided grants and loans through the First Right Purchase Program (FRPP), using federal and, eventually, local funds to purchase buildings for the creation of limited equity cooperatives and affordable rental housing. These funds were offered on a rolling basis, meaning that, unlike a traditional Request For Proposals process that opens once or twice per year, FRPP funds could be accessed as the buildings were offered for sale. While the program worked across the city, agency staff cited gentrifying neighborhoods such as Adams Morgan, Dupont and Shaw as targeted areas where funds were most needed.

In the 1980s, homelessness, as an issue, grew in prominence across the country – but particularly in DC. This pressured the council and the Mayor continued to provide support for affordable housing in the District, largely using federal funding. As one long-time organizer explained:

> When homelessness is on your radar, other housing is related to preventing homelessness by helping people buy their buildings or whatever. And the City Council – I mean, Marion Barry had a passion for it – so there were people who had come out of the Civil Rights movement [who] were primarily what the City Council was. The idea of organizing was in their consciousness. Now [organizing is] a dirty word for a lot of people.

However, through the 1980s, District government also focused on downtown development, leaving the neighborhoods outside the core with assistance of local housing and community development funding and programs, rather than targeted investment and political support. While there were small investments in neighborhoods during this time, preservation of affordability through TOPA and new construction through federal funding sources were the primary investments in housing and community development. This approach allowed the District to provide basic neighborhood-based funds to serve families. At the same time, the District used the goal of growing the tax base to support large-scale projects like the redevelopment of the Gallery Place/Chinatown neighborhood, where an arena, museums and other entertainment became a primary focus to bring tourists downtown. This split politically facilitated a neighborhood-focused image while keeping developers engaged and supportive of the administration[33]

In 1995, the District had amassed more than $700 million in debt, due to a combination of heavy social spending and the structural problems faced by the District in being both a city and a state. These challenges included paying high shares of social service, infrastructure and education costs and limits on revenues such as commuter taxes as well as the high share of untaxed federal properties in addition to the large number of nonprofits, university and church portfolios across the District. The newly Republican-controlled House of Representatives created the DC Financial Responsibility and Management Assistance Authority, referred to locally as the "Control Board". Signed into law by President Bill Clinton, the president also appointed the board members and created the Office of the Chief Financial Officer. Initially focused on balancing the budget, the Control Board could ultimately override the decisions of the local government, including contracts, appointments and other budget-related decisions. After the election of Anthony Williams – and a balanced budget for four years – the Control Board was dissolved. Yet, this period marked a change in the approach to District government, shifting toward a primary focus on development and financial strength that ultimately impacted the ways that housing policy was implemented.

Community-Powered Policy in a Changing Landscape

In 2002, at the urging of advocates from the Coalition for Nonprofit Housing and Economic Development (CNHED), then Mayor Anthony Williams created the Housing Production Trust Fund (HPTF) to supplement the existing funding from the federal government. In doing this, the District more than doubled its housing resources, exceeding the roughly $30 million from HUD programs, such as HOME and the Community Development Block Grant, and $3.6 million annually in Low Income Housing Tax Credit allocations. The HPTF is funded through a dedicated 15% portion of the tax on real estate sales, yielding between $12 million and $65 million annually from 2004 to 2015. Supporting both new construction and preservation, the fund set targets for affordability focused at those earning less than 50% of the Area Median Income (AMI). Across the total, 40% has to serve those earning less than 30% of AMI, 40% for those earning between 30 and 50% of AMI and the remainder can serve households earning up to 80% of AMI. Those targets have not been met since inception, but the rules have been tightened to increase the percentage of the trust fund going to households earning below 30% of AMI.

In 2004, the District allocated Community Development Block Grant funds to support tenant organizing and technical assistance to community-based organizations (CBOs) through DHCD's Division of Neighborhood Based Activities. While legal services have been supported through District government since the initial federal grant in 1978, organizing and other technical support had not been available, meaning that organizing was often done ad-hoc through attorneys and development consultants who were working with the residents to purchase the building. This change would become critical in more effectively operationalizing TOPA.

Two years earlier in 2002, the Columbia Heights neighborhood, located two miles north of the White House, became the first of an ongoing series of major redevelopments outside of the downtown core. The neighborhood had been slowly gentrifying since the early 1990s, with new residents at that time attracted to the neighborhood's cultural diversity and sense of community. However, the opening of the Metro Station and plans for redevelopment changed the pace across the neighborhood. After a lengthy neighborhood charrette-based planning process and contentious disposition agreement starting in 1998, developers broke ground on a new, relatively high-density commercial and residential development, including the District's first Target retail store and several other big box retail options that had not been available outside of downtown or DC's suburban shopping centers (Figure 4.1). Development was underway across the neighborhood in the midst of a housing bubble and growth of subprime lending, as well as increased demand from young, white and upwardly mobile residents for city living.

The results were dramatic. Between 2000 and 2010, the white population of the neighborhood increased by 330%, African American population fell by 26% and Latinx population fell by 11%. At the same time, neighborhood household

Figure 4.1 14th Street NW in Columbia Heights

income shifted from one concentrated at the low end of the distribution to a bifurcated distribution with incomes increasingly above $100,000 per year and below 50% of the regional median. As part of the redevelopment, the District required approximately 250 units be set aside for affordable housing as part of an affordable dwelling unit negotiation. Yet, as those buildings broke ground, that number decreased as developers negotiated with the National Capital Redevelopment Corporation (NCRC), the agency that replaced the Redevelopment Land Agency.

At the same time, more than 2,100 units were preserved as affordable – many using TOPA to remain rental or become limited equity cooperatives. For some, like Hubbard Place discussed in Chapter 2, the residents used TOPA as a critical negotiation tool that improved their position in discussions with a developer. Others, like Claiborne Apartments, became Limited Equity Cooperatives. Claiborne Cooperative is a 92-unit building located on 16th Street on the border between the Columbia Heights and Adams Morgan neighborhoods. Formerly rent controlled, Claiborne houses a population that building residents argue is representative of the surrounding community – including African American and white residents, as well as Ethiopian, Latinx and West Indian immigrants. Meetings are conducted in up to three languages – English, Spanish and Amharic. The residents purchased the building in 2006 when it was offered for sale using the local Housing Production Trust Fund, and it was rehabilitated in 2017 using private financing.

Courts also played a role in preserving affordable housing in the District. Columbia Heights specifically was the testing ground for TOPA and the District's human rights law. In response to neighbors frustrated by buildings lagging behind the rapid gentrification in some neighborhoods, in the early 2000s, the District's Department of Consumer and Regulatory Affairs (DCRA) created the Hot Properties Initiative. Through the initiative, housing inspectors identified multifamily properties with significant housing code violations, resulting in a list of 75 properties that was then pared down to 27 buildings.

Melissa, a veteran tenant organizer in the area explained that the owners of the properties in the neighborhood saw the economic boom coming after Metro opened in the neighbourhood:

> Owners were holding onto their properties – no point to vacate them when they had Latinos willing to pay even though they had no heat at all – so you might as well keep getting the rent, but they were just holding them because they saw the writing on the wall.

Emily, who represented some of the tenants in a condemned building explained, "we estimated that [the landlord] was taking in $30,000 a month with renting to immigrants who do not question – they simply pay their rent. They were not savvy – until they got representation." This pattern of milking properties is typical in low-income and minority neighborhoods. It also remains a key challenge to preservation.

These buildings would be condemned and closed by city agents due to the poor conditions. All were located in neighborhoods where the share of Latinx population was at least 4.1 times that of the city as a whole. Five of these buildings were located in Columbia Heights, where the Latinx share was 4.4 times that of the city as a whole. After notices were posted on two buildings in Columbia Heights, the tenants filed a motion for a temporary restraining order. However, for residents of another building in the neighborhood there was no such restraining order, and the tenants were evicted with no relocation assistance. Moreover, the violations were not new. After citing the owner for significant violations, the city failed to act until more than a year later. Further, the city had a policy of using a special fund to abate the violations, putting a lien on the property that has to be paid by the owner, but this was not used in any of these cases. In a lawsuit, three tenant associations claimed disparate treatment and impact under the Fair Housing Act (FHA) and the District of Columbia Human Rights Act (DCHRA). Some tenant advocates argue that closing the buildings was intentional, paving the way for developers who wanted to convert the buildings into high-end condominiums in rapidly gentrifying neighborhoods. The court found that although the tenants did not demonstrate disparate impact on the Latinx population, the Hot Properties Initiative "(1) intentionally discriminated against them on the basis of national origin in violation of the FHA and (2) discriminated against them on the basis of place of residence in violation of the DCHRA"[34].

While the other condemned buildings had already been sold to private developers, the tenants of 1458 Columbia Road were given the right to purchase the building. Residents received $1.5 million in acquisition funding in 2003 to purchase the 50-unit building, and $1.8 million to rehabilitate it – both from the Housing Production Trust Fund. The building has a 20-year covenant – with ten units serving households earning less than 50% of Area Median Income (AMI) and 40 units serving those earning between 50% and 80% of AMI.

One outcome of this process was that advocacy organizations and pro bono lawyers successfully pushed for more involvement opportunities for the non-profit sector, as well as relocation assistance for tenants. The result was that when a building was to be closed for poor conditions, organizers would be notified, and tenants would be put up in hotels in emergency cases and assisted in their relocation. Melissa explained:

> So, we at least got them to say that we could go in a few days in advance and tell the tenants "it's looking like the city might condemn your building. We've tried to get the landlord to turn the heat on. He hasn't. We believe that this is too dangerous for you." So, we would be supporting the city and saying "yea – this building is horrendous." If you can't get the landlord to make these repairs immediately, someone will die in this building. And then we could go in and say "hey – we're concerned, here's what we can do. We want you to know – we want you to prepare." And so, we got a system going, but Columbia Heights had the majority of these buildings.

Tenant organizers also wrote form letters to the owners for the tenants to sign stating that they were moving out against their will and would retain their TOPA rights, rather than allowing the landlord to benefit from a vacancy exemption to avoid complying with TOPA.

In addition, in the midst of the legal proceedings, the Office of the Tenant Advocate (OTA) was created within the Department of Consumer and Regulatory Affairs (DCRA) as a part of the backlash from advocates. The Chief Tenant Advocate explained:

> As a result of that ... the questions surrounding the incompetence of public service delivery on the part of DCRA on inspections brought us into ... properties within the Columbia Heights area where the tenants were crying foul with respect to landlords' ability to maintain the properties as safe and sanitary.

DCRA was critiqued in news articles of time for being managed by outside interests including developers and law firms representing developers. The OTA has since become an independent agency, which has allowed the office to both critique the city and act as a liaison between city agencies and the tenants.

The redevelopment of Columbia Heights and the concurrent changes to policy reverberated across the District. First, this redevelopment proved that there was demand outside the downtown core for high-density housing and retail. When the redevelopment of Columbia Heights was planned, the District and the local Development Corporation of Columbia Heights had to convince developers and anchor retail. After Columbia Heights, high-end, nationally-anchored neighborhood redevelopment became ubiquitous in DC, with new shopping districts emerging throughout the eastern and southern parts of the city where Black households were in the majority and unsubsidized affordable housing was the norm. Second, this redevelopment illustrated the need for more support for affordable housing across a range of needs. DC was changing, and it became clear that the existing funding and regulatory environment would not be sufficient to prevent displacement and maintain the existing subsidies. Finally, it showed the District that affordable housing within redevelopments was possible. Though it was not the first time that affordable dwelling units (ADUs) were required as part of a development, it was the first time it was used at such a scale, driving home the need for consistent rules on inclusionary zoning and city-owned property dispositions.

Changing the Preservation Landscape

In the early 2000s, local jurisdictions like Washington, DC were losing subsidized and market-rate subsidized units as many of the HUD subsidies began to expire and redevelopment became profitable in downtown-adjacent neighborhoods. At the same time, the growth of the housing market and delayed family formation among millennials and young generation Xers, created demand for new rental housing, further pressuring the existing subsidized housing stock. In 2006, DC's Comprehensive Housing Strategy Task Force released a report detailing the growing need for affordable housing. They argued for the preservation of 30,000 existing units of housing, including all subsidized housing units, the creation of 55,000 new units by 2020 and the creation of a locally-funded voucher program to supplement the federal program. The recommendations also supported the transformation of public housing through the District's New Communities Program[35]. With advocacy from the Coalition for Nonprofit Housing and Economic Development (CNHED) members, the District government created the Local Rent Supplement Program (LRSP), which can be either place-based or for individual households to use in the private market, which focused attention on preservation, increased resources for affordable housing and built a network based in data development.

Data for Preservation

One of the challenges to responding to the recommendation for preservation was a lack of data. There was no comprehensive, publicly available data source with which to track the location, expiration dates, opt-outs or REAC inspection scores. In 2007, the National Low Income Housing Coalition (NLIHC) initiated pilot programs in Washington, Florida, North Carolina, and Washington, DC using a grant from the MacArthur Foundation's Windows of Opportunity initiative, which would help them build their national database of subsidized housing. This database would also have a component of local knowledge from "housing monitors" to provide direct data about the conditions at the buildings with a goal of improving preservation efforts. Washington, DC was the first pilot by NLIHC, selected partially because NLIHC is located in the District. DC also had an existing network of tenant organizers, legal advocates, housing policy advocates and nonprofit developers who had been working on preservation issues using DC's powerful tenant protection laws.

The DC Preservation Network (DCPN), as it came to be known, meets monthly and discusses preservation at the building level. In 2010, it was transferred from NLIHC to the CNHED and the Urban Institute, which convene and manage the data, respectively. Its participants include local agency staff from the District's three housing agencies, as well as regional HUD staff, tenant organizers, attorneys, policy advocates, technical assistance providers, affordable housing developers and funders. The data, based initially on HUD's multifamily database, has grown to include locally-funded housing and has notes about the building to provide a brief history for future discussions. The data has also become an agreed-upon source for the participants and a space to share critical data about buildings that are at risk of losing their subsidies.

The work of DCPN highlighted the need for a stable large funding source and focused policy for preservation. The total funding amount in the Housing Production Trust Fund was both insufficient to address the needs of preservation and inconsistent. When the market was strong and property transfers were swift, the trust fund had more than $60 million in annual funds. But in 2009, when the market slowed, the fund had less than $12 million. This unpredictability of the funding for affordable housing, combined with the rapidly growing need for housing, drove a change in the approach. In 2010, the Coalition for Nonprofit Housing and Economic Development released a report, *An Affordable Continuum of Housing...a Key to a Better City*, which made the case that affordable housing in the District was connected and needed to be approached holistically[36]. Later that year, CNHED initiated the Housing for All campaign, aimed at stabilizing the trust fund at $100 million. However, while the District had targets for affordable housing preservation and production, there was no comprehensive policy to curb the loss of affordable housing. The primary mechanisms they had for development were TOPA and the RFP process but both were reactive and did not necessarily result in the preservation of the buildings at risk of loss.

Based on their lessons learned in the first seven years, DCPN participants wrote *Maintaining Economic Diversity and Affordability: A Strategy for Preserving Affordable Rental Housing in the District of Columbia* in 2014[37]. The report created a proactive policy approach to preservation, including priority criteria for preservation and tools for implementation. Specifically, the strategy recommended the creation of a senior staff position that would coordinate responsibilities for preservation, at least $100 million in the trust fund and the creation of an interagency committee to address preservation. The report also recommended repairs to public housing, one-for-one replacement of units as the communities are redeveloped and critical repairs. In February of 2015, after three years of sustained advocacy in rallies, council hearings and individual meetings with agency staff, DC Council passed a budget that included $100 million for the trust fund. When finally, this was passed by the council in 2015, this increase created a predictable resource through which to support preservation and new construction. Increases in local funding have made preservation more realistic in DC.

In 2018, DHCD hired a preservation officer to coordinate preservation policy and find ways to improve preservation processes. The agency also created a leveraged affordable housing preservation fund to facilitate quick acquisition that did not need to await a Request For Proposals timeline, administered by the Local Initiatives Support Coalition (LISC) and Capital Impact Partners (CIP). In its first year, DC added $10 million to the fund, which was leveraged to create a $40 million fund. While this fund moved money more rapidly, the loans were short term, could be made quickly, had higher loan-to-value ratios and required permanent financing, leaving smaller or low-income cooperatives or those with greater capital needs at a disadvantage. This shift from the more permissive First Right Purchase Program frustrated advocates and was seen as another example of the District's change away from community and rights approaches to housing that funded buildings with whom the agency built relationships. By contrast, District agency staff felt that this approach improved access for qualified buildings and was more efficient.

Affordable Housing and Development

At the same time that the District was increasing the funding for affordable housing, local government also focused on market-based approaches to the creation and preservation of affordable housing. Yet the underlying assumption of this approach was that the District could both facilitate rapid, high-cost development and gain some affordable units from these developments. This approach shifted from a resident-centered approach that – both explicitly and implicitly - acknowledged the need for community and housing stability as well as right to remain. Instead of starting with community, these approaches started with development and added the existing low-income residents back at the end if there were adequate resources.

Inclusionary Zoning, ADUs and Other Negotiated New Units

When the District used the power of city-owned land in Columbia Heights to require income restrictions in new development, the city responded to the neighborhood's demand for support for long-term residents within the context of ongoing development. They had previously used overlay districts in neighborhoods like Shaw and Logan Circle, nearer to downtown, to require the construction of affordable dwelling units (ADU) through the Office of Planning, as well as set-asides similar to those in Columbia Heights, in District-owned land dispositions.

Unfortunately, these overlays and set-asides had no management or enforcement other than title searches for owner-occupied units. This lack of enforcement was complicated by a lack of standard language, affordability standards or percentage of the units that could be set-aside. Though set-asides were an important innovation, the long-term management was not considered. The Department of Housing and Community Development was designated as the entity to manage ADUs after residents trying to sell their affordable condominium units needed to know how what price they could list the unit.

Inclusionary zoning (IZ) was put into law in 2007, but regulations were not published until 2009, and the program was not implemented until 2010. IZ codified the creation of ADUs and provided an entity to track units, including the management of income limits, regulatory updates and the creation of a lottery for new units. The lottery was centralized and required that anyone who wanted to get an IZ unit had to register with the goal of preventing discrimination by individual landlords and increasing access to information by tenants. When a unit became available that suited the household's needs, they had to income certify with a designated community-based organization. The goal was to centralize the administration and improve access by residents who may not be aware of the opportunities across the city. Inclusionary zoning in DC codified an existing process, and in 2013, the DC Council passed a law requiring a 30% set-aside of affordable units in any property owned by the District.

Public Housing

At a 2012 meeting in the NoMA (North of Massachusetts Avenue) neighborhood, staff from the Deputy Mayor's Office for Planning and Economic Development (DMPED) presented the basic tenets of the New Communities Initiative (NCI) as part of a presentation about the Northwest One project. Created in 2005, NCI is the local program developed to redevelop public housing and their surrounding neighborhoods, following the assumptions of HOPE VI and, in many ways hearkening back to the goals for the Northwest One Urban Renewal plan, specifically underlining the poor housing and neighborhood conditions, specifically concentrated poverty[38]. The program has four "guiding principles": one-for-one replacement of existing affordable units, right of return, mixed-income housing and a commitment to building before demolition[39]. The District has four NCI areas: Barry Farm (Ward 8), Park Morton (Ward 1), Lincoln Heights (Ward 7) and Northwest One (Ward 6), where the meeting was held. Yet, sitting in two tables toward the back of the gym where the event was held were former residents of Temple Courts, a Section 8 property that was demolished in 2007. Temple Courts has not been replaced, though ground was finally broken in late 2020 on the first phase of replacement housing.

The Northwest One (NW1) New Community shares the same general boundaries of the Northwest One Urban Renewal Area, designated in 1963. Located eight blocks north of the Capitol, the neighborhood has become a part of the central city.

After it was designated, the NW1 Urban Renewal Area became home to several affordable housing developments, including Temple Courts (Section 8), Sursum Corda (Section 8), Carmel Plaza (Section 8), Sibley Plaza (Public Housing) and Tyler House (Section 8). After taking criticism from the Southwest Urban Renewal project about the lack of housing for existing residents, specifically low- and moderate-income households, the District used this Urban Renewal Area (URA) to rehouse. In a response to Congress, National Capital Planning Commission Director William Finley wrote:

> In June of this year, this commission adopted the boundaries of the first residential renewal project in the close-in Northwest area. This 80-acre tract is to be dedicated to public housing and private housing for the lowest possible income group[...] We are attempting in this first northwest project to make use of every possible device, both private and public, to bring down the cost of new housing for families of lower income, the majority of which will most assuredly be Negro[40].

Yet HUD admonished RLA for concentrating housing in the area in a letter to the agency. This critique of the high levels of concentration of public housing would continue through the URA's lifespan. Between 1968 and 1974, six apartment buildings, a grocery store and a nursing home opened in the neighborhood, rehousing just over half of the neighborhood's previous residents. All but one of the apartment buildings had a nonprofit sponsor – primarily churches – and four were sponsored by African American institutions. The neighborhood also held schools, libraries and a community center. Yet by the 1980s, the neighborhood was also experiencing a rise in violence and increasingly poor housing conditions, reflecting broader trends in DC and cities across the country. Cuts in social services and housing support combined with incentivized moves to the suburbs by middle class households to create high demand and low funding for services at the local level.

Bush Construction, owners of Temple Courts and Museum Square One three blocks away, had threatened to opt out of their Section 8 contracts and failed repeated HUD inspections for poor housing conditions. In 2004, a murder in the neighborhood – a teenage girl was murdered in Sursum Corda, next door to Temple Courts – lead the District to look for solutions to the neighborhood's challenges, particularly the ongoing violence throughout the neighborhood[41]. The Williams administration (1999–2007) developed the New Communities Initiative and named Northwest One the first NCI area arguing that concentration of poverty and poor neighborhood conditions made mixed-income redevelopment necessary. In 2007, the residents of Temple Courts were given Housing Choice Vouchers to use in the private market as their building was purchased by the District for $22.5 million and was subsequently demolished. Since its demolition, the District has rebuilt Golden Rule Apartments nearby and added affordable units to market-rate developments, not yet replacing all the demolished units. But Temple Courts remains an empty lot, in spite of NCI's "build first" goals.

The pattern of NW1 has been repeated across the District, with local agencies arguing that the only way to preserve these units is to redevelop into mixed-income, mixed-use developments, while residents, fearing loss of community and shelter, fight against the policies for redevelopment. The New Communities Initiative reprises for many residents the mistakes of HOPE VI and pathologizes low-income, largely Black neighborhoods as toxic and irredeemable. This framing serves to justify a total redevelopment of neighborhoods, rather than community-centered redevelopment and preservation. In 2018, the Housing Authority, a quasi-public agency, was allocated $30 million for critical repairs of public housing in response to advocate goals to retain public housing, even as DCHA has released a plan for the transformation of public housing, yet advocates fight for more funding to rehabilitate the existing buildings and keep the residents in place.

Conclusion

Preservation can be a clear conflict between the logic of market development and tenant rights and power. Preservation, in a rights-based approach, can remove affordable housing from the speculative market, meaning that the highest and best use calculous must be reconfigured and that rights to property are more than a financial determination. A market approach suggests that the adage of Wall Street do-gooders – "Do well by doing good" – is possible. One can make money on redevelopment *and* incorporate a percentage of affordable housing into the deal. In DC, like the US as a whole, this is a fight playing out between policy and laws, funding and implementation, and between new and old residents, practitioners and policy-makers.

In 2013, the Urban Institute released a report on available and affordable housing by income sectors. What they found was that DC was one of the top cities for meeting the needs of the lowest-income households – those below 30% of Area Median Income (AMI). Given DC's high level of gentrification and rapid increases in home sale prices and rents, this seems strange. But perhaps the most incredulous group on hearing this finding were tenant organizers. They watched affordable housing disappear, heard from displaced residents, advocated to keep existing buildings and fought against landlords who tried to shirk the laws. But what they did not entirely see was that, while all of this was true, there were laws to enforce, funding to access and buildings that had long-term covenants. And more importantly, compared to other jurisdictions without this infrastructure, DC had significant resources. In short, DC did not rely on existing stock alone, but developed policy backstops.

Specifically, the District's focus on tenant rights through rent stabilization, the Tenant Opportunity to Purchase Act (TOPA) and other anti-displacement measures passed in the early years, in concert with the federal interventions discussed in the previous chapter created a foundation for residents to demand rights to remain in the city. At the same time, the District began to fund attorneys to assist residents in purchasing their buildings and fighting unfair housing practices, helping to build a connected advocacy network that understood the needs of residents. The legislation passed and the policies they implemented, particularly in the decade after Home Rule, created a policy infrastructure that provided long-term protection for low-income residents in the District and institutionalized the idea that renters – not just homeowners – had a right to be in their communities, a key element of tenant-focused preservation.

Yet, at the same time, the District underwent a transformation in approach after the Control Board and subsequent mayoral administration. Whereas the Barry administration and the council in the post-Home Rule period saw a first priority of developing needs-based social programs for low-income households, the post-Control Board period continues to look for ways to use the fast pace of development to negotiate for affordable housing. Economic efficiency as a guiding logic becomes a powerful driver of policy. However, it is DC's historic policy infrastructure, prioritizing rights-based affordability, that has facilitated the preservation of affordable housing for low-income households.

Notes

1 "Oversight Hearing and Markup on H. Con. Res. 420 – To Disapprove Rental Housing Conversion and Sale Act of 1980," Pub. L. No. 96–18, § Committee on the District of Columbia (1980).

2 Chris Myers Asch and George Derek Musgrove, *Chocolate City: A History of Race and Democracy in the Nation's Capital* (Chapel Hill: The University of North Carolina Press, 2017).
3 Brandi Thompson Summers, *Black in Place: The Spatial Aesthetics of Race in a Post-Chocolate City* (Chapel Hill: University of North Carolina Press, 2019).
4 Adrian Fenty was an African American mayor in Washington, DC from 2007 to 2011 and remains a divisive figure in the recent history of the city – seen as a reformer by new residents and a symbol of the larger gentrification and "negro removal" of new, white DC by many African-American residents.
5 Marion Barry was the mayor in Washington, DC from 1979 to 1991, and went to prison briefly after being caught smoking crack cocaine during an FBI sting operation in January 1990. He returned as mayor from 1995 to 1999. He has been the council member for Ward 8 since 1999.
6 Johanna Bockman, "Home Rule From Below: The Cooperative Movement in Washington, DC," in *Capital Dilemma: Growth and Inequality in Washington, DC,* ed. Derek Hyra and Sabiyha Prince (Routledge, 2016), 67–85; Summers, *Black in Place.*
7 Summers, *Black in Place*; Derek Hyra, "Race, Class, Culture and the Federal Government: The Rise, Fall and Legacy of DC's Black Political Machine," in *Community Inclusion and Conflict: Multiracial Gentrification in Washington, DC's Shaw/U Street Neighborhood*, ed. Derek Hyra (Chicago: University of Chicago Press, 2013).
8 Carolyn Whitzman, "Rights Talk, Needs Talk and Money Talk in Affordable Housing Partnerships," *Journal of Planning Education and Research*, December 3, 2018, 0739456X1881596, https://doi.org/10.1177/0739456X18815964; Rachel Bratt, Michael Stone, and Chester Hartman, "Why a Right to Housing Is Needed and Makes Sense: Editors' Introduction," in *A Right to Housing: Foundation for a New Social Agenda*, ed. Rachel Bratt, Michael Stone, and Chester Hartman (Philadelphia: Temple University Press, 2006), 1–19.
9 Whitzman, "Rights Talk, Needs Talk and Money Talk in Affordable Housing Partnerships."
10 Karen S. Christensen, "Both Process and Outcome Are Essential to Planning," *Journal of Planning Education and Research* 35, no. 2 (2015): 188–98, https://doi.org/10.1177/0739456X14566277.
11 Derek Hyra, *The New Urban Renewal: The Economic Transformation of Harlem and Bronzeville* (Chicago: University of Chicago Press, 2008); Asch and Musgrove, *Chocolate City.*
12 Summers, *Black in Place.*
13 Asch and Musgrove, *Chocolate City*; W.E. Finley, "Correspondence from W.E. Finley to Hon Frank Thompson, Jr.," September 20, 1960, National Archives.
14 Columbia Heights Citizens' Association, "A Statement of Some of the Advantages of Beautiful Columbia Heights: A Neighborhood of Homes" (Washington, DC: Columbia Heights Citizens' Association, 1904).
15 Sarah Jane Shoenfeld and Mara Cherkasky, "A Strictly White Residential Section," *Washington History* 29, no. 1 (2017): 24–41.
16 Cameron Logan, *Historic Capital: Preservation, Race, and Real Estate in Washington, D.C* (Minneapolis: University of Minnesota Press, 2017); Amanda Huron, *Carving out the Commons: Tenant Organizing and Housing Cooperatives in Washington, D.C*, Diverse Economies and Livable Worlds 2 (Minneapolis: University of Minnesota Press, 2018).
17 Department of Licenses and Inspections, Government of Washington, DC, "Housing Code Enforcement: Progress and Plans 1956–1965" (Washington, DC: Government of the District of Columbia, 1958).
18 Jerome S. Paige and Margaret M. Reuss, *Safe, Decent, and Affordable: Citizen Struggles to Improve Housing in the District of Columbia, 1890–1982* (Washington, DC: The University of the District of Columbia, 1983).

19 Catholic University Law Review, ed., "Tenant's Remedies in the District of Columbia: New Hope for Reform," *Catholic University Law Review* 18, no. 1 (1969): 24; David Tiplady, "Recent Developments In The Law Of Landlord And Tenant: The American Experience," *The Modern Law Review* 44, no. 2 (1981), https://doi.org/10.1111/j.1468-2230.1981.tb02742.x.
20 Huron, *Carving out the Commons*; Logan, *Historic Capital.*
21 Harry S. Jaffe and Tom Sherwood, *Dream City: Race, Power, and the Decline of Washington D.C.* (New York: Simon and Schuster, 1994).
22 In 2017, after a series of government shutdowns stopped local activity, Congress began to allow the District to spend its own money during government shutdowns, but no federal funds. This made it possible for DC to pick up trash on the National Mall, keep its schools open and pay its local employees. While Congress continues to have veto power over local legislation, it rarely intervenes unless the issue has some national relevance.
23 The Committee, on the District of Columbia, House of Representatives, Ninety-fourth, and Congress, "Rental Accommodations Act of 1975, (Council Act No. 1–46) and Report of the Council of the District of Columbia as Referred to the Committee on the District of Columbia," Legislative Report (Washington, DC: U.S. Govt. Print. Off., 1975), 23.
24 Oversight Hearing and Markup on H. Con. Res. 420 – To Disapprove Rental Housing Conversion and Sale Act of 1980.
25 Kerry Dougherty, "Tenant Power: Growing Number of Tenant Groups Fight to Buy Buildings," *Washington Post*, July 26, 1979, sec. DC.
26 Blair Gately, "Tenant Rebellion Fueled by Increases in Rent, Evictions," *Washington Post*, December 21, 1978.
27 Oversight Hearing and Markup on H. Con. Res. 420 – To Disapprove Rental Housing Conversion and Sale Act of 1980, 4.
28 Dougherty, "Tenant Power: Growing Number of Tenant Groups Fight to Buy Buildings"; Wendy Swallow, "Tenants' Rights To Buy Angers Sellers, Brokers," *Washington Post*, April 7, 1984, sec. F.
29 Bockman, "Home Rule From Below: The Cooperative Movement in Washington, DC."
30 Swallow, "Tenants' Rights To Buy Angers Sellers, Brokers."
31 Patricia Camp, "The Battling Tenants: Associations Help Once-Voiceless Victims Gain Victories in Some Conversion Fights," *Washington Post*, November 19, 1979, sec. A; Dougherty, "Tenant Power: Growing Number of Tenant Groups Fight to Buy Buildings"; Swallow, "Tenants' Rights To Buy Angers Sellers, Brokers."
32 Camp, "The Battling Tenants: Associations Help Once-Voiceless Victims Gain Victories in Some Conversion Fights."
33 Asch and Musgrove, *Chocolate City*; Jaffe and Sherwood, *Dream City: Race, Power, and the Decline of Washington D.C.*
34 2922 Sherman Avenue Tenants' Assocation et al., v District of Columbia (District of Columbia Court of Appeals April 14, 2006).
35 Alice Rivlin, "Testimony of Alice M. Rivlin On the Recommendations and Final Report of the DC Comprehensive Housing Strategy Task Force," June 13, 2006, https://www.brookings.edu/wp-content/uploads/2016/06/20060613_Rivlin-1.pdf.
36 CNHED, "An Affordable Continuum of Housing...a Key to a Better City" (Washington, DC: Coalition for Nonprofit Housing and Economic Development, 2010), https://www.dropbox.com/s/fzs2zl74z91w13u/Continuum%20of%20Housing%20Report.pdf.
37 DCPN, "Maintaining Economic Diversity and Affordability: A Strategy for Preserving Affordable Rental Housing in the District of Columbia" (Washington, DC: DC Preservation Network Preservation Strategy Working Group, 2014), https://www.neighborhoodinfodc.org/dcpreservationcatalog/Preservation%20Strategy%20Dec2014.pdf.

38 NCI, "About NCI" (New Communities Initiative, 2019), https://dcnewcommunities.org/about-nci/.
39 DMPED, "New Communities Initiative (NCI)" (Deputy Mayor's Office for Planning and Economic Development, 2019), https://dmped.dc.gov/page/new-communities-initiative-nci.
40 W.E. Finley, "Correspondence from W.E. Finley to Hon Frank Thompson, Jr."
41 Serge Kovaleski and David Fahrenthold, "NW Housing Complex A Tangle of Drugs, Despair," *Washington Post*, February 1, 2004.

5 Strange Bedfellows

Governance Infrastructures for Preservation

In 2010, the residents of Mass Place Apartments (Figure 5.1), located just north of downtown Washington, learned that the owner of their building was trying to transfer their property without giving them a notice under the Tenant Opportunity to Purchase Act (TOPA). The community was a mix of Latinx immigrant, Black and white households. Instead of the required timeline, the owner posted a notice that said they had 30 days to challenge the decision. The owner of this 201-unit building was planning to sell this and four other properties, Petworth Station Apartments, Ft. Stephens Apartments, Brookland Place and Takoma Place, across the northeast quadrant of the city 10 years into their first 15-year compliance period for the Low Income Housing Tax Credit. Quickly, Mass Place residents formed a tenants' association with the help of

Figure 5.1 Mass Place Apartments

tenant organizers funded by the DC Department of Housing and Community Development (DHCD). One resident described the early process, "the first time [the building was sold] was disastrous. It was very difficult because we did not have the knowledge of how this works. We didn't know about any of the rights that we were entitled to." They credit the organizer with helping them understand the process and, just as importantly, believe that it was possible to exercise their rights under TOPA because the residents at Mass Place, like low- and moderate-income households across the District, expect to be displaced and believe they have no power to change the situation.

When the portfolio dump was announced at the monthly meeting of the DC Preservation Network (DCPN), advocates collaborated to find solutions that would ensure residents could improve their negotiation power and choose the outcome that would work best for them. Instead of treating the buildings individually, organizers worked across all five buildings to build a network to challenge the owner and successfully demand their TOPA rights. Before the sale, residents at Mass Place reported rats, bed bugs, leaking ceilings and other critical housing conditions issues. At the same time, residents at the other buildings faced similar levels of deferred maintenance, as well as faulty security, poor resident management and overcrowding. The tenants of Mass Place decided to remain rental, and two purchasers put in bids. Unfortunately, the other four properties were not faring as well as they were in neighborhoods where speculation, but not gentrification, were underway, meaning that there were not many buyers interested in the properties in the neighborhoods outside the core of the District.

However, Mass Place had a prime location where rents were rising and rapid redevelopment was underway. The residents of Mass Place used that desirability to make demands of would-be purchasers. Specifically, they demanded that any purchaser buy the entire portfolio of five properties or none of them. One tenant leader, an elderly white man who has been at Mass Place for more than a decade, admitted to being reluctant to support the other buildings. He explained:

> Do you know what really decided me, pulled me on board for that, 'cause I was sort of apathetic about that? I was in such a state of fear and feeling so defensive that I just wanted to get what we needed and then see what else there would be. But I met [a leader at Petworth Station Apartments].

The Petworth Station leader is a vocal advocate who explained the conditions across the portfolio, including her building. They formed a partnership that has resulted in both of them participating in the Coalition for Nonprofit Housing and Economic Development (CNHED) resident board, frequently testifying before Council and being known to residents, organizers and policy-makers in housing in Washington.

A buyer who was experienced with Low Income Housing Tax Credit (LIHTC) properties accepted the terms, which gave the tenants of all five buildings time to organize tenant associations, build leadership and make decisions outside of the timeframe of TOPA. The buyer hired a nonprofit that worked with residents across the portfolio to find appropriately-sized units. This was particularly critical at Mass Place where units were relatively small and overcrowding was common. While conditions at Mass Place improved over the next few years, the other buildings received little investment from the new buyer. However, the residents were on firmer footing, had built relationships with technical assistance providers, knew their rights and mobilized their membership.

When the building came up for sale 5 years later – at the end of the first 15 years of tax credit affordability, things were different. First, the market in Washington, DC had changed. Not only had the District come out of the recession relatively unscathed, but property values had increased across the city, meaning that there was more demand for all five properties regardless of their location. Second, the residents had changed. Over the intervening five years, the tenant associations, which were newly formed at the first sale, had worked with organizers to build stable organizations. Finally, the advocacy community had grown, and preservation had become a priority of actors across the network, including District government. These organizations had developed their information-sharing networks, put out a report and recommendations for preservation to the District and had successfully advocated for changes in the local government around preservation that resulted in an increase in the local housing trust fund support to $100 million annually. In short, these buildings had resources in the form of negotiating power, technical assistance, funding and visibility.

While Mass Place and two others remained affordable rental, two opted to purchase and become Limited Equity Cooperatives. The negotiating power coming from TOPA and the established tenant association facilitated partnerships with the affordable housing developers who purchased the rental buildings. They were able to make critical decisions about the futures of their buildings' physical development as well as the long-term implementation of programming and implementation. But they also relied on the knowledge and support from organizers and attorneys who helped them work through the process of negotiation and purchase. They had support from advocates – both from nonprofit organizations and from other resident boards – who showed up for more funding. Finally, they benefitted from the broad network of affordable housing lenders and developers who could purchase and rehabilitate the buildings.

Since the early 1980s, affordable housing creation and preservation has rarely been done with government alone. Over the past four decades, the share of government-provided housing has continued to shrink, replaced by private developers and management companies[1]. Similarly, housing services rely on grants to nonprofit organizations who can support the needs of households across the housing continuum, including housing counseling, wrap-around special needs services, housing search, direct cash assistance or program administration. As a result, external governance plays a critical role in organizing, advocating and providing oversight to government agencies. These organizations ensure the ongoing function of housing at the local, state and federal levels.

DC's housing governance structure serves three primary purposes: service and housing provision; organizing; and citywide advocacy. Within each of these, approaches differ. As was discussed in Chapter 3, the ways that housing is framed – right, need or macro-economic necessity – change the ways that governance is organized, both within sectors and across them. The ecosystem implementing housing work in DC includes collaborative, consensus and confrontational methods that can be critical to both pushing policy toward a rights framework while addressing basic needs and maintaining relationships and information-sharing with government agencies and private sector actors. Though the details of service provision – specifically the development of affordable housing – are discussed in other chapters, this chapter will focus on the advocacy and organizing networks in DC and how they interact with other actors in the ecosystem.

This chapter investigates the role of governance networks in promoting preservation work in DC. Because of preservation's complexity and the local policy landscape of tenant protections, a mix of actors, beyond just service provision, has engaged on this issue. The governance that has developed around affordable housing is imperfect and, like all governance, relies on personalities and knowledge of council members, advocates and agency staff members. They make awkward bedfellows. Lenders, organizers, developers and government actors are not known for their great partnerships. However, in the ecosystem of DC's affordable housing preservation, successful tenant-focused preservation has been able to rely on access to capital, expertise and development ability through advocacy networks. However, these networks also embody conflicts, risks of cooptation and the potential for reproduction of power relationships. Yet these conflicts have also created a wide continuum of actors who can play different roles in affordable housing advocacy, provision and organizing.

DC's Housing Governance Network

In 2008, the District, like the nation more broadly, experienced a real estate slow down, though not a collapse. Home prices dipped in some areas, but due to the stability – and even growth – of government-related employment during this period, home prices across the board stayed stable. However, at the same time, the Housing Production Trust Fund, which relied on 15% of all deed and recordation taxes as a dedicated source, faced a more than $50 million decline from the previous year. These external changes in the housing landscape, combined with shift in the approach of District government as a whole after the Control Board, caused advocates to demand clear underwriting guidelines for the rolling application process for tenant purchases through TOPA. Until that time, decisions were made by the program manager who would meet with the residents and development team and decide what buildings would receive funding to become limited equity cooperatives. While the process was thorough, it was opaque to the development consultants and organizers working with residents. As DHCD staff presented their plan to advocates in a meeting, they tried to explain the constraints, and what advocates perceived was a system that made underwriting for tenant purchases impossible due to the loan-to-value ratio, reserve requirements and the maximum percentage of the total development cost the agency would lend. Limited Equity Cooperatives (LECs) would also only be able to get acquisition funding and would have to compete in the Request for Proposals (RFP) process for rehabilitation funding.

As we presented our fully developed and completed regulations without engaging with practitioners, or seemingly listening to the needs of affordable housing developers, the room grew increasingly tense. One organizer, frustrated, said, "It's like you don't care about affordable housing *at all*." Organizers saw the effective shut down of tenant-led preservation in this policy. LECs would struggle to compete against large projects with experienced developers because many of the buildings came with decades of deferred maintenance and a resident board with no experience in development. Its effect was a dramatic decline in the number of Limited Equity Cooperatives created since 2010. Figure 5.2 shows the change in the number of Limited Equity Cooperatives over time in DC. Even after the $100 million annual commitment to the trust fund started in 2015, advocates struggled to explain the importance of this type of housing to agency staff who had no experience with it. Many of the staff members had worked in other jurisdictions or private banks that rarely saw this type of housing, inherently focused on the tenant power, non-conforming from a financial perspective and lacking clear guidelines. This was exacerbated by growing fractures in the governance structure as nonprofit developers seeking subsidy for affordable rental housing found the new funding to be advantageous to their model, while those

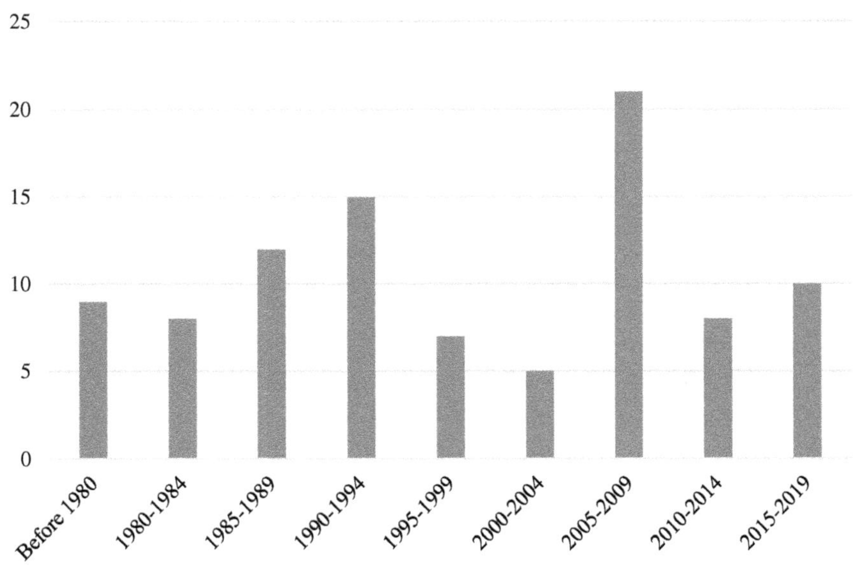

Figure 5.2 Number of Limited Equity Cooperatives Created by Year

who engaged in preservation – particularly through TOPA or in public housing developments – felt that the shift to a model of professionalization and efficiency did not serve the residents with whom they worked. Exacerbating this was the ongoing turnover in the Office of the Director of the Department of Housing and Community Development (DHCD) that did not end until the most recent mayoral administration. Until this point, the longest serving director of DHCD only served for 3 years, a notably long tenure compared to the previous decades where directors often left after 18 months, on average.

Figure 5.3 shows the housing governance ecosystem in DC, including the three housing agencies and other District agencies, service providers, funded and unfunded tenant organizers, mission-driven developers, funders, advocacy residents, the council and the DC Preservation Network. These groups interact in a number of ways, including funding relationships, advocacy relationships and partnerships. I will discuss these roles and relationships throughout this chapter.

Government Actors

There are three housing-specific agencies: the DC Housing Finance Agency (DCHFA), DC Department of Housing and Community Development (DHCD) and the DC Housing Authority (DCHA). Of those, only DHCD is a public entity. While HFA and DCHA have boards that are appointed by elected officials, they do not report officially to the DC Council or the Mayor. This means that, even when the District gives money to those agencies – as was the case recently with $30

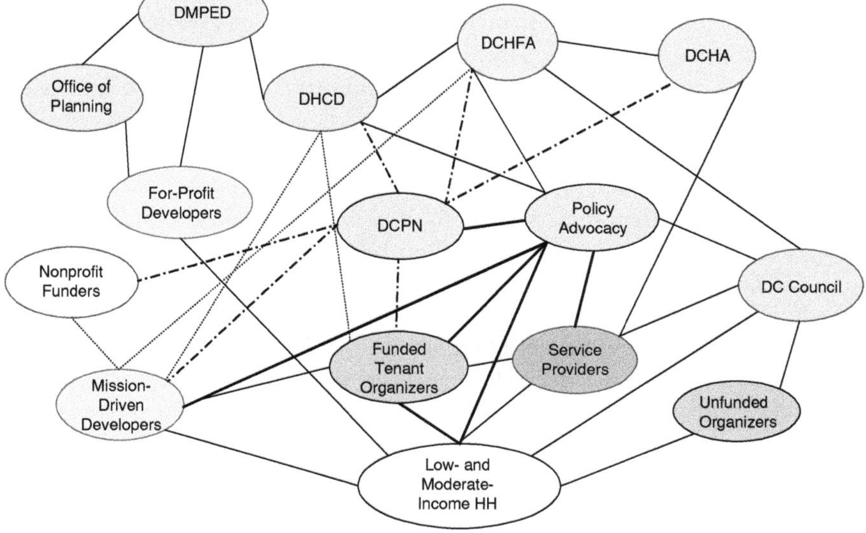

Figure 5.3 Washington, DC's Housing Governance Ecosystem

million to rehabilitate public housing – Council and the Mayor have limited oversight beyond appointing board members. HFA implements the tax exempt bonds, mortgage programs and the 4% Low Income Housing Tax Credit Program (though DHCD is responsible for the Qualified Allocation Plan (QAP) and the 9% credits). The Housing Authority plays a traditional role of administering both local and federal vouchers and managing public housing.

DHCD is responsible for all federal affordable housing programs outside of public housing and vouchers. It also administers the local Housing Production Trust Fund (HPTF) and the Affordable Housing Preservation Fund (AHPF). DHCD implements the various activities that are funded through the Community Development Block Grant (CDBG). This includes grants for neighborhood-based activities, including housing counseling, tenant organizing and technical assistance. They also implement programs like the single-family rehab program, lead abatement and the Home Payment Assistance Program (HPAP) for down payment assistance. DHCD manages the inclusionary zoning (IZ) program, rent control and condominium sales and conversion – which specifically includes the Tenant Opportunity to Purchase Act notifications. Finally, the agency also manages small District-owned properties – such as single-family homes – for disposition.

Two additional executive agencies warrant a note in the preservation landscape. The Office of Planning (OP), though not responsible for direct production, does have housing planners, responds to planned unit development applications and conducts research to create plans for housing, particularly zoning, the master plan and small area plans. They have intermittently reported on the impacts of redevelopment and created target areas for affordable housing preservation in gentrifying neighborhoods. DHCD and OP report to the Deputy Mayor for Planning and Economic Development (DMPED) which manages large-scale redevelopment projects involving city-owned land. Most recently, this was the Southwest Waterfront redevelopment in what was Urban Renewal land. The redevelopment included affordable housing through the District's requirement for inclusionary zoning, as well as the set-aside required for city-owned property. DMPED also houses the New Communities Initiative to redevelop public housing communities. DMPED emerged in 2006 out of the National Capital Redevelopment Corporation (NCRC), a transactional, quasi-governmental agency that was responsible for disposing of large properties, specifically in Columbia Heights. NCRC, as discussed in the last chapter, replaced the Redevelopment Land Agency, which was housed in DHCD, amidst critiques that the agency moved too slowly. DMPED, as a result, has grown into a development-focused agency to which all other housing and economic development agencies report.

The District has two independent agencies that have roles in housing: the independent Office of the Chief Tenant Advocate (OTA) and the elected Office of the Attorney General (OAG). OTA was created in the wake of the Hot Properties Initiative discussed in Chapter 4 to ensure tenants had support and information to level the playing field. In 2010, 75% of DC voters approved a ballot measure creating an independent attorney general's office and in 2014, the first independent AG took office. While OTA may seem like a clear part of the housing landscape, OAG has taken on a critical role in the prosecution of slum lords and landlords trying to circumvent TOPA.

These diverse responsibilities can lead to siloed funding relationships between advocates, developers and city agencies. While DHCD engages with mission-driven developers and small nonprofits engaged in organizing, service provision and economic development, DMPED has relationships (and occasionally a revolving door of employment) with large-scale market-rate developers, specifically those who are politically connected.

Non-Governmental Actors

In 2010, during a monthly meeting of the Coalition for Nonprofit Housing and Economic Development (CNHED), the organization introduced their new campaign: Housing for All. The goal of Housing for All was to push the District to invest in the full continuum of housing as a unified voice for housing. In contrast to an approach that often pits housing providers against each other, Housing for All was intended to unify the demands for affordable housing by "maintaining a strong coalition, building a wide base, seizing opportunities, and supporting the leadership of those impacted"[2]. Specifically, the campaign pushed for $100 million in the District's Housing Production Trust Fund (HPTF). The goals were broad, bringing in residents of affordable rental housing, organizers, lenders and affordable housing developers, among others.

CNHED was created in 2000 from two organizations, focused on economic development and affordable housing, respectively, as a way to grow effective advocacy in Washington that addressed a more complete set of needs. The first director was a former DHCD director and long-time housing advocate in the District. Within two years of CNHED's creation, they had proposed a housing trust fund supported through a portion of deed and recordation taxes. This passed and was funded in 2002, fundamentally shifting the possibilities for affordable housing creation and preservation. In 2004, they released a study on limited equity cooperatives in Washington, DC, recommending, among other things, support for tenant organizers to support tenant organizations hoping to purchase their buildings[3]. This recommendation similarly shifted the opportunity to purchase and made the preservation of buildings through the Tenant Opportunity to Purchase Act stronger. The latter shift also helped to create a coalition of strange bedfellows at CNHED.

Members include large- and small-scale nonprofit affordable housing developers from both local and nationally-affiliated organizations, economic development organizations, traditional community development corporations, homeless services providers, tenant organizers, development consultants, and lenders from local and national financial institutions. The majority of these organizations have some relationship to the city as a contractor or a grantee. As a result, the creation of an umbrella organization facilitated significant advocacy at a reduced risk to the individual organizations. The Housing for All campaign was an effort to pull together these disparate members around a common cause, which was ultimately $100 million in funding for the Housing Production Trust Fund. Because the housing organizations were engaged in some facet of affordable housing provision, this common cause resonated.

The members, as well as the residents with whom they worked or for whom they provided services, rally annually at a local church, bringing together elected officials and housing organizations of all types in support of housing. They testify at and attended council hearings at the Wilson Building (DC's main government building that houses the DC Council) wearing yellow Housing for All t-shirts. They packed the council agendas and filled the rooms, leading council members to don their own yellow t-shirts – often over their button-down shirt and tie, as former Mayor and Ward 8 council member Marion Barry did. The support of Housing for All became a bellwether for council members. Their advocacy was ultimately successful and has been a successful building block atop the base of laws and organizing in the city.

Yet CNHED – and, indeed, Housing for All - did not encompass the full range of affordable housing actors in Washington, and these divides revealed conflicts of interest between groups focused on consensus organizing and confrontational organizing. Community organizing can be defined in three primary ways: confrontational organizing as a means to system transformation; consensus organizing to improve neighborhood outcomes; and community-building organizing, which focuses on creating or remediating relationships within the community with the goal of community-based control[4]. CNHED's efforts focused on consensus organizing partially because they are also focused on building support for their members. However, two of the organizations focused on confrontational organizing in Washington – Empower DC and ONE DC. ONE DC emerged out of a community development corporation working in the Shaw neighborhood in the 1970s and 1980s. Neither organization takes money from the District or other government sources and often functions in direct opposition, organizing protests, challenging decisions in court and holding rallies to preserve affordable housing communities. ONE and Empower have engaged primarily in public housing communities and a handful of large Section 8 buildings around the city at risk of loss through redevelopment.

Conversely, CNHED rarely engages in discussion about public housing, which illustrates conflicts in the membership. While tenant-based preservation is a key tenet of the organizers engaged in CNHED, other members have been actively involved in the redevelopment of public housing through programs like the Rental Assistance Demonstration Program (RAD) and New Communities, creating conflicting goals for advocacy that echo conflicts in how housing is framed and, indeed, how advocacy is conducted. What ultimately unites CNHED members is their shared relationship to District government, particularly an agreement on a need for local funding to make affordable housing possible, rather than a shared approach to housing.

Conflicted Governance

When Brentwood Village Apartments were built, starting in 1937, the development, which would grow to 738 units over more than 15 three-story buildings, was the first large building to be built by non-governmental organizations using Federal Housing Administration guaranteed loans. Located in the all-white Brookland neighborhood near Catholic University, Brentwood Village Apartments housed white residents, including young working families, medical students, small business owners and married football players from George Washington University after WWII. It was one of five federally insured housing projects underway across the region, and:

> all projects [...] bear a close similarity in planning, land use, construction and location. All are located in suburban neighborhoods which are, however, easily accessible to employment, shopping and amusement centers by means of cheap, regular accessible transportation facilities. The placing of projects in outlying areas has made it possible for sponsors to acquire relatively large tracts of land, and careful land use has made it possible for each family unit to receive maximum light and air[5].

The development was celebrated as a model over the next decade, part of a larger planned community of new single-family homes and a large shopping center, including a bowling alley, movie theater and shopping followed over the next few years[6]. Over the next 80 years, the building would change hands seven times, largely owned by investment firms as the neighborhood desegregated in the 1950s and 1960s. When the building finally desegregated in 1963, the new owner "pointed out that Brentwood Village has been surrounded by private housing and apartments mainly occupied by Negroes but occupancy at the building had been restricted to whites," suggesting the decision was about the ability to rent the units in a highly segregated Washington, DC, rather than an effort to make housing available to African Americans[7].

After the 1963 desegregation and sale, a series of owners let the building fall into disrepair, and by 1967, the buildings had amassed more than 1,000 code violations that were not repaired until the building was subsidized through "Project Rehab," an HUD program focused in Washington, DC, among a select few cities. The program used federal loans to rehabilitate and preserve affordable buildings. However, it caused significant controversy. Because it was not part of the Model Cities or Urban Renewal Programs, HUD and the District government argued that residents did not qualify for relocation money while the development was under construction and, similarly, did not qualify for rent subsidies that would make the rehabilitated units affordable to them. The argument was that because it was a private owner, they were not subject to the regulations that would have been in place with government-owned buildings. The residents at Brentwood Village challenged this in court, and the court sided with them on the relocation. The rent subsidy, meanwhile, required an additional fight by residents who would be locked out of the new building[8].

The project came under criticism in outcomes as well. The number of units at Brentwood Village would decrease to 535, and across the District, "although the greatest need here is for large family units, there is a heavy emphasis on small apartments." The rehabilitation was not completed until the mid-1970s[9]. After the rehabilitation, the active tenant association of Brentwood Village presented a proposal to the owner for shared governance. It would have required the owner to give full monthly financial accounting to the tenants, pay all utilities and bill the tenants, and allow the association to hold hearings about lease violations before an eviction action could be undertaken. This was similar to the structure of Clifton Terrace Apartments a mile away in Columbia Heights. The owner rejected it. Meanwhile, the funding had run out for rehabilitation, and hundreds of units remained vacant, promised recreation spaces unbuilt and residents displaced[10].

The neighborhood continued to suffer the effects of white flight and disinvestment over the next three decades. The neighboring shopping center was set on fire in 1983, and many of the storefronts were vacant. Throughout the 1980s, Brentwood faced many of the challenges of the District – and segregated African American neighborhoods across the country – including evictions, disinvestment, violence and poor housing conditions.

Yet Brentwood Village – renamed Brookland Manor in the late 1980s – had a new owner who would become Mid-City, a for-profit mission-driven local developer with nonprofit roots. They focused on community-building activities, including outreach coordinators, a Boys and Girls Club, volunteer activities and public spaces such as a pool and basketball courts. The tenants' association was active, with residents engaging in neighborhood organizations, including one resident who was elected as an Area Neighborhood Commissioner. However, by 2016, there were growing tensions between the residents and management.

In 2014, Mid-City applied for a planned unit development (PUD) permit to redevelop the 20-acre site into a dense mixed-use, mixed-income community including a total of 1,760 units and new retail and public spaces. Of the 535 units in the development, 162 were supported through an HUD 236 loan, which kept the rent increases low, while the remaining 373 units had a Section 8 subsidy. Most of the households living in the 236 units have Housing Choice Vouchers to keep them affordable. In 2017, Mid-City paid off the 236 mortgage for the building, releasing them from affordability covenants for 162 units. DC's inclusionary zoning law would require the new development to have 165 units affordable to households earning less than 50% of Annual Median Income (AMI). The plan includes 440 affordable units, keeping the Section 8 subsidy to rehouse existing residents and adding additional units as part of the PUD application. Mid-City has also hosted job fairs and community events to provide information and build support for their plan.

The tenants' association claimed that the owners hired private security to cite residents for small infractions that would justify eviction from the building ahead of the redevelopment. The tenants' association, supported by pro bono attorneys and organizers from ONE DC appealed the zoning commission's decision to build. The association also filed a lawsuit arguing that the development violates the Fair Housing Act and DC's Human Rights Act because it discriminates based on family structure by excluding intergenerational families, resulting in their displacement.

This argument is based on a critique of the structure of the new development. Much of the housing will be inaccessible for current residents, the association argues, because 200 of the Section 8 units are to be part of an age-restricted senior building, meaning that no children will be permitted to live there. Additionally, the loss of 95 affordable units from the total number of affordable units and the loss of the number of family-sized units will reduce the affordability of the building for families. The new development will eliminate five-bedroom units and reduce the number of three-bedroom units to 64, a primary issue for intergenerational households. They argue that households where a grandparent, parent and children live in the same unit will have to choose between splitting up or being homeless.

The tenants' association argued that the developers should preserve all 535 affordable units with the same sizes and levels of affordability – particularly the large family-sized units. They also argue all residents should have a right to remain during a build-first process of redevelopment. They have further demanded a first source agreement that gives Brookland Manor residents priority in hiring for jobs related to the project. In short, they argue that this building should support affordable housing as a platform for economic and social power: first for the existing residents, but also should not contribute to the shortage of affordable housing across the District by reducing the total number of units.

The developers believe that they have met the requirements of the residents. They are building first by constructing the 200-unit senior building and a 131-unit affordable building, which will house all existing residents. They have ensured a right of return for all existing residents, and have built up their community services – including job fairs – to build support for the project, provide information and improve the services they have been providing. However, they also contest the need for large units, and believe the number of large units would be difficult to fill in a city where family sizes are shrinking. This has created a split among residents, of which more than 70% support the change. In 2017, almost 200 residents signed a letter of support for the redevelopment, and in 2018, the Zoning Commission approved the plan to begin construction of the 200 senior units and 131 units for current residents. The tenants' association filed an appeal, arguing that the developers have not proven there will be no displacement of residents. In response, the owners have threatened to build a by-right project that maintains current density and does not include affordable housing beyond the 165 units required by inclusionary zoning.

However, the redevelopment plan immediately received criticism from residents and advocates who feared potential displacement due to the new mix of housing units, residents and the redevelopment process. In this process, which did not trigger TOPA, tenants had no official power to determine their collective future. A *Washington Post* editorial board commentary framed the debate around the responsibility of private land owners:

> How far should private companies be pushed to solve public problems? How far can – or should – a developer building on private land with private money be pushed to address the shortage of affordable housing in gentrifying Washington, D.C.? Is it sufficient to meet, even exceed, the requirements of city law? Or is it fair to demand even more because of the city's great needs? Those are questions being raised in a contentious, and increasingly ugly, controversy over a redevelopment proposal for an aging housing complex in Northeast Washington. The answers could have implications that reach beyond whether this one project gets built.[11]

While individual members of CNHED – particularly attorneys – have expressed support for the Brookland Manor appeals and lawsuit, the organization as a whole has not engaged in the project. For those who are concerned about the loss of Section 8 and other federal subsidies, this redevelopment is successful. At the same time, for many affordable housing developers, the precedent set should the tenants be successful has the potential to make their work more challenging. They would have to prove there will be no displacement, and they would be required to replace units exactly, regardless of the feasibility or their read of the market. Conversely, ONE DC and the Brookland Manor Tenants' Association start with the needs of residents – both inside and outside of the development and believe that policy should focus there first, rather than starting at the top and working down to make the residents fit the plan.

Brookland Manor demonstrates the often-conflicting definitions and actors of preservation, the role of tenants and the potential tools that can or should be used to make preservation possible. This fight is common in discussions of public housing redevelopment, where the government has control over the pace, type and affordability of the redevelopment. Requirements for one-for-one housing and build first remain a challenge as localities, trying to respond to funding gaps, political pressure and deteriorating conditions negotiate between developers and banks and the capacity of local funding tools as affordability is lost. However, this fight has gained less traction in the redevelopment of privately-owned publicly financed affordable housing and illustrates, in many ways, the limits of the American approach to affordable housing creation. As Mid-City and District officials continue to stress, the developer is only required to provide the 165 IZ units under a by-right scheme. But the use of the PUD creates an additional layer that requires the District to define the public benefits and how they will be employed. PUDs require the development to be better than what would arise from a by-right development. The residents argue that the District should use this power to guarantee that there is no displacement and that the District loses no affordable housing – particularly for intergeneration and large families. Over the long term, this also illustrates a key challenge posed by the Rental Assistance Demonstration Program's structure for the redevelopment of public housing. The move toward the privatization of public housing, while solving an immediate funding problem, creates a long-term problem of shifting the power over preservation to the private sector, which has limited formal responsibility to the public to provide housing outside of the requirements of inclusionary zoning.

Brookland Manor also illustrates that how housing is preserved is as important as what is preserved – and that affordable housing is clearly a planning matter requiring deep community engagement with tenants. Residents are ultimately arguing that the process should start with residents who have a right to housing. While TOPA processes in DC start with this premise, the residents of Brookland Manor have, over the past decades, had to respond – or, typically, acquiesce – to the actions of the building owners who, over time, reduced the number of units from 783 in the 1940s to 535 in the 1970s and now, to 440. The lack of resident engagement in the most recent design and development process suggests that the building, not the community, was the aim of preservation. While Mid-City's intention to avoid displacement of existing residents addressed one level of frustration, the lack of early engagement meant that there was no acknowledgement of the needs, preferences or existing structure of community at Brookland Manor. As a result, the current community events appear to some tenants to be ways to coopt through inclusion as a way to build support for a project they had already determined[12]. The dwindling group of residents opposed to the redevelopment, therefore, are using the only power they feel they still have – appeals and lawsuits to stall the process.

This approach exemplifies the fundamental gap between organizations in housing governance. Those who see housing as a right of tenants and those who see housing as a social service are often at odds – and this is on top of the challenges of time, money and finance availability that builds in limitations on projects. CNHED's silence on this and other large-scale redevelopments that do not have clear TOPA implications illustrates the growing gap between different types of organizations. Over the decades since the passage of Rental Housing Conversion and Sale Act, the network of tenants that successfully advocated for the law has weakened and fractured. At the same time, CNHED's network has grown to focus on primarily production and preservation of affordable housing units, rather than displacement. While residents and organizers remain committed to anti-displacement, the growth of affordable housing development – partially due to the high volume of affordable housing funds – brought in large scale players focused on units, rather than power. This subtle, yet important, change has shifted the focus to reflect the interests of affordable housing developers within the governance network – and remains supported by the development interests outside the network. At the same time others groups responding to issues surrounding DC's real estate boom include more radical organizations such as Empower DC and ONEDC, both of whom take no city money and focus specifically on grass roots-level action to prevent displacement. They do not work with – and, at times are at odds with – many CNHED members whose models depend on District or federal funding for housing development, organizing, community services or economic development work. Attorneys from the Washington Legal Clinic for the Homeless and Bread for the City tend to cross the lines between groups because of their focus solely on tenants.

Where there are laws, as in TOPA, the lines are clear, and nonprofit developers work with the tenants to build affordable housing, but the conflict between the confrontational organizers and others can create significant challenges. At Museum Square One (discussed in Chapter 1), there were significant conflicts that arose in the process because the confrontational organizers were not willing to work with those funded by the District or with District officials.

As one white female attorney who represents low-income residents explained:

> I don't know who to blame. Not that there is blame, that's maybe not the right word but, like I thought ONE DC was organizing out there and I offered to come out and they said, "no we've got it." And, you know ... are there other groups who aren't participating in the network that need to be participating? Because I think two of the biggest organizing groups, Empower and ONE DC, aren't at the table and I wonder why.

This issue illustrates a clear conflict of interest for the housing governance network itself around its willingness to engage in anti-displacement work and invite more confrontational organizing groups to the table. At the same time, it illustrates the challenge of radical organizing's unwillingness to engage with more consensus organizers.

Policy Advocacy

While CNHED advocates generally on affordable housing, the focus on the preservation of subsidized housing was supported through the data and focus of the DC Preservation Network (DCPN), a meeting of stakeholders from organizers to funders and local and federal agency staff who discuss preservation at the building level convened by CNHED. In the early 2000s, local jurisdictions were losing subsidized and market-rate subsidized units as many of the HUD subsidies began to expire. At the same time, the nascent back-to-the-city movement was gaining momentum with the growth of the housing market and delayed family formation among millennials and young generation Xers, putting pressure on the real estate markets in some of America's fastest growing areas like Washington, DC. However, there was no comprehensive, publicly available data source with which to track the location, expiration dates, opt-outs or Real Estate Assessment Center (REAC) inspection scores. Meanwhile, there were also few federal initiatives to address the preservation of affordable housing. In 2007, the National Low Income Housing Coalition (NLIHC) started pilot programs in Washington, Florida, North Carolina and Washington, DC that would help them build a national database of subsidized housing. This database would also have a component of local knowledge from "housing monitors" that would provide direct data about the conditions at the buildings. The goal of this type of data was to provide more direct housing data that could aid in preservation efforts.

When the foundation funding ended, NLIHC transferred the project to CNHED and the Urban Institute. CNHED's executive director at the time explained:

> We took it to our board because [...] it wasn't necessarily a fit [...] with our members and so I pushed it and it got okayed which is great. So that was it. From then on, you know, I was just kind of the convener, followed up on issues and worked with The Urban Institute and tried to keep the agencies involved and I think that was pretty successful. I mean it's kind of a unique process because [of] others in the process, other rehab agencies participating, advocates, lawyers, legal services kind of people, housing services kind of people. It was kind of a tricky little dance to maintain all of that.

DCPN was focused on more than just getting funding for affordable housing or services, as had been CNHED's primary mission. This shift meant that CNHED would engage in policy around particular buildings, tenant rights and power, ultimately resulting in a report and recommendations for the preservation of affordable housing in Washington, DC.

Meetings have been held monthly since 2007 when the group was constituted. Initially, the group was conceived as a space for on-the-ground tenant organizers and legal advocates to interact with government agency staff and provide early-warning information in both directions. However, as the group has evolved, funders and mission-driven developers have joined and provided another layer of data about buildings: the discussions on the market about buildings, the potential funding sources and interested buyers. Participants discuss buildings that have been flagged by the conveners as at-risk, which include bankruptcy or foreclosure, an opt-out notice, a notice of sale of the building, conditions complaints, condominium conversion, expiring subsidy, failing REAC, or more information needed. The flagged properties are added to the monthly agenda of properties, which also includes any information currently available from the database or participants. The agenda, which includes running and often lengthy narratives about each building – is sent out before the meetings by CNHED staff to give participants a chance to find additional information about the relevant properties. Agency staff particularly appreciated seeing the agenda early in order to better prepare information from a variety of sources.

Elena, a legal advocate who was involved in the network from the beginning said, "I remember that the purpose was to get ahead of the game on preservation – up until that point we had been pretty reactive – the point was to see what we can do to get ahead." Since 2008, almost 200 buildings have been on the Preservation Network meeting agendas, representing more than 20,000 federally or locally-assisted affordable units and approximately 22,000 total units, including those under rent control, market affordable and market rate. DCPN has played three critical roles: data sharing, connections to power and relationship-building among participants.

Data in Governance Networks

A central goal of the Preservation Network has been what can be characterized as building vertical and horizontal networks. Vertical networks, or those across different sectors of the network – such as between residents and funders or organizers and agency staff – can build power through equitable data access and data sharing. Horizontal networks, or those amongst actors within the same sector, can build strength and efficiency – while also improving broader outcomes. One of the primary goals of the network was to facilitate data sharing across networks. Vertical sharing was most frequent between HUD staff members and tenant organizers to clarify expiration dates, REAC scores or opt-out notices. However, tenant organizers also provided important data to government agencies about the actions of landlords, conditions within the buildings and plans by tenants to purchase their buildings. This type of information sharing was the primary reason participants cited for continuing to participate in the network. John, a tenant organizer and meeting convener explained:

> I went to the first meeting and then I kept going because it is useful as a means of occasionally getting information from government about properties. It was also useful to get information from other non-governmental participants who happened to know something about particular buildings or developers, owners, management companies – it's ideally for issues and information sharing.

Through this vertical sharing, government agency participants used it as a way to both acquire and share knowledge about buildings, acting as a warning system about projects that are troubled. They further have a better understanding of the organization level and interests of the tenants living in the buildings. Finally, as both conveners and agency staff stated, they learn about bad actors and loopholes exploited in tenant protection laws. Ben, a government agency staff member explained that he started to participate because his agency was receiving tenant complains about buildings and did not always know what was happening. He also saw his role as a connector to information and other parts of government. He explained, "Because a lot of the information is confidential, I have to educate them about how to go around to get the accurate information ... My contribution was more in setting the record straight and getting the information and understanding the solutions." He explained that many times tenants and advocates had incorrect or incomplete information that made action and advocacy difficult. In 2012, he offered an early warning about a series of buildings owned by the same entity that served special needs populations. Because he worked directly with owners, he was able to let the organizers and other government agency staff know – albeit obliquely at times – that there were issues with the management that may impact affordability in the buildings.

Organizers similarly found this access to government data important. As Hannah, a legal advocate stated simply, "I think it's beneficial to clients because we have access to various government officials [through the network]." John, a tenant organizer, commented that "knowledge is power," and that having a better equity of information between grassroots organizers, government and developers leveled the playing field.

In 2010, during the market downturn when few landlords issued notices of sale for TOPA, Anna, a tenant organizer and a colleague went to DHCD's files on evictions and rent control to search for anomalies in order to proactively reach out to tenants. At The Gregory Apartments in Southeast DC, they found a high number of evictions for amounts exceeding $20,000 per tenant. After approaching the building, the owner refused to allow the tenants to meet on the premises or in a local church, so Anna brought the building to the network to see if there was additional information. She explained:

> What we ended up finding out through the network was that the Housing Authority, DHCD, and DCHFA were all involved with the building and all had different plans for the building. The housing authority had just stopped paying on the vouchers [due to] failed HQS [Housing Quality Standards] inspections ... And then DHCD, I think, was currently reviewing a loan application and the Housing Authority was trying to force a change in management and asset management because of mismanagement at the building. And DHCD was looking to give the current management a loan. And, there was also, I forget who, well maybe it was Housing Authority, but maybe it was one of the other groups as well, [who] was working to like pull some subsidy which would have jeopardized the loan [...] So, essentially, I mean, it was kind of easy, at least from our, organizing perspective or whatever, it was just like, "you all just need to sit in a room together and figure this out." And literally, I mean, I said that and people were like "oh!" And the next month they were like "that was such a good idea," so, it was just kind of like, an obvious idea ... just whoever was looking at Housing Authority wasn't understanding how that would impact the subsidies that DHCD and HFA had in there.

This use of both horizontal and vertical networks ultimately kept the building affordable and brought agencies into more direct contact with both the owner and the building residents.

Building Deep and Wide Networks

To make the network work effectively, frequent and effective participation by a diverse set of actors was necessary. NLIHC conveners argued that this broad-based participation was due to the championing of the network by key stakeholders, including city government actors. But time also played a role as government actors began to see the importance of participation for getting information, sharing information and building trust. On the other hand, organizers explained that they found out about properties that they visited through the Preservation Network typically because there was an expiring subsidy or a failing REAC score. However, while the participation by advocates was regular and significant, the quality and regularity of public sector participation was unpredictable, largely dependent on the priorities of the directors of the relevant agencies. Participation has taken two forms: direct attendance and email responses to agenda items. Some of the agency participants reported that while they may have initially been told to attend by their directors, there was often little or no interest in the results – meaning that the frequency of the participation was based on individual-level interest in the issues discussed. For instance, in a previous administration, the director of the Department of Housing and Community Development, new to District government and the advocacy community, prohibited his staff from attending DCPN meetings, arguing that it was a conflict of interest. However, more recently, agency directors have sent both more relevant and more frequent reports to the network.

Many interviewees specifically cited the participation of HUD as a key source of information. In the first few years of the network, participants had to file Freedom of Information Act requests to acquire the REAC scores of Section 8 properties, a key indicator of risk for loss from the subsidized stock. When HUD participated, staff members were able to share the information, a particularly important element given the risk of termination and loss of a property as a result of multiple failed REAC scores. Additionally, due to delays in data reporting and the renewal process, having an HUD representative to clarify the status of particular properties was important. HUD was also an important source of information for properties in the process of redevelopment. Building owners in negotiation with HUD over refinancing or applications for new sources of funding may have buildings with expiring subsidies. Rather than being a sign of risk in this case, it could lead to a more stable building. However, having agencies like HUD at the table allowed members to better discern risks to affordability.

In early 2013, the owner of Tyler House Apartments in the rapidly changing NOMA (North of Massachusetts Avenue) neighborhood received federal Low Income Housing Tax Credits to significantly renovate the 42 year-old 284-unit building while retaining a long-term place-based Section 8 contract. Tenants received notifications to recertify their incomes and eviction notices due to items that had been on their background checks for many years, and felt they were being intimidated to leave the building by the management company. The tenants of Tyler House had a history of negative interactions with the landlord, including a failed REAC inspection in 2009 and an unwillingness to allow the tenants to work with organizers in 2010. The active tenant association tried to get meetings with the owner in 2013 when rumors surfaced about a redevelopment. Tenants called HUD's toll-free number to complain about the issues at the building with no success. When both of these efforts failed, the tenant board president, tenant organizers and legal advocates attended DCPN meetings to discuss the issue with HUD staff. Both during and after the meeting, HUD staff worked with the tenants and organizers to better understand the issues. Although HUD was not involved in the rehabilitation, which used 4% Low Income Housing Tax Credits, HUD staff used its position from the ongoing Section 8 contract on the building to initiate meetings between the DC Housing Finance Agency (DCHFA), the tenants and the owner. HUD's involvement facilitated significant dialog between the owner and the tenants. In addition, the DC Housing Finance Agency (DCHFA), who provided the tax credits, asked for a relocation plan and a renovation plan from the owner. Since that time, DCPN has monitored the ongoing preservation work, and both HUD and DCHFA have remained in contact with the tenants and their attorneys about the ground-level challenges as the rehabilitation has continued.

Building Trust within Governance Networks

An important input and output of the network is relationship building and trust. Elizabeth, a government agency participant, argued that over the years the network has been in place:

> the meetings became more productive and more action-oriented ... and it was less of trying to figure out who was responsible and who should take ownership, and even in a negative way where to point a finger. It was more, toward the end, how to problem-solve.

Advocates like John talked about relationships built with particular agency staff members who engage in dialog about properties outside of meetings. Meanwhile Hannah, a legal advocate, argued that the relationships built during the meetings give her greater access to government actors outside of the meetings. Ben sees part of his role as a government participant as providing access to other parts of his agency and the local government more broadly. This trust, participants felt, was because meetings were focused on data sharing. From the standpoint of tenant organizers and other nonprofits, the very act of greater transparency on the part of government actors improved the relationships and trust. Government actors felt that the fact that they would not be blamed or attacked in meetings improved the relationships and trust among participants and led them to being open to working with organizers, legal advocates and other nonprofits outside of the meetings to focus on particular properties.

Elizabeth explained that she was not supportive of the network when it first began because of the potential for conflicts of interest due to the advocate participants in the room:

> So I think that caused some of the public sector representatives ... to feel less comfortable about the conversations being held in the room. I think as the years passed, and definitely within the last four to five years, I think that there was a sense of trust that was built ... I've seen it go from

> something that could've been seen purely as an advocacy tool that turned into a problem-solving tool which, if that is the future of the network, that would be a positive thing.

This trust typically extended beyond the individual participants to the organizations they represented, supporting ongoing work amidst turnover.

Shared Learning and Governance

Technical learning and brainstorming proved to be important to the empowerment of organizers and the tenants with whom they worked. For many organizers, the various financing programs such as Section 8, the Low Income Housing Tax Credit (LIHTC) and Section 236 – some of which are obsolete – were relatively unknown. Anna, a tenant organizer who has been involved since the inception of the network explained:

> For the first year I went I was pretty lost most of the time because I didn't have a finance background, and so you know people would just be like, "202 mortgage" and then you know all these – particular HUD terms and HUD mortgages that … only exist for a few properties … I think in particular at the time there was a lot of folks in the room that were really useful so government, attorneys, HUD came really early at the beginning … so I think both just having that mix to be able to coordinate and also just for learning since I was working on subsidized buildings.

The imbalance of information can leave many organizers out of the policy discussions and make it difficult to find the appropriate levers to make preservation activities happen.

This type of learning was illustrated in the ongoing discussion of Low Income Housing Tax Credit (LIHTC) compliance periods. Properties subsidized through LIHTC since 1989 have two 15-year compliance periods. However, their expiration dates are often set for the first 15 years in the HUD database, causing confusion among participants. As Anna explained, much of the learning was facilitated through the diversity of participants – many of whom were not previously experts in housing finance or housing policy. But learning the rules of funding sources, affordability periods for programs, and impacts of prepayments, failed REAC inspections and other issues related to housing finance, gave them the tools to address many challenges facing their clients.

In the case of Elsinore Apartments, a building that had gone into monetary default with DCHFA, the attorney representing the tenants often brought housing finance questions to the network to better understand the impact of foreclosure on the existing LIHTC and Section 8 covenants. Originally a 12-unit Section 8 contract created in 1970, the project expanded in 2004 using a Low Income Housing Tax Credit subsidy that added 152 units to the project by adding a neighboring building. When the owner defaulted on the project in

2010, the building was in good condition. DCHFA faced a loss of $5 million to repay the HUD-insured mortgage on the property and hoped to minimize that amount. The building was sold at auction in 2012 without any tenant involvement in the decision-making in spite of repeated efforts by the tenants, attorneys and organizers to be involved.

Because the new owner was only required to maintain LIHTC for three years after the auction, and the fate of the Section 8 contract was unclear, the attorney worked with other participants to find alternative solutions. At several points during the process, the attorney representing the tenants brought an issue to the network stating that she was not a housing finance person and needed assistance in both understanding the complex issues around compliance and continuation of Low Income Housing Tax Credit covenants, the impacts of layered subsidies and the potential solutions in this project. The group – particularly participants working for the DHCD and nonprofit developers – worked together to both explain the program and propose solutions.

Ultimately, they were able to pressure DCHFA to require the continuance of the partial Section 8 contract in the auction of the building. The building reverted to rent control after the loss of LIHTC, and those rents were comparable or lower than the tax credit rents. Although the building was a loss in terms of the subsidized stock, the knowledge gained through the network allowed the attorney and others in the network to advocate better for tenants in other buildings and to ensure that tenants in Elsinore had the best outcomes in the circumstances. It also served to build relationships with DCHFA to improve the outcomes for similarly situated buildings in its portfolio. More importantly, through this project and others, housing advocates were, as Anna and others argued, able to better advocate for their clients using information learned over the course of the network's existence.

Conclusion

Preservation that focuses on tenants necessitates a broad and deep set of actors who may not always agree. Both CNHED and DCPN have been effective at connecting residents to power. One attorney working at a nonprofit organization explained about her engagement with DCPN:

> I think it's beneficial to clients because we have access to various government officials. I would like to see more of more participation by tenant leaders at the various properties. Because I think to build a unified voice around preservation and around affordable housing in the city, I think it really has to be driven by the folks who [are] affected most by it so part of what we talk about is how to mobilize that population, how to get our clients there.

For her, and many other organizers who directly engage with residents, the governance that specifically includes DCPN has facilitated the connection of resident needs to policy-makers. This was particularly acute in buildings across the city where local government agencies rarely knew about conditions, landlord abuses or opt-outs of Section 8 contracts until they became emergencies. DCPN facilitated early engagement and coordinated responses – if not as quickly as advocates hoped.

These connections have led to a shift to a focus on preservation – both at CNHED and District government. At the same time, CNHED's Housing for All campaign, starting in 2010, engaged all members in the community to think about affordable housing across the housing continuum with a specific demand for a $100 million annual allocation to the local Housing Production Trust Fund (HPTF). CNHED hired a community organizer who developed materials, organized rallies and phone banks, trained resident advocates and organized testimony to encourage residents to voice their own needs at council hearings, rallies and one-on-one meetings with decision-makers.

One nonprofit developer explained:

> I've heard the mayor talking about preservation, I've heard DHCD talking about preservation, I've heard a lot more than I think I've ever heard at that in previous administrations. I'm not saying that they, that preservation wasn't funded, but it was sort of, it was never really something distinct we discussed in the political, you know, council.

In 2014, DCPN members developed *Maintaining Economic Diversity and Affordability: A Strategy for Preserving Affordable Rental Housing in the District of Columbia* [13] outlining recommendations for preservation in DC. The following year, the Mayor convened the Preservation Strike Force, which made recommendations that echoed the DCPN report, specifically calling for zero losses in the subsidized affordable housing stock, that is, 100% preservation. Over the next five years, the District implemented a number of the recommendations, including hiring a preservation officer to coordinate policy and practices to facilitate preservation, developing an acquisition fund, improving asset management and increasing the trust fund. These recommendations, in conjunction with the ongoing Housing for All campaign pushed the District to center preservation as a policy, and the Strike Force's recommendations made them an official Mayoral goal.

At a 2018 Housing Rally, CNHED's current executive director welcomed the assembled tenants working with member organizations and iterated what was always underlying the advocacy missions of CNHED's work – "We are a trade organization." This statement highlighted CNHED's overall goals – advocacy with the goal of supporting members' access to funds that would help them continue their existing work. This shift in priorities is changing the connections to power as residents are no longer organized en mass to testify at council hearings, and most often the organization focused more on preservation and production funding for affordable housing – a clear demand from the affordable housing developers working in DC.

It has also left a gap in the governance that connects residents directly to power. The resulting space has been filled by confrontational organizing, which, while changing the conversation, is less focused on partnerships to address policy development or implementation. It further leaves no room for collaboration between residents and agencies for shared goals in contentious redevelopments such as Museum Square or Brookland Manor – and little space for policy advocacy that will improve outcomes and support improved policy in TOPA projects.

Notes

1 Alex F. Schwartz, *Housing Policy in the United States* (New York: Routledge, 2015).
2 CNHED, "Housing For All Campaign Case Study," Coalition for Nonprofit Housing and Economic Development, 2015, http://h4all.cnhed.org/.
3 CNHED, "A Study of Limited-Equity Cooperatives in the District of Columbia" (Washington, DC: Coalition for Nonprofit Housing and Economic Development, Spring 2004).
4 William Peterman, *Neighborhood Planning and Community-Based Development: The Potential and Limits of Grassroots Action* (Thousand Oaks, CA: Sage, 2000); Randy Stoecker, "Understanding the Development-Organizing Dialectic," *Journal of Urban Affairs* 25, no. 4 (2003): 493–513.
5 Franklyn Waltman, "Private Housing Projects in Capital Set Example for United States," *Washington Post*, November 28, 1937.
6 "Display Home Open Today on Channing Street: Six-Room Colonial House on Display in Brentwood Park," *Washington Post*, December 3, 1939; "New Shopping Center in Northeast Washington Underway," *Washington Post*, February 11, 1940.
7 J.V. Reistrup, "738 Unit Brentwood Village Is Sold and Desegregated," *Washington Post*, July 11, 1963.
8 Eugene Mayer, "Tenants Win Eviction Stay in Northeast," *Washington Post*, April 15, 1972; Eugene Mayer, "'Best Tenant' Has Problem: Income Too Low to Stay in Rebuilt Unit," *Washington Post*, June 4, 1972.
9 Eugene Mayer, "Renewal Projects Scored: Critics Charge Relocation Aid Not Adequate," *Washington Post*, March 19, 1972.
10 Eugene Mayer, "Brentwood Pact Is Rejected," *Washington Post*, August 19, 1972; Judy Nicol, "Brentwood Village Hopes Rekindled by Fund Grant," *Washington Post*, August 18, 1973.
11 "How Far Should Government Push a Private Company to Serve the Public Good?," *Washington Post*, May 1, 2017, sec. Opinion.
12 Faranak Miraftab, "Making Neo-Liberal Governance: The Disempowering Work of Empowerment," *International Planning Studies* 9, no. 4 (2004): 239–59.
13 DCPN, "Maintaining Economic Diversity and Affordability: A Strategy for Preserving Affordable Rental Housing in the District of Columbia" (Washington, DC: DC Preservation Network Preservation Strategy Working Group, 2014), https://www.neighborhoodinfodc.org/dcpreservationcatalog/Preservation%20Strategy%20Dec2014.pdf.

6 Housing for Community Power and Voice

> I feel now as if I unwittingly perpetrated a shell game on the public ... we've destroyed more low-income housing than we've replaced and haven't relocated the people. If Urban Renewal is to continue, it will have to center on people and not on buildings.
>
> Senator Paul H Douglas, Chair of the Presidents National Commission on Urban Problems[1]

> People started asking me "do we still belong here?" This was after we bought the building. And I was really angry. I was like "yeah, we fought to be here, why don't we?" And I didn't realize I was feeling like that myself. You know I was just so gung-ho about it. This is ours.
>
> Resident leader, 1417 N Street NW

The Shaw neighborhood, located approximately between 14th and 7th Streets and centered around U Street NW, has changed dramatically over the past two decades. Built by African Americans after the Civil War, Shaw, home to Howard University, played host to some of the most illustrious Black entertainers over the past two centuries. It was also home to one of the few hotels open to African American travelers in the country. During the mid- to late-20th century, Shaw was a center of community organizing and activism, with organizations such as the Model Inner City Community Organization (MICCO), the Student Nonviolent Coordinating Committee (SNCC), Pride, Inc. and others providing social services, demanding community voice in Urban Renewal projects and providing jobs and job training to youth in the community. Former DC Mayor Marion Barry got his start as the first SNCC chairman in the 1960s and continued by starting Pride, Inc., an organization focused on youth employment and empowerment in 1967. In 1968, 14th and U Street NW was where organizers started to march after the assassination of Dr. Martin Luther King, Jr. to request that businesses close out of respect. The march grew into an uprising, ultimately destroying blocks of 7th Street in Shaw, 14th Street in Shaw and Columbia Heights and H Street NE.

By 1968, Shaw was already in the middle of an Urban Renewal planning process centered around the creation of a new school, in which the Redevelopment Land Agency (RLA) had started to acquire land for affordable housing creation and preservation. A 1966 Urban Renewal Report by RLA stated:

> Shaw renewal will strongly emphasize rehabilitation of existing structures [...] Physical renewal will be tied in with job training, health services and other economic opportunity programs, and the entire endeavor will be planned with the full participation and involvement of neighborhood residents[2].

MICCO was intensely engaged in this process, organizing meetings and responding to proposals, raising the ire of agency staff in the area who felt that the community groups were too intense.

On 7th Street NW, four blocks south of U Street, Kelsey Gardens residents experienced a very different type of preservation and loss. Kelsey Gardens was built in 1972 by the Deliverance Church of God in Christ with a Section 236 loan to keep the rents affordable. At that time, churches were major sponsors of US Department of Housing and Urban Development (HUD)-funded housing – particularly in the Shaw neighborhood and Northwest One Urban Renewal Area. The church, originally located at 14th and P Streets NW, seven blocks from Kelsey, has since moved to Ward 7, eight miles away, following its members who have been displaced from the community. Kelsey Gardens was a set of garden-style buildings located between Q and R Streets NW, housing 54 households with balconies and large rooms facing the street and interior courtyard. Kelsey housed several multi-generational families – many with deeper roots in the Shaw neighborhood spanning generations.

As one elderly African American woman explained:

> So we three [families] moved in at the same time [in 1975]. On that weekend, Miss [Neighbor] was supposed to have third floor ... we switched because she was elderly ... And I so I took the third floor and she took the second floor. Us three never moved. On that other side, everybody moved in and out but us three was the original ones for 32 years, we never moved.

Another resident summed it up by saying, "we were like family" with block parties in the parking lot, arguments between neighbors and support networks to watch children or help with daily chores.

Over the next three decades, Shaw, like much of DC, would change dramatically as the Metro system expanded and the District began to explicitly try to attract new residents. Meanwhile, the owner made few improvements to the building, resulting in increasingly poor conditions. In 2004, the same year the District started funding tenant organizing and technical assistance, residents learned that the church planned to redevelop their building. At the time, many of the original residents still lived in the community, serving as leaders of the tenants' association. The church, no longer located in the neighborhood, issued a Tenant Opportunity to Purchase Act (TOPA) notice. The same year, after failing multiple failing Real Estate Assessment Center (REAC) scores, HUD began the process of terminating the Section 8 contract that supported the building's operating funds. The church made critical repairs, meaning that the building could pass subsequent REAC inspections.

In the midst of the TOPA process, the owners began to pay tenants to sign away their TOPA rights and agree to let the owners sell without restrictions. This practice, common throughout the gentrifying neighborhoods of Shaw, Columbia Heights and Adams Morgan at the time, gave tenants as much as $30,000 per household to give up their rights. However, at Kelsey, the owners offered $1,000, and many residents did not understand their TOPA rights or what they agreed to. As many as 30 households signed away their rights because they expected to be displaced anyway and believed they would be unable to obtain a Tenant Protection Voucher (TPV) if they did not agree to move, which was untrue as federal TPV are not related to the local TOPA process. One tenant, an African American woman, explained:

> It was very conflicting. You could tell, the first set of information that was coming out, they weren't initially just trying to make people just move. They were offering the folks that they knew would take a check and that was not a part of the tenant association.

Over the next months, local community organization ONE DC, at the invitation of tenant leaders, initiated an education process, which prompted some tenants to revoke their assignation of rights and return the money. Yet the lack of capacity by the organizers, the inconsistency of resident attendance at meetings and the speed that the owners tried to sell made the process difficult to understand. Ultimately, the tenants registered for their rights under TOPA. However, the competing offer for the building, which included a 10% share by the current owners, could not be matched by the tenants, and their offer was not accepted. The tenants went to court, arguing that this was not legal, and the court mandated negotiations between the tenants' association and the owners. This led to a settlement, giving all 54 tenants a right of return, but no guarantee of how they returned and when. In addition to the right of return, 54 units would remain affordable but at Low Income Housing Tax Credit rents, rather than Section 8 because the owners ultimately opted out of their Section 8 contract. This meant that the original Kelsey residents would be required to use their Housing Choice Vouchers to afford the rent, and new residents who wanted to live in the affordable units would have to pay rents that were affordable to those earning 60% of the Area Median Income, rather than the deep affordability available through the Section 8 subsidy.

By late 2008, the building was emptied, and residents expected to be back within two years. However, the housing crisis put the financing into disarray, pushing demolition back to 2012. Residents had to find housing across the District, with several small households finding units in clusters in Southwest and Northwest, far from the community where they had lived for decades. Large families had greater challenges in finding and keeping a home that would safely house them. One family reported moving five times in six years due to poor conditions and landlord disputes.

Construction was not completed until 2014. The new building included the 54 units of affordable housing and another 227 market-rate units. There is a stylish community room that can be rented for a fee – with TVs, a pool table and couches and tables – a rooftop pool, concierge and a gym. Of the 54 families that left Kelsey Gardens, only 18 would return to the newly developed Jefferson Marketplace (Figure 6.1). While 15 remained in their relocation units, the reasons were mixed. In some cases, the families were settled and did not want to move, but in others, their credit would not allow them to get through the screening process at the new building. Two other households lost their vouchers and three died or moved into nursing homes in the intervening years. Another 16 lost contact with their neighbors and could not be found for interviews.

At the groundbreaking for the building, residents felt they had built some trust with the owners, and the owners were conciliatory, even suggesting that the photo of the groundbreaking with the old Kelsey residents might be placed in the lobby. Yet after the building opened, the residents felt frustrated that the fight they had undertaken and the community they had built was not respected in the building. The 18 households who returned, overall, did not report satisfaction with their new building. One resident leader explained that the rules were excessive, but they tried to play by the rules. She said:

> When we moved in here we was so excited and I'm speaking for myself. We was so excited to move back. We said, we're gonna follow the rules and regulations, right. We're not gonna do anything to make us lose our

Figure 6.1 Jefferson Marketplace

> place. We fought too hard for eight years. Well, 12 years. Four years before they put us off the property. Eight years while we was gone. We fought 12 years to make a reality and come back.

Several other residents expressed similar views, but quickly found that management singled them out and enforced rules and norms that did not support the community they expected at the old Kelsey. One elderly African American woman whose grandchildren often visit her apartment said management harassed her over having too many people living in the unit:

> At first they was telling me that people couldn't spend a night or nothing. They can't tell me who I can have in my house. Long as they don't live here, their name is not on lease I know they can't live here.

She explained that while her grandchildren were often in the home, it was typically after school and on the weekends to help care for her or so that she or her daughter could care for them.

The fact that the Kelsey residents were African American and did not fit the age profile of the majority of the residents in the building – most of whom were white singles and couples between 25 and 35 years old – made them visible to management. Residents felt that management unevenly enforced nuisance rules or assumed that the Kelsey residents were perpetrators of nuisance violations. One resident's adult son lives off site and uses medical marijuana outside, but after repeated incidents of harassment by management because he smells of smoke, he no longer visits his mother at Jefferson Marketplace. Although marijuana is legal in DC, individual buildings regulate it in the same way they regulate cigarette smoking. Another who lives on the first floor near the courtyard says she was accused of smoking in the courtyard when in actuality it's staff from a neighboring restaurant who come to smoke in the alley behind her first floor apartment. In addition, children are allowed to use the building computer room, but "they'd call the kids out after a certain time," as one parent explained. More importantly, mistakes by management about the Housing Choice Vouchers often fell on the tenants, who received threats of eviction and insults from management while the DC Housing Authority rushed to intervene on the residents' behalves.

Though eighteen households moved back after the redevelopment, only nine households remain, and others are considering a move. While technically, the subsidized stock as a whole did not diminish – 54 units were preserved – they were preserved on very different terms. Though the residents had the right to return, the terms under which they returned did not respect the culture they had built or their right to be an active part of the community. Low- and moderate-income residents had no control over their space at Kelsey Gardens and were subsumed into a race-neutral approach that punished the African American residents disproportionately.

While many of the preservation projects in DC's affordable portfolio were saved through some form of tenant engagement, others – particularly those before the District engaged directly in preservation, funded tenant organizers or participated in the DC Preservation Network (DCPN) – had little to no engagement with residents. Kelsey's initial fight came just as organizers were funded and before DCPN first convened. Buildings were, in many cases like the Geraldine discussed in Chapter 2, redeveloped or lost with very little notice to residents. At the same time, Kelsey Gardens could be considered a victory in a situation where the baseline was to redevelop without any keeping existing residents in place or affordable units. However, this logic sets up a default: either they accept displacement as a result of their demands or they accept whatever ownership or engagement structure that the owners give them. Yet this choice ignores the possibility for partnership and the rights of tenants to shape their futures. In this case, it was only the work of the residents, organizers, attorneys and the courts that made it possible for the residents to move to Jefferson Marketplace, yet it was no longer "the old Kelsey Gardens," as most of the residents called it.

The models of preservation that evolved out of DC's policy and advocacy framework have illuminated significant opportunities and challenges both in the fight to initially preserve their communities and the ongoing effort to maintain them. Preservation, importantly, acts as a tool of anti-displacement – both physical and cultural. One cannot resist cultural displacement in the community or city if one is no longer able to afford housing there. But, as has been discussed throughout the book, preservation – as anti-displacement – is more than just the housing unit as an end. Rather, preservation, as this chapter will discuss, is about the process – an approach that starts with the residents and ends with deeper ongoing engagement and empowerment.

Though this book has been preoccupied with the process of preservation, this chapter looks at how those tools look from resident perspectives. The tools discussed throughout the book are critical to addressing the complexity of affordable housing development, overcoming gaps in trust by residents who have been repeatedly displaced and supporting long-term stability. However, while preventing physical displacement is necessary, it is not sufficient. Specifically, in this chapter I ask why residents moved to the building and remained in the midst of poor conditions and management; how the preservation process impacted their lives; and whether the way that preservation was achieved – including the subsidy, building, community and ownership structure – impacted the way they view their building and community to understand the way that particular approaches to preservation change the way residents perceive their role in the community, the stability of their housing situations and the way the approach translates into an acknowledgement of rights of renters both in the building and in the broader community.

Though this orientation to preservation is challenging, it may enable residents to build stronger communities through control over space, knowledge of the existing context and ground-based problem identification. This chapter illustrates that the orientation toward a tenant-based preservation policy, including sustained funding and technical assistance, can be a strategy for long-term affordability with lower turnover and higher tenant satisfaction than in buildings in which tenants have had limited – if any – control over their building's preservation. This is embedded in a substantially different view of renters – one that suggests they have a right to be part of their own futures, have a stake in their communities and have the capacity to engage. The erasure of renters' contributions to their communities often serves as a default position and justifies a top-down approach to affordable housing. I argue that tenant-centered preservation acknowledges their collective rights to the city and builds and maintains critical community networks that enable power, visibility and day-to-day support.

Challenges for Tenant-Based Preservation

In practice, tenant-led preservation faces significant challenges in Washington, DC, despite laws and, increasingly, funding and practice that requires engagement with tenants. These challenges are primarily due to speculative behavior in the real estate market, a sense of inevitability of displacement, amassing the financing, experience and timing to respond to immediate needs, and laws beyond the local context that override TOPA. While not unsurmountable, these challenges illustrate the clear need for ongoing advocacy and vigilance on the part of residents, organizers and advocates.

The housing market in DC has changed quickly, and yet, the challenges facing low- and moderate-income residents are similar: speculation driving poor conditions and disinvestment, followed by sales and a cycle that repeats across the city. The local government, new homeowners and outside investors intensely develop a neighborhood, low- and moderate-income households are displaced by rising rents and owner opt-outs, and they move to another neighborhood that has been disinvested from decades of racist policies. Speculators purchase properties and milk the property, leaving residents living in poor conditions. If the property owner is "lucky," the process repeats. In DC after 2000, redevelopment and gentrification has not been a case of if – but *when* and *how* it happens. What is clear, however, is that losses in the affordable stock are not only the result of gentrification in DC or anywhere else. Many of the losses – such as the Geraldine, Elsinor or Congress Heights – occurred before the first dog park opened or the first latte was poured.

Why Stay?

The majority of residents I have interviewed over the past decade lived in buildings where conditions before preservation were alarmingly bad, regardless of whether or not they were subsidized. These conditions ranged from threats to physical safety, including poor security and inadequate physical infrastructure, to threats to health, including infestations, poor weatherization and abundance of lead, mold and other toxic substances. In other cases, a lack of accessibility for those with limited mobility or other impairments made the buildings non-navigable. As was discussed in Chapters 4 and 5, the District was sued for its Hot Properties Initiative in 2000, which used code enforcement purportedly as a mechanism to reduce blight – but in largely Latinx buildings. The District, like other local code enforcement agencies had to balance evicting at-risk tenants through code enforcement or allowing slum properties to continue. However, they typically foreclose the possibility of using receivership or another repair program to address these conditions. This issue of unsafe conditions could be compounded in buildings where undocumented or other low-income families did not report code violations out of fear of deportation or retaliation by their landlords. While efforts starting in 2018 by the elected Attorney General have brought code enforcement to the fore with more resources for receivership, it was too late for many residents.

At 1417 N Street NW (Figure 6.2), an 84-unit market-affordable building near Logan Circle, a gentrified neighborhood near downtown Washington, DC, residents – a mix of documented and undocumented working class Latinx and Black households – were aware of the neighborhood's changes, even as they faced significant housing conditions issues. A Latinx woman living in the building explained management raised rents in spite of poor conditions that were never repaired:

> I remember one night, we were already in bed and a piece of debris fell beside our bed from the ceiling. It was a big heavy piece. I couldn't even

Figure 6.2 1417 N Street Cooperative

imagine if it had fallen on top of us. It could have killed us. So, I didn't pay the rent for that month and I called the office and told them to come and clean it out but they never came. I had to do it myself and it was really heavy. They never fixed it. So, we started a fight on this.

Alexa, another former tenant leader explained that this was widespread throughout the building:

> We had a massive bed bug infestation, mold along walls, kids with asthma, rats, mice, roaches, no heat, leaks, everything you could think of in a slum building we had. And our goal was let's just get it fixed. We wrote letters, nothing. We called, nothing. So then after we tried all those things we were like "so now what do we try?" And so, we started doing some outreach to different organizations and we found LEDC [the Latino Economic Development Center] ... we also found TENAC [the DC Tenants Advisory Coalition], another organization. We found the tenant survival guide and we read it like a bible. We were like "okay, we're gonna do all this."

This led to a seven-year fight, including rent strikes and public campaigns and mobilization to improve conditions and, eventually, preserve the affordability of their building. In July of 2007, after the landlord refused to fix both the air conditioning and the elevator, the residents staged a lemonade stand sit-in, handing out cold drinks to residents trudging up the seven flights of stairs to their apartments. In 2008, after major bedbug infestations plagued the building with no response, they built partnerships with community-based organizations to conduct city-wide public outreach on bedbug prevention and treatment, garnering news coverage and support.

The residents organized very publicly, getting significant press and local government attention. The board president finally met with the building owner who was trying to convert the building into condominiums in spite of recommendations by both legal teams not to do so. Ultimately, after a protracted fight and multiple meetings with the board president, the owner relented and sold the building to the tenants, who were awarded Community Development Block Grant (CDBG) and local funding for acquisition and rehabilitation of their building, which is now a Limited Equity Cooperative (LEC). Yet these poor conditions can prevent tenant-led preservation. First, residents are more likely to move out before their building is sold due to the poor conditions. Second, those who remain often have more to lose by complaining about conditions. In many cases, the housing in which they lived was a last option – needed for affordability, a lack of a credit check or because they were undocumented. Organizing is a risk. Finally, if the residents are successful, amassing the funding to support both acquisition and rehabilitation of a building that has decades of deferred maintenance, even in a city with $100 million in local funds, is no small feat.

When asked why they stayed in spite of the building conditions, residents of this building and many others cited access to their jobs, the growth in neighborhood businesses, the support they received from their neighbors and the challenge of finding affordable housing. A resident at another building explained:

> I used to live in number 6 and she used to live in number 4. That's where I had [my son]. I couldn't go out for a month to do my shopping. So, a neighbor downstairs offered to help with the baby so that I could do my shopping. My husband used to leave to go to work at 6:30 am and wouldn't return until 10:30 at night because he had to work a second job so that we could pay the bills. It was difficult for me to use the stairs and the elevator didn't work.

Residents of other buildings, particularly those in central locations like 1417 N Street, discussed their access to work. This was particularly true of Latinx residents working overnight shifts cleaning buildings or on the many construction sites throughout the cities.

The reasons for staying also included a desire for housing security after several previous moves due to displacement, and poor conditions or other housing insecurity issues. One resident in Northwest Washington explained that she was displaced twice in the six years before she moved to her building – once when the building was redeveloped and rents slowly rose and later after the landlord was cited for illegally renting his units. Other building residents reported similar stories. One Latinx resident moved to her building after experiencing foreclosure during the financial collapse. Michelle, an African American woman living in a large building now in the midst of massive redevelopment explained that she was about to move due to the poor conditions in the neighborhood and the building in the early 2000s. However, a coworker convinced her not to move because she would lose the housing security of her Section 8 building:

> So, she said "just listen to me, let me tell you something" […] I raised all my kids right there in Immaculate Conception, I raised all my kids there. And guess what, all my kids they grown and gone and married and everything. Guess what, I'm still there though." She said "I'm still up there, yeah I see," she said "so you don't let where you raise your kids … where you live at, you know what I'm saying? … disturb you or how you raise your kids." And hopefully that your kids when they get to … and sometimes that's true, when they get to a certain age in their life, point in their life they start branching out and doing other things and following their peers and other structures to do things that they chose to do. So, I ended up staying, I ended up staying. I never had any problems with my children being in there because that was my main and my biggest focus – that my kids might get mixed up with what's going on with their surroundings and what they're growing up to see, and I stayed there. And thank God, ya know I was just really worried about my family and thank God we didn't run into any of those situations. So, I stayed there. I looked for no other home.

Disbelief

Another central barrier in the interviews when discussing process was previous displacement or future displacement and its impact on organizing and engagement in the preservation of the building. The fear of – and in some cases the inevitability of – displacement played a role in both disempowering residents and leaving them vulnerable to outside interests. It also played a critical motivational role for many residents who knew this was the only opportunity to remain in their communities. In a predominantly Black neighborhood that was undergoing significant reinvestment east of the Anacostia River, Ciara, the board president of a 148-unit development explained that it was often difficult to get people to support the tenant association and the TOPA process. She explained:

> At first it was like you had some that was like "oh, y'all listen, they tried this before, it ain't gonna work. Call me when it gets done." They were just sort of like negative, you know what I'm talking about? "But no, but really this time it's gonna happen."

This challenge was frequently discussed by board leadership throughout the city. In order to exercise any rights through TOPA, 51% of the residents have to vote and support the decision. The ability to organize was sometimes stymied by the lack of previous organizing or sense of community and previous displacement from other housing. Many residents – particularly those who had not been in their buildings for long – simply expected to have to move at some point due to eviction, rent increases or condominium conversions. Many had been displaced more than once due to poor conditions, redevelopment or eviction. For this reason, as Ellen, an attorney who works with tenants, explained, even when residents plan to buy their buildings:

> The control isn't the first thing people think about. The first thing they think about is "I want to have security in the place that I live." That in and of itself is a stabilizing factor. I mean, huge. I mean it's probably the biggest factor. People have a place to live, and they can afford it, and they have some control over the economic forces around them.

Typically, resident leaders, who often learned they had the right of first refusal from an organizer or someone else who had gone through the process, drove the process to stay. These leaders often talked about the determination to stay due to the impact of the rapid changes occurring in their communities. Gerald, the new president of an affordable cooperative in Southeast DC had to be convinced that it was possible to stay. Then he explained:

> Me personally, I don't know if it's actually going to come to pass but I look around, right up the street here by the Metro that they started

> building stuff [...] I thought of, you know, this is gonna be like a prime spot, it's gonna be a nice spot [...] and like I said, originally, I loved this spot, so if we can find some kind of way to hold on to the spot, then people are gonna come in, they're gonna develop it, they're gonna ... not necessarily run us out but they'll price us out.

This determination often drove the process for building leaders like Gerald and Ciara, among others. But overcoming resistance required significant information and support from organizers, family and social networks to overcome the disbelief.

At Hubbard Place, discussed in Chapter 3, residents had faced significant housing conditions and safety issues, including prostitution, drug dealing and violence, and explained that many of them did not have other options and stayed because it was affordable. Ella, an African American tenant leader said that it was difficult to organize the residents – many reported keeping to themselves to stay safe. When the tenants received a TOPA notice, they worked with tenant organizers who had worked with the developer on other buildings and helped them organize and negotiate with the new building owners. She explained:

> Some of the people were scared, didn't know what to expect. They thought that [the developer] would play games and then eventually put them out but that wasn't [their] intention so that was the biggest challenge but we finally got the people to come around.

She, along with several other women in her building explained that people were afraid to move into the building due to reports of violence, but that they needed affordable housing and, in many cases, had few options. As a result, they had difficulties organizing their neighbors. Organizing residents to support the new buyer, a mission-driven developer, required almost two years of engagement with the residents to prove legitimacy. The new buyer met frequently with the board and shared plans and discussed community needs. However, the need to build legitimacy quickly can stymie a project in a system where time is tight. In buildings where residents have not been organized previously, not only do organizers and tenant leaders have to form an organization, but they have to convince their neighbors that they do not have to be displaced, have rights and can change the course of their housing situation.

Beyond TOPA

While the District's position as both a city and a state facilitate a greater ability to control how preservation occurs and where the money originates, federal law continues to trump the local. When the Office of the Attorney General put the Sanford Property portfolio – including Elsinor Apartments (Chapter 5), Sayles Place (Chapter 2) and the Congress Heights Planned Unit Development (PUD)

(Chapter 2) – into receivership and barred them from doing business in the District, the company went into bankruptcy, putting 18 properties, 7 of which were subsidized, at risk of loss from the affordable stock. While a traditional sale would precipitate a notification of rights under TOPA, when the owner filed for bankruptcy, the residents of these buildings no longer had TOPA rights, meaning that the buildings could be sold to any new owner – as was the case with Sayles Place, discussed in Chapter 2. This was because the goal of a bankruptcy was to satisfy debts owed, not address the needs of affordable housing residents. Similarly, foreclosure proceedings canceled TOPA rights. While, in the District, foreclosure is not a legal justification for eviction, it could result in displacement if the owner demolishes, redevelops or increases rents at the building.

In the case of the Sanford Portfolio, the buildings faced a broad range of fates based on the court, the new buyers and the financial and physical conditions of the building. Those that had already been placed into receivership were secured – but had not yet been renovated. In some cases, the residents were able to negotiate with the new owners to remain in place, and to make repairs. Other lucky residents were able to retain existing subsidies, while others continued to wait on decisions. However, for all buildings, the process meant ongoing instability of housing, poor conditions and an uncertain future, compounding existing fears of displacement.

Opportunities in Tenant-Centered Preservation

Community Networks and Stability

The Parkway Overlook Apartments East and West (Figure 6.3), was a 266-unit Section 8 community with a preservation process that both built and built upon nascent relationships among networks. It was in alarmingly poor condition by the time the residents moved out. But it, like the Temple Courts residents who continue to show up as a block to New Communities public meetings, had residents fighting to stay. Parkway Overlook, like the Congress Heights PUD, is one of the communities surrounding the St. Elizabeth's Mental Hospital redevelopment. Residents described their community in loving terms. They were aware of and impacted by the violence and drug dealing that happened outside of the community, but they described proms, graduations and other community celebrations that were part of daily life in Parkway Overlook.

In the early 2000s, the management company began to turn over frequently, raising the alarm among tenant leaders. Conditions deteriorated until the building failed five REAC inspections. In 2005, HUD terminated the place-based Section 8 contract at Parkway Overlook due to repeated failed REAC inspections. The DC Housing Finance Agency (DCHFA) staff, tenant organizers and legal advocates recall the property as extremely troubled with gang activity, poor conditions and isolation. There were also concerns because, despite the tenant community, need for affordable housing and pending redevelopment,

Figure 6.3 Parkway Overlook Apartments

Parkway Overlook was located in a census tract that, in 2000, had a poverty rate near 65%, and in 2010, the rate remained at almost 50%, marking the neighborhood as high poverty and adding to the justification – including housing conditions and neighborhood violence – for its demolition. However, as discussed in Chapter 2, this justification was questionable given the redevelopments surrounding the area. The HUD termination resulted in foreclosure of the property. Because the project was a DCHFA risk-share project[3], and the agency had issued bonds totaling $14.9 million four years earlier, DCHFA was named mortgagee in possession by 2007. The terrible conditions of the building and surrounding neighborhood was their justification to focus on recovering their losses over the tenants' rights to stay.

The DCHFA called a meeting with the tenants to discuss the agency's plan for the building, which was to demolish and for the residents to receive Housing Choice Vouchers. This triggered engagement from community organizers who called a meeting of the residents at a local church. Parkway Overlook residents began to organize, strengthen their tenant association and show up to meetings, call agency staff and council members, and disrupt events to be heard. DCHFA continued to move forward on their plans, arguing it was the only way to recoup the money they had in the project. DCHFA began to empty the building and asked the DC Housing Authority (DCHA) to issue vouchers for the tenants. However, the tenants showed up to the HFA board meeting, disrupting it and angering some board members. One tenant leader said, "I asked them, all the board members, I said: 'What you need us to do? Because whatever you need us to do we can go do it. 'Cause we have no problem talking to the mayor.'" They continued to fight, long after they had to leave the building, attending frequent meetings, lobbying their council member and the mayor's office, and making frequent calls to HFA. Between 2008 and 2013, DCHFA issued and rescinded multiple Requests for Proposals (RFP) for the redevelopment of the property citing vague concerns. HUD participants explained that there were concerns about the site because of its adjacency to a new development that would require changes to the road grid and new housing development in the area.

Early in the process, the relationship between advocates, tenants and DCHFA were adversarial, and because the quasi-public DCHFA and the public Department of Housing and Community Development (DHCD) were also not coordinated, there was very little transparency about the affordability requirements of the RFP, the development teams contending for the property, or the potential outcomes for the tenants.[4] Government agency staff members did not understand why the residents wanted to return to a high-poverty neighborhood and a building that had years of deferred maintenance. Residents focused on the critical networks among residents and sense of community that existed in the building. Elizabeth, a city staffer engaged in the property, and others engaged in the process, admitted that the DCHFA staff did not understand the importance tenants placed on maintaining their community for several years, focusing solely on the condition of the property and the need to make sure they did not lose money. The result was what a tenant leader described as "a vinegar and oil relationship."

As the building sat vacant and was vandalized and squatted in 2011, staff continued to complain about the slowdown of the process by residents engaged in the process. It was not until 2013, after announcing the building would be sold in a foreclosure auction and in response to pressure from on-going engagement from tenants and tenant advocates as well as local council members, that DCHFA coordinated with DHCD and other District agencies to identify gaps in financing for the project. The DC Housing Authority won the project at auction and was awarded money from the District's Housing Production Trust Fund to rehabilitate the project. They have also worked with the tenants, who have remained engaged in the process, thereby retaining their right to return, to determine the design and affordability mix.

Elizabeth explained:

> It started off as a very adversarial relationship between the district government, the residents and the advocate community and the topic of conversation was supposed to be about the people. But instead it was about, you know, who was going to take responsibility for why the project didn't succeed and why did the families have to relocate. And I think that took about three years to overcome [...] and I think partly that was because of some of the things that other colleagues and myself saw in the network [DCPN] – [... that] there were benefits working with the tenant advocates,

> the tenants, and trying to see what the overall success needed to be where we started working together.

Advocates and agency staff still working with tenants at the building argued that, as a result of the work of the DCPN, the project would be different if it happened today. Not only would they have had an early warning system when the building failed its first REAC inspection – or before when tenants complained about conditions – but they would have relationships and trust with the relevant organizations engaged in the building.

Over the next decade, the residents held reunions and worked to maintain community outside of the physical building. They had ongoing meetings with DCHFA staff and continued to partner with community-based organizations. Ten years after the building was demolished, they awarded the contract for redevelopment to the Housing Authority. Shaundra, a 30-year resident of Parkway Overlook said, "I told DC Housing Authority when they was awarded, I told them that I felt like it was a child of mine that I decided to go ahead and entrust to you all. So, you take care of my child." Though Shandra had already purchased a home near to Parkway Overlook, she and her fellow residents continued to advocate for their neighborhood. DCHFA broke ground on the new Parkway Overlook in 2018 and residents moved back at the end of 2019.

The fight to stay is rarely just about having an affordable place to live. Residents continue to fight and return because there is more to housing than cost. Over the years, residents, like those at 1417 N Street, Mass Place and Hubbard Place, have testified at council hearings and explained in interviews about the poor conditions, dangerous communities and limited access they have endured for affordability and community. Community is, however, not merely a reason to stay, but an opportunity to create a sense of safety, survival and power.

Josephine, who is visually impaired and in a wheelchair, explained that it was hard to find an affordable accessible building so she was living in an unsafe unit. She explained:

> Well you know where I was my neighbors were really bad and they were stealing stuff, it was a really bad building. So, to be in a secure building is a blessing to me, to be able to get around a lot without assistance and to know the neighbors is significant. I know the neighbors here … I lived in my [old] building for 12 years and I knew one who was a tenant in the building and it was only one person in that building I could trust and then they moved out. Everybody else was in the building trying to see what they could get off of you, from you. So yeah, it's a drastic change.

For her, a sense of a trustworthy community and safety was necessary for her survival. Often those outside of buildings fail to see the role that networks and history – community – play in the fight to stay. Affordable housing and low-income communities are often pathologized as toxic, particularly when they are located in high-poverty neighborhoods, leading public officials to assume that all change is good change. As a result, to many agency staff and developers, any slowdown to that is just fear of change, lack of security or internalized self-deprecation – suggesting the residents do not know they deserve somewhere better to live. If the building is troubled, unsafe, high-poverty, toxic or in poor condition, it is difficult for outside actors to imagine it has value. Yet it is clear from the work on preservation that, while residents want better conditions, they do not want it at the expense of community – but *with* community. The Kelsey Gardens residents moved back into a modern luxury building with market-rate amenities available to them in a neighborhood with restaurants, grocery stores and access to transit. Yet, their affordability came at a price. Painting redevelopment of affordable housing as an either/or prospect – *either* we redevelop as a mixed-income development or with significant displacement on terms developed outside of the community *or* you continue to live in poor conditions – is a false choice. There are models that engage residents in their own futures, but that takes time and trust. There are reasons low-income residents in poorly maintained public housing fight to stay. Community matters, and whether decades, years or months, these renters have the right to engage in the direction their community moves. Given that residents often *expect* to be displaced – or threatened with displacement – by city agencies, developers and homeowners, it should be no surprise that this type of engagement takes time. But for residents, preservation is not just about the ability to stay, but an acknowledgement of a fundamental right to engage in their own futures.

Right to the City

The idea of the right to the city has been used as a way of defining uses of public space. Starting with Henri Lefebvre, geographers, planners, anthropologists and others have used the concept to explore protest – direct, in the case of something like *Occupy Wall Street* or the *Black Lives Matter Movement*, and perhaps less direct, as people discuss homelessness and the right to *exist* and *live* in public space. Yet, the concept of the right to the city – or, as Harvey put it, "the right to remake ourselves by creating a qualitatively different kind of urban sociality,"[5] has critical implications for housing. Harvey's argument is not merely that residents should, as many DC residents with whom I have discussed displacement believe, "get to stay." Rather, it raises critical questions about *how* they stay, as I have argued throughout this book. With the fight to pass TOPA in the late 1970s, organizers demanded their right to the city be enshrined in statute. Yet, that right was incomplete without the realistic means to take that right when the District set aside funding for organizing, legal services and redevelopment.

As DC's housing market began to take off in the late 1990s, affordable housing came under fire again. Neighborhoods like Columbia Heights, where decades of shelved plans had told of development that no one believed would happen, became hotbeds for house flipping, condominium conversions and preservation fights. Deborah, a tenant leader in the Columbia Heights neighborhood explained how she became clued into her rights:

> I'm saying look how they moved in so quick. But I was warned, [cousin's name] came down here, my cousin down in Clifton Terrace. 'I had something I need to tell you, I have something you need to learn. They're coming your way.' And I said I didn't want to go down there and sit around her and learn but she said, 'You gonna learn something, you need to know what's going on. It may help you save your building. If you save your behind, you save the rest of them.' So, she kind of educated me with Empower DC ... a lot of different coalitions I was involved with, still am by email. And because of my age we got a lot of young legs and can let them do the work. But I can advise, I've become more of a consultant than anything. But there's so much positive, smart, educated [people]. I always say this, we have so much to offer one another ya know?

She and her fellow residents assigned their rights and kept the building affordable, adding resident services and organizing their own community groups, including a women's circle and youth activities. Their self-advocacy also translated to engagement outside the building. Residents share their knowledge with friends and neighbors, testify at public hearings and tell their stories at rallies across the District. Many of these residents understand the necessity of being part of the conversation.

Rights are not given, but taken. They may be institutionalized by others, as TOPA was, but the taking of rights is a proactive decision to act against the dominant narrative of economic efficiency and exchange value, suggesting that housing is an anonymous social service based on the units available and the income of the applicants[6]. But this also means that a meaningful right to the city is not without an ongoing struggle. Most of the buildings discussed in this book have gone through multiple processes of organizing, preservation and challenge. The ongoing financialization of the housing market – whether through rising costs, declining conditions or speculation mean that precarity will likely be an ongoing cycle for affordable housing.

In the late 1980s, the building at 1425 T Street NE was home to a community of African Americans and Salvadoran immigrants who had moved to the District in the wake of the Civil War starting in the late 1970s. It was built in 1904 as The Windsor Apartments and rented for between $22.50 and $50 per month by 1915. By the 1970s, the building had ongoing conditions complaints, garnering attention by the DC Council and the Department of Consumer and Regulatory Affairs in 1983. Over the next seven years the tenants partnered with Washington Intercity Self-Help (WISH) and the Harrison Institute for Public Law at Georgetown University to successfully sue their landlord for poor conditions, winning a $365,000 settlement. The court transferred this amount to a lien on the property, forcing a foreclosure sale in 1990. The 1425 T Street tenants' association was the only bidder, and they won the 30-unit building, finalizing the sale and forming a Limited Equity Cooperative in 1992. In 1996, after two years of rehabilitation, the building reopened and the residents moved back into the cooperative. To do this, they had loans from private lenders, permanent financing from the Department of Housing and Community Development and a Housing Assistance Payment (HAP) contract to facilitate Section 8 payments that made costs affordable. Over time, the resident population became increasingly Spanish-speaking, but the bylaws were never translated to Spanish, meaning the board followed custom, not bylaws in practice. The limited English proficiency generally, along with violation of the bylaws, left the cooperative vulnerable to exploitation by outside parties.

By 2011, the surrounding neighborhood had changed dramatically, and the 15-year Section 8 contract had to be renewed, or it would be lost. Meanwhile, the management company approached the tenants about becoming a condominium. Over the past decade, several similar companies and consultants who do not see Limited Equity Cooperatives as a viable option have carved out a space in the landscape, taking fees and often serving as the management company and development consultant with renovations. One of these consultants explained:

> But the bottom line is that the owners – who are the declarants/developers in this area – they will be getting their units totally free with no mortgage debt, and very low condo fees. So, we're talking in that case of instant equity – because the units have sold for upwards of $250,000 – and that was for smaller one-bedrooms. And there are some three-bedrooms in the building.

Across the District, he and others have worked with several buildings, yet, like 1425 T Street, the promises rarely came to fruition – particularly for residents who did not have the money to pay the ongoing costs of buying into and living in a market-rate condominium.

At 1425 T Street, the way to make buying-in affordable for the existing residents was to open up the building for a mixed-income population. The board voted to opt out of their Section 8 contract and prepay their loan from DHCD and convert to condominium in 2011. However, the management company that convinced them to convert did not explain all the costs of converting, which would have displaced the low-income households of the building. The organizers working at the building were able to help the residents cancel the conversion and remain a cooperative.

However, they had already updated some of the units in the building and had to support the debt through sales of those units at a higher cost, now serving households at up to 120% of the Area Median Income (AMI – $105,850 for a one-person household) and offering a higher equity return. While many of the original residents want to keep the units for households earning less than 80% of AMI, the cost of buying a share is too high for low- and moderate-income households to pay cash and too small for many banks to lend, averaging between $20,000 and $50,000. They are working with a local Community Development Financial Institution (CDFI) to be creative, but the building also has low reserves available to finance these loans.

This change in affordability has meant that the building has changed, sidelining many of the original residents, including the board members. Long-serving board members report that new members do not listen to long-term board members. Yet there are other clear changes. When asked if she speaks with her neighbors, Luisa, a Latinx woman, explained, "Well with the newcomers no but with our old neighbors, yes. They [new residents] don't even say hi to us when we were the ones that welcomed them here." The fights between old and new were common in communities that used mixed incomes to cross subsidize and be financially stable.

Another T Street leader explained the hope she has for the building in the midst of this change in the population:

> I would like to see if one day after we die, for my kids to have their families here. To see the building to stay affordable because we don't want to lose this. Because, I think, at the end of the day, since we won the building, we're hoping things, after we die, that things keep on [...] It's changed but it's still ours.

The changes in the building represent the ongoing challenge of continually taking and retaking rights. The residents fought for their building in the 1990s, but as the neighborhood changed, outside pressure increased on the community to convert and resist a logic of quick financial gain. But through the engagement of organizers and mission-driven lenders, they have been able to remain an affordable cooperative.

Tenant-centered preservation recognizes that renters, like owners, have a right to be part of the city's change and development. Research on homeownership argues that homeownership is a means for intergenerational wealth, a source of improved childhood outcomes and in indicator of a more engaged community. These findings have led to debates about where the benefits of ownership originate: homeownership itself, stable tenure, equity or control over one's surroundings. Yet it has been clear from my interviews that, whether residents have lived in a building a year or 50 years, they have an interest in having control over their tenure and may have a clear stake in the building or larger community.

The Kenyon Yes We Can Cooperative is an 18-unit building overlooking the large-scale New Urbanist development in Columbia Heights. The building is two blocks from the Metro, a Target, a variety of bars and restaurants, and the central plaza where events, including a farmers market and holiday celebrations occur. Like Hubbard Place, it was built in the early 20th century as a high-end apartment house. It experienced a similar trajectory in terms of conditions, reflecting the change in the neighborhood that surrounded it. In 1963, it was part of the portfolio of a landlord that had amassed thousands of code violations – including 44 at Kenyon Street[7]. In 1966, four households, representing the tenants, purchased the building from the landlord.

However, by 1979, the residents realized repairs needed to be made, and they did not have the capacity to rehabilitate and maintain the building financially. They made a deal with a new ownership entity – a group of investors – who purchased the building and rehabilitated it with a combination of an HUD-insured mortgage, new HAP contract and bonds from the newly formed DC Housing Finance Agency[8]. In exchange, the tenants' association continued to manage the building and retained a 0.5% share in the ownership. More importantly, they retained a right to purchase the building should it be sold at the end of the 20-year term[9].

The residents described the building as close-knit and connected with generations growing up and remaining connected. Residents moved in because their friends already lived there, and their children grew up and moved into units in the building. They made decisions about management of the buildings. The disinvestment in the neighborhood – and resulting violence, lack of services and drug trade – was a challenge for families in the building, but the community within the building was a strength. In 2004, the owner attempted to sell the building without notifying the tenants of their rights. However, with the assistance of a pro bono attorney, the tenants notified the owner that they would exercise their right to purchase. The owner rejected the tenants' right to purchase, and the tenants sued for breach of contract. Ellen, one of the attorneys who assisted the tenants said:

> This was an attempt ... to pretend the tenants had no rights ... to assume that nobody knew what they were doing, this low-income group of people who are just ignorant of their rights – and take the building back without ever telling anybody. This happened to be a very savvy group of people ... and the long-term nature of the population there was very important to the stability of that building.

Pearl, who has lived in the building for more than 30 years, explained:

> Well, we had the building and we hired this guy to manage the building. He ended up buying out the other – there was three partners. He ended up buying the partners out and never discussed it with us. So, what he was trying to do was to throw us out on the street. So, he sent us a little letter tellin' us everybody had to be out, like 90 days or so we had to be out. And uh not one person moved. We had a little meeting – we discussed it and we discussed trying to stay. Then we got to diggin' in things and findin' out stuff and uh we hired uh – not hired – we found some pro bono lawyers who's very good and they got to diggin' in to the situation and found out that we were already .5 [percent] owners.

The court acknowledged both the rights of the tenants to purchase and their original agreement with HUD and the owner. This agreement stipulated a price, minus depreciation. As a result, the tenants purchased the building for $586,000 using a loan from an intermediary lender and retaining the Section 8 subsidy for operating expenses for the low-income residents. According to the DC Tax Assessor's Database, the cooperative has been assessed at $1.8 million, meaning the residents have significant equity in the high-cost market of Columbia Heights.

Studying preservation – and rental housing more generally – calls into question the relationship between homeownership and neighborhood engagement. The idea is that only those with an exchange value stake in the neighborhood will want to take care of it. Yet it is clear from the buildings where long- and short-term renters have invested time and energy into their communities that this is a false assumption and may be a part of a larger system of disempowerment related to instability. Landlords often create feelings of instability and powerlessness through lack of communication and engagement with residents. These practices, carried out by a wide range of owners, are supported by a narrative that suggests tenants do not care and have no right to stay. This then makes tenants less likely to stay and engage in the building.

At Tyler House, discussed in Chapter 5, the residents have been frustrated with the lack of communication about the relocation plan during the recent renovation, as well as the repairs that now need to be made due to the poor quality of the repairs. At a tenant association meeting, board members and residents complained about a lack of access to community rooms and playground areas – that also have no benches on which parents can sit while their children play. The residents wanted the playground to remain open after 5 pm when many parents would be available to bring their children after work. As the tenant board member complained, "They just don't want to open up the playground to the children. They want the playground to open up on management hours, 9–5, what good is that gonna do for the kids, 9–5?" The uses of space, communication about important elements of the building and punitive actions for tenant complaints were common in buildings where residents did not have a role in the building's future. These residents complained of feeling disrespected or frustrated and did not have a strong sense of ownership or connectedness to the building. They did not feel confident of their ability to remain in their building or its long-term affordability.

Conclusion: Tenant-Led Preservation for Visibility and Power

Two of the most important lessons from a tenant-based understanding of preservation are, first, that most tenants expect to be displaced because they have rarely had the chance to determine their futures, and second, their fight to stay is partially about affordability, but most often, it is about community-based networks for quality of life, survival and family. Taking a tenant-based approach to preservation is ultimately about acknowledging the rights of tenants to determine their futures in the building and, ultimately, in the communities in which they live. To do this, however, it is critical that the actors discussed in Chapter 5 include tenants as partners, acknowledge the collective stake of renters and use those understandings to operationalize a right to the city.

Tenant-led preservation opened broader opportunities for residents beyond their buildings and individual household stability. The approach also created an opportunity for residents to engage and connect more directly with other low- and moderate-income tenants in what I call horizontal networks, or networks across the same sector. Tenant-led preservation also enables access to vertical networks with city leaders and decision-makers. This engagement ultimately increased the visibility, profile and understanding of the need for affordable housing preservation in Washington. The key to being able be part of the conversation about redevelopment was the combination of motivated leaders and tenant organizers. Organizers responded to tenant organizations who called them to address complaints and understand their TOPA rights. They also proactively visited buildings where problems were reported at the DC Preservation Network (DCPN) to determine what was happening and provide a link between the residents and city government. However, organizers also visit buildings where there have been tenant rights complaints, building code violations and challenges with ownership. This approach put tenants at the forefront of the process.

Access to Information and Horizontal Networks

Housing instability for many households can be a solitary challenge. In some cases, residents commiserate with neighbors or family members, but the ongoing housing instability of low- and moderate-income households – particularly households of color – can keep residents from looking outside for options. Instead, as with other types of forced moves such as eviction, residents move, rather than waiting on the notice. Yet, in the District, like other places with histories of organizing, the ongoing and hard-won focus on resident power means that they can build horizontal networks that facilitate power, visibility and information-sharing. Like Mass Place, and its fellow associations where residents were able to work as a block to prevent displacement, these networks changed the course of the future for many communities.

Ada, a tenant leader at a building in downtown Washington explained that they were fearful when they received their first TOPA notice, "But since then it's been so much better because we learned what our rights were and we have that voice and we're more united and so that is what keeps me a bit more … considerably more confident in the building." Organizers helped tenants to organize when there were no sales, but their work was even more challenging when the buildings received notices that the owner was selling. They visited the buildings and provided information about rights and options and knocked on doors to help tenant leaders get signatures and members for the tenant association. They then helped them through the process of deciding how to proceed, negotiated with the new owner or worked with the city to secure funding. In addition to the work they did before and during the sale, technical assistance providers continue to work with resident boards dealing with succession planning, financial management and relationships with management companies.

Access to Vertical Networks

In many cases, organizers also helped residents gain access to vertical networks – that is connections between sectors. In this case, it meant that tenants could access city government agencies, funders, advocates and nonprofit developers that could provide clarity, enforce tenant protections or discuss possible project financing. One of participants from a nonprofit engaged with tenants at Tyler House explained that she was able to facilitate access to city agencies. Expressing a common view among organizers she explained, "I think to build a unified voice around preservation and around affordable housing in the city, I think it really has to be driven by the folks who affected most by it." This approach was critical in challenging preservation situations like Parkway Overlook. Organizers were able to provide expert knowledge and access that tenants could use to advocate on their own behalves with city agencies, the council and funders.

However, the power residents were able to gain – and the networks to which they had access – opened the door to advocacy on their own. Residents from across the city who had been threatened with displacement became frequent participants in council hearings and public rallies. One leader expressed his appreciation for the space created through the vertical networks to learn and be a voice for affordable housing residents, in spite of his chronic health challenges that he felt could have sidelined him. He said:

> That whole process was a life changing event for me and … so I'm gonna continue to do what I'm doing and I'll do more if it turns out that there's a need. If the council is willing to hear from us more often […] I'm not nervous about getting in front of the council, I would love to have an hour or more sitting at a table with [Mayor] Muriel Bowser. Just to explain what's going on with people in the city.

These residents keep preservation and resources for affordable housing on the front burner in council, in the press and in the District's policy landscape.

Notes

1 Jim Hoagland, "Urban Panel Inspects Squalor of D.C. Ghettos," *Washington Post, Times Herald (1959–1973)*, October 28, 1967, 143112145, ProQuest Historical Newspapers: The Washington Post.
2 DC RLA, "Urban Renewal – 1966 Annual Report D.C. Redevelopment Land Agency," September 30, 1966.
3 Risk share projects are authorized by HUD under Section 542(c) and provide enhanced credit to projects that have been underwritten, processed, serviced and disposed of by a local Housing Finance Agency.

4 The District has three housing agencies, the Department of Housing and Community Development, The Housing Authority and the Housing Finance Agency. Only one, DHCD, is public. The other two are quasi-public. The agencies often did not share data or information about buildings in which they were engaged.
5 David Harvey, "The Right to the City," *International Journal of Urban and Regional Research* 27, no. 4 (December 2003): 939–41, https://doi.org/10.1111/j.0309-1317.2003.00492.x.
6 David Harvey, *Justice, Nature, and the Geography of Difference* (Malden, MA: Blackwell, 1996).
7 Rasa Gustaitis and Leslie Whitten, "Housing Code Is Virtually Suspended For Landlord in District Slum Areas," *Washington Post*, May 16, 1963.
8 "Transfer, Lease and Option Agreement Between the 1372 Kenyon Street NW Tenants Association, Inc. and Kenyon Limited Partnership" (DC Recorder of Deeds, October 13, 1982).
9 "Transfer, Lease and Option Agreement Between the 1372 Kenyon Street NW Tenants Association, Inc. and Kenyon Limited Partnership."

7 Lessons Learned

In the process of finishing this book, I met with a former student in Richmond who wanted to hear about the project. She works in housing policy in the nonprofit sector, and when I explained the project, she became really engaged. She explained that her organization has started to track expirations of Low Income Housing Tax Credit (LIHTC) properties through the National Low Income Housing Coalition's National Housing Preservation Database. She explained that, as Richmond, Virginia gentrifies, more market-affordable housing is being lost to speculation and redevelopment. She also told me that they are trying to understand how to convince owners to keep the buildings affordable, and, more importantly, who should provide that support.

Richmond, as a region with few affordable housing resources, faces a dilemma. The region is growing quickly, yet Richmond is the second highest evicting large city in the country, has only 30 units for every 100 people who earn less than 30% of Annual Median Income (AMI) that need them, and the combined state and local support for affordable housing is less than 15% of DC's local trust fund allocation. It is a city that struggles with centuries of inequality baked into its built environment – from devastating Urban Renewal and Highway Projects to redlining and foreclosure. And in spite of that, Richmond, like Washington, DC, has to start somewhere to build the infrastructure.

Our conversation echoed conversations I have had with activists and government agency staff in communities across the country, where the two largest sources of affordable housing – market-affordable and LIHTC – are being lost to expiration, poor conditions, speculation and redevelopment. While I wrote about DC in this book, it is not the only city with a broad range of housing and neighborhood conditions, widening income inequality and rampant speculation across all contexts. The ongoing financialization of housing in the US and around the world has put low- and moderate-income housing at risk beyond the cyclical trends of building-level deferred maintenance in an aging stock. Not only are there very few places where investor activity is not underway, meaning that whether it is expiring LIHTC projects, market-affordable housing or Section 8 communities, there is a lot at stake in large and small cities across the country.

The preservation context has changed over time starting with the crowded and deteriorating conditions of legally segregated neighborhoods, the dual conditions of gentrification and deterioration of the late 20th century and the rapid, state-supported and financialized gentrification of the 21st century. But across contexts, preservation has been viewed concurrently as a tool for resident stability, anti-displacement, retention of subsidies and community power, mapping onto understandings of the role of housing for households and community, including the broad goals of needs, economics and rights. Practitioners may approach preservation through a needs-based housing lens as a way to improve family stability and household outcomes, prevent homelessness and reduce rent burdens. Housing through the economic lens justifies preservation through the comparative cost of displacement in getting people into employment, paying for homeless services and the long term costs for education. Perhaps most measurable, preservation makes a strong economic argument that new construction will never move the needle if a jurisdiction continues to lose housing to redevelopment, conversion or demolition. Finally, preservation as part of a right to the city, sees housing as a means to political power, identify formation and visibility. These approaches play out in policy where, like the story of Parkway Overlook, the goals are the same – preservation for the residents – but the process and implications for community power can be dramatically different. Yet, like Parkway Overlook, putting all the stakeholders – residents, funders and organizers – together in a room over time can help all parties remember what the end goals are.

How Do We Get There?

DC's context was unique – in the way that Richmond, Newark, Minneapolis, Los Angeles or Dayton are unique. They all come with histories, norms and methods of acting in the public space. But when I speak to practitioners, activists and academics about the DC case, after explaining the proximate issue, they ask "What can we do?" It would be easy – and not entirely helpful – to point to the Tenant Opportunity to Purchase Act (TOPA) as a quick response. But TOPA itself, while a useful piece of the policy toolbox, is part of a larger approach to preservation. As I have explored through the book, preservation comes down to three basic areas:

1 Existing building stock
2 Funding and policies that support flexible, comprehensive responses
3 A network of organizers, developers, funders, advocates, agencies and residents who can work at many scales

These three arenas are interrelated and serve to do more than preserve one building at one time. Rather they are part of an increasingly intentional policy that makes preservation of housing a priority. The complexity of preservation – at the building, community and jurisdictional levels – means there is no single answer or approach. Rather, the approach is to prioritize it and see how those three arenas function in one's own jurisdiction – state or local – to preserve housing.

DC's existing stock was a critical resource for preservation. The base of existing, subsidized Section 8 buildings arguably was a source of "low-hanging fruit" for preservation. It came equipped with a building-based subsidy determined by tenant incomes, which facilitated both flexibility to address a broad range of needs and depth to reach the incomes of the lowest-income households. But that was not the only source of preservation in DC. The District had large stocks of market affordable multifamily housing developed over decades. Starting with the development of multifamily housing in the early 20th century to address the District's growing population, and zoning decisions made over the decades since then, the built environment was formed and, in many ways crystalized to both help and hinder preservation 100 years later. This was because the ways that these tools were deployed were intentionally uneven, creating a landscape where white and upper-class communities became insulated from multifamily housing after zoning allowed them to restrict it. Other communities became spaces of concentration and containment of African Americans. Within this uneven landscape, the preservation and development of new deeply subsidized affordable housing during the mid- to late-20th century created a base of existing affordable housing that could be preserved as the District changed over the past 20 years. The public subsidy means that these buildings can be tracked through the work of the DC Preservation Network.

Though having buildings to preserve was necessary, housing does not remain affordable without a policy and funding infrastructure to work comprehensively across many types of buildings – particularly in a speculative landscape. The District's Tenant Opportunity to Purchase Act (TOPA), rent control and other regulations facilitated tenant-focused engagement in the process, opened access to the market and took units out of the speculative market. At the same time, the District used its Community Development Block Grant allocation to fund tenant organizers and others working with low- and moderate-income tenants. Finally, the creation of large, flexible funding sources, specifically the $100 million Housing Production Trust Fund and the leveraged Affordable Housing Preservation Fund, have made preservation possible, in spite of rising costs.

These two tools would not have been supportable without the work of the ecosystem of affordable housing actors across the District. With a full range of organizing styles, engagement with District government and roles, DC's governance network is multi-scalar and multi-sector. Residents, organizers and council members pushed for the laws and policies that support preservation. They also continue to create spaces to share information and collaborate around particular buildings while challenging decisions and advocating for policies that recognize residents' collective rights to the city.

Lessons

While DC has a particular set of policies and practices that have emerged over time, this book is not meant to be a step-by-step recipe – but rather a set of lessons based on experience about how to develop a housing policy that preserves not just units, but communities.

Lesson 1: Know Your Context

Local context can be both limiting and freeing. This means understanding how we got here, what currently exists, who the players are and the current political reality. But it is also critical to realize that while the context helps to understand where you are, it is not necessarily predictive. What it does do is help to develop the path to achieve your goals for affordable housing. Working in Richmond, I spend a lot of time doing two things: 1) thinking about how to get around the Dillon Rule and 2) apologizing for not giving examples in Virginia and points south. The former often leads people to close the door to possibility and the latter allows people to imagine that communities do not evolve. Bicycle advocates remind skeptics that Amsterdam was not a bike-friendly city until community members demanded it, and it evolved in response. Housing is the same. While this does not mean that Richmond will have the same housing landscape as DC, there is space for change if you know the context in which you are trying to make change.

In the past two years, DC-focused research organizations have focused on the ways that white neighborhoods retained "community character" through racially discriminatory single-family zoning in the early 20th century and maintained it through protests, court cases and ongoing pressure of elected officials and agency staff. This conversation has been critical to understanding the opportunities available for the preservation and creation of affordable housing in the District. But until that point, the vast majority of actors in the affordable housing space, like former Mayor Williams, had written off Ward 3 as a non-starter for density, much less affordability. Learning the context has opened up this possibility and made residents whose neighborhoods have been up-zoned to make space for new high-income residents demand a more fair-share approach to planning.

Lesson 2: It's All About the Data

It is impossible to preserve a building if you do not know where it is. Many local governments have spotty knowledge, spread out over multiple agencies, about affordable housing in their communities. It may be that Code Enforcement knows a building very well because they visit monthly, Human Services knows another building well because the families they serve live there or the Housing Department knows it because they subsidized it. Individual organizers and service providers know the conditions at buildings where they have worked. These data often are dispersed and rarely pulled together. Yet brokers and investors are all-too aware of where to target resources. Addressing this inequality of data must be a priority.

But what does that mean? We have to redefine how decision-makers and other practitioners define data. Even those who contribute to the DC Preservation Network (DCPN) often say to me, "we need actual data, not stories," effectively denigrating the data points that their organizers and residents bring about individual buildings. As anyone who has ever done research will tell you, anecdote is not truth. But neither does one line on a spreadsheet tell you about the population. Qualitative data about the conditions of buildings, experiences with management or affordability are triangulated to represent bigger pictures about individual buildings. The data from the National Housing Preservation Database are a necessary base, but all they tell us is where the buildings are and when they expire. As the members of DCPN explained, the expiration date was often just one indicator that did not explain much about the actual risk to the building's long term affordability. Instead, they had to physically visit, speak to the residents and match that with other data about funding, inspections and sales.

Data also have unifying power. While data are never neutral or, arguably, uncontested, they are a cause around which to convene. Government agencies are restricted in advocacy conversations, but they can show up and share public data about buildings that can be used by advocates. Just as importantly, they can show up and listen to on-the-ground data about the buildings that they have funded or are in search of support. These data have the power to influence both building and jurisdiction-level approaches to preservation.

Finally, having a central, accessible data source on preservation can level-set on the housing landscape, elevate the conversation and bring new actors into the space. By taking a data-driven approach within the visible context of a changing city, the network was able to make policy recommendations that have changed the conversation and, ultimately, make preservation a public priority.

Lesson 3: Create Awkward Situations (Convening)

Preservation, quite honestly, does not work in a system-wide scale without some really awkward groupings of strange bedfellows. If, as I argue, preserving affordable housing requires an amassing of building-level knowledge, financial resources, development and public funding, then it is clear that we cannot sit within silos and hope for the best. Preservation necessitates the convening of both horizontal and vertical networks. It means that, instead of fighting for resources amongst similar groups, they are coordinating. In DC there are three separate agencies focused just on housing, and in most jurisdictions, not only are there at least two housing agencies at the local level, but there are also housing agencies at the state level. Each of them may have an interest in one building with no mechanism through which to communicate concerns and shared or conflicting goals. Similarly, within the nonprofit sector, the shortage of resources often results not in collaboration, but territoriality over projects, funding or information. Yet, these agencies are frequently overlapping geographically, are seeing the same trends and can develop pictures of larger trends that, alone, would not sway decision-makers.

Horizontal networks are awkward at times, but far more complicated is the development of vertical networks. Organizers, focused on systems change, rarely work comfortably with developers, lending organizations or government agencies. Similarly, high-level advocates, lenders and government agencies may be interested in hearing information from community-based organizations to support their work, but that is different than engaging on terms of equality to preserve a building. These awkward groupings are necessary, not because everyone will always agree, but because within the system where we live, the resources available in the majority of communities come from these broad-based groupings collectively.

In both cases, this work requires trust-building in more than just individuals – but in the institutions they represent. This does not mean that the institutions work together on everything, share an approach or even always share goals. What it does mean is that they are willing to work together toward shared goals. These partnerships can be fragile, with each broken trust by individuals chipping away at the networks. Changes in leadership can challenge the trust of institutions, even if individuals are trustworthy.

Lesson 4: Prioritize Preservation

Preservation should be a policy, not a project, regardless of the type of organization engaged. In the ideal world, preservation is a state-wide or District-wide policy that engages all agencies in preserving housing for the most vulnerable communities. But this is rarely where housing policy – much less preservation policy – begins. Instead, it might start with organizers who are helping residents form an association, attorneys who are counseling tenants facing rising evictions, social service providers trying to help households find new housing, policy advocates watching the macro numbers of units fall or elected officials receiving calls from displaced residents. Regardless of the genesis, the next step is to bring all the resources you can currently muster to bear. In DC, stakeholders were originally organizers, attorneys and policy advocates who brought data to the table and used tools such as the funding for organizers and TOPA to preserve buildings. Over time, as momentum has built, new resources have been developed and partnerships formed that have supported preservation.

These resources brought to preservation have come from partnerships forged through DCPN and other advocacy organizations with lenders, organizers city government and developers. One of the Community Development Financial Institutions (CDFI) helps to fill gaps for buildings in exchange for long term covenants on the property, similar to a land trust model. These gaps may include things like buying down share prices in Limited Equity Cooperatives to make the building more financially stable, paying for repairs or contributing to the reserve fund. Other innovations like the District's Affordable Housing Preservation Fund responded to the need to get financing to buildings purchasing through TOPA quickly and off-cycle. The District partnered with two local banks to offer loans that facilitate immediate critical repairs while waiting for the next Request for Proposals (RFP) cycle. Organizers have worked together for more than a decade to divide up buildings that have requested help to ensure effective and even distribution of work. They have also partnered with attorneys, local government and others to engage in proactive education in impacted neighborhoods, training for Limited Equity Cooperatives and finding pro bono services for tenant associations.

Lesson 5: It Takes Money

Possibly the only prescriptive policy recommendation I have about preservation is to create state and local housing funds. There is no way around the reality that affordable housing requires public sector support. Jurisdictions that think the private sector will make it happen are fooling themselves. The state and local governments are going to have to make hard decisions that literally put their money where their mouth is to preserve affordable housing. DC now has more than $100 million in affordable housing money annually, yet it is still one of the fastest gentrifying cities in the country, displacing African Americans and Latinx residents at a high rate and seeing rents at rates that require incomes of almost $90,000 annually to make them affordable. This may be why I speak with DC residents who have no idea that the District is a leader in affordable housing preservation. But this $100 million annually is competing with a multi-billion dollar housing market that has turned housing into an investment. It means we have two options: wait for the system to change or invest local and state dollars into the problem. Though it is clear that the answer to this question is "Yes!", there is an immediacy to the funding problem.

How does this happen? For some jurisdictions like the City of Austin, TX, another impacted community, there have been multi-year housing bond measures. The challenge, which was finally overcome, was that these bond measures had to go to the voters. In other places like the State of Virginia, the allocation to the trust fund has gone through budget appropriations. After more than a decade of lackluster support, Governor Northam allocated more than $60 million over two years, with a plan to add another $20 million in the third year. Other places look to dedicated funding sources like the District's syphoning of 15% of the transfer taxes on property sales. The result was that, even at its lowest, DC's annual amount was still higher than most state allocations for affordable housing. It also tracked to the growth in the housing market. Yet it also fell with the slow-down in the market. In the past five years, the Mayor and the Council have topped the trust fund off to $100 million. Last year, the trust fund was supported at $130 million, and this year the Mayor's proposal for the trust fund tops $200 million.

Lesson 6: It Takes a Movement

Few elected officials are going to be affordable housing champions alone, and even fewer will be successful alone. It takes the ongoing work of activists, residents and advocates. More specifically, it requires the broad range of activists. Effective advocacy is not when organizations speak *for* and create platforms *for* impacted communities – but when residents are part of the power that develops policy and engages in change-making. The DC Council or Mayor did not create a preservation agenda, a large trust fund, TOPA or rent control in isolation. These policies were built through the work of a coalition of residents, community-based organizations, policy advocacy organizations, nonprofit developers, lenders and others who showed up. They showed up to council hearings in bright yellow shirts, sat-in at government offices, rallied outside government buildings, and called and went to the offices of council members. They were so successful that council members and the mayor show up to their annual rallies to prove their housing credibility.

They then used the knowledge they collectively built to promote policy agendas. The recommendations created by the DCPN in its 2014 report have been almost wholly adopted, and the District is slowly working through the process of cleaning up records, building a funding base, proactively working with developers and building owners, and engaging with tenants. It is, by no means perfect, but it is a start that could not have happened without folks showing up in a coordinated way.

Lesson 7: Process Matters – But So Do Outcomes

After trying to understand how we preserve, it became clear that *how* we preserve matters. Residents who had the opportunity to be part of the decision-making felt more confident in their housing, built broader networks in the building and engaged with advocacy more directly. New construction *should* be informed by the needs of low- and moderate-income households. But preservation should necessitate engagement before the first plan is created. We also know that housing is fundamental, and that instability does not just arise from an eviction notice, demolition or redevelopment. The threat of loss can destabilize families because they *expect to be displaced*. One organizer, speaking about this challenge, explained that she went to a building recently to help them respond to a TOPA notice. She told the attendees at the meeting twice that they did not have to move. Then midway through the meeting she said, "Pop quiz – who thinks you have to move?" More than half of the attendees raised their hands. This echoes the experiences of residents facing eviction who move before they go to court. They know they will be displaced and prefer to move when they can.

Not engaging residents in the process of redevelopment suggests that renters have no stake in their community, which, we know is not true. We know that renters have a variety of tenures – from 5 minutes to 50 years in the same unit or longer in the same neighborhood. But regardless, they have a highly vested interest in making sure their community is a stable, safe place to live, raise children, age-in-place and build community. They want a good outcome, but they also have knowledge that should be incorporated about the type of community they want.

There is a perceived risk for those in power of engaging in this type of process approach. Research suggests that there is a fear of losing control over the process[1]. But arguably, buildings that do not engage can similarly lose control in the form of resident protests, as at Brookland Manor, and resident turnover and dissatisfaction, as at Tyler Housing. In DC this engagement is mandated in the TOPA process, but when there is no sale, or the jurisdiction does not have a right of first refusal, this has to be mandated in other ways. The most obvious approach would be to require community engagement in any Notice of Funding Availability (NOFA) for city or state funding. This type of requirement would go a long way to acknowledging the stake and right that existing residents have to the future they desire.

Lesson 8: Preservation Is a Long Game – Deal With the Root Issues

My students often ask about how to deal with work in communities when the residents do not trust your institution. My answer is short – start sooner. It is the same with preservation. The need for affordable housing is rooted in deep issues of inequality and marginalization of low- and moderate-income renter households that have to be addressed over time. This is only a little helpful when you are a community staring down massive losses in the affordable stock, rapid gentrification and limited resources. But preservation is a long-game activity that starts with the buildings that were created decades earlier.

Yet you have to start somewhere. It means you may miss some at the beginning – that you would likely never have known about absent the new preservation policy – as the District did with buildings like the Geraldine or Lincoln Westmoreland II. In the first few years of the DC Preservation Network, many of the participants began asking what we were really doing and if we were effective. But you have to start and make plans that will take years to realize. When I first spoke to the former director of the Coalition for Nonprofit Housing and Economic Development for my dissertation in 2011, he lamented the District's lack of preservation policy. He saw the housing agencies as approaching each deal individually without thinking about the big picture. In nine years, his vision is being realized – and that vision was built on decades of activism to get a trust fund, TOPA, rent control, multifamily housing and more.

It takes time to build trust, create new units, develop networks or spark a movement. Preservation policy – rather than one-off wins – can't be a quick ribbon-cutting, but is, in fact, a form of infrastructure. There is a lot of risk and typically little reward for marginalized communities to engage in advocacy, partnerships with traditionally powerful entities or speaking on behalf of their policies and practices. There is also a perceived risk on the side of government agencies in changing their approaches. The space to make those changes must be created.

Preservation, like so much of the work of planners and policy-makers is the work of decades while also working with the immediate needs of those residents facing displacement in the moment. Thus, the bigger challenge is working on multiple fronts. Because preservation requires buildings, policies, money and people, if you want to keep preserving, you need to keep creating. This means new production through existing funding sources, Inclusionary Zoning programs, set-asides in redevelopment and zoning that permits the creation of multifamily housing. It also means connecting residents who are displaced to new units and resources, including local vouchers, housing search services and relocation assistance. This is why the District hired an Affordable Housing Preservation Officer to coordinate resources, the DC Preservation continues to meet monthly to discuss buildings, the Office of the Attorney General has prosecuted landlords and organizers continue to fight with residents to keep their buildings affordable and in good condition. It is real for both current and future residents in affordable housing.

Looking Forward

In January of 2019, Mayor Bowser announced her plan to increase the District's total housing stock by 36,000 units by 2025, the District's share of the regional need estimated by the Metropolitan Washington Council of Governments at the end of 2018[2]. The plan for new units includes 12,000 new affordable units across the city, with the highest shares going to neighborhoods where affordable housing has typically been unavailable due to prohibitive zoning and neighborhood resistance, particularly in the northwest of the city. As part of this plan, the Mayor adopted the recommendations of both the Preservation Strike Force and the DC Preservation Network of zero losses to the subsidized stock. This means that if they lose any affordable units, they must be replaced, adding to the 12,000 total units.

In May of 2019, she signed a Mayoral order to direct all DC agencies to bring their policy and practice tools to bear on her plan. The Office of Planning has made a goal of making 15% of all areas of the city affordable[3]. This plan promises critical outcomes for the District – in the form of an increased supply of affordable housing – on the magnitude of the influx of new and preserved housing created during the mid-20th century. The plan, on its face, seems to be a win for those who live in and build affordable housing *and* market-rate housing developers. By opening access to high-value neighborhoods through density, while not planning to add more affordable units to neighborhoods where affordable housing has been concentrating, the Mayor seems to have created a win-win plan that pushes the boundaries of the District's traditional socioeconomic lines while facilitating development in new areas of the city.

But the plan is not uncomplicated. Even beyond asking the critical questions like *affordable to whom?* and *what size units?*, those who execute the Mayor's goals must also ask *how will we define successful preservation?* This new housing supply will be both a product of and will create new forms of infrastructure for the next century. Preserving and creating this much affordable housing will require significant tools in the form of zoning, existing units to preserve, funding and actors within the governance structure. As discussed early in this book, new creation requires one set of tools and actors, while preservation will necessitate both existing and, perhaps, new approaches to be successful.

And so, we return to my initial questions: What are the roots of these policies? What are the goals? Who has voice? What is the nature of that voice? Who has the power to make decisions? Who has the power to originate ideas? These questions should be driving this preservation process if it is to be effective in not just housing, but in supporting the ongoing social, economic and cultural contributions of a broad range of residents. These questions are not what policy-makers and developers are always trained to ask, and, arguably, there are schools of planning thought that still see these questions as distracting. But these questions are at the base of not just what, but *how* we preserve. More importantly, these should be the driving questions as residents, advocates, nonprofit practitioners and government agencies take on the challenge of preservation.

Notes

1 Judith E. Innes and Judith Gruber, "Planning Styles in Conflict: The Metropolitan Transportation Commission," *Journal of the American Planning Association* 71, no. 2 (2005): 177–88; Karen S. Christensen, "Both Process and Outcome Are Essential to Planning," *Journal of Planning Education and Research* 35, no. 2 (2015): 188–98, https://doi.org/10.1177/0739456X14566277.
2 Metropolitan Washington Council of Governments, "New COG Analysis Recommends Increase in Area Housing Production" (MWCOG, September 12, 2018), https://www.mwcog.org/newsroom/2018/09/12/new-cog-analysis-recommends-increase-in-area-housing-production/.
3 DC Office of Planning, "Housing Equity Report: Creating Goals for Areas of Our City" (Washington, DC: DC Office of Planning, October 2019), https://housing.dc.gov/sites/default/files/dc/sites/housingdc/page_content/attachments/Housing%20Equity%20Report%2010-15-19.pdf.

Index

Figures are indexed in italic.

For Product Safety Concerns and Information please contact our EU representative GPSR@taylorandfrancis.com
Taylor & Francis Verlag GmbH, Kaufingerstraße 24, 80331 München, Germany

www.ingramcontent.com/pod-product-compliance
Ingram Content Group UK Ltd.
Pitfield, Milton Keynes, MK11 3LW, UK
UKHW020004200926
475702UK00015B/2465
* 9 7 8 0 3 6 7 7 7 1 8 0 5 *